T0354879

Life on a Roller Coaster

Ralph G. Mendoza

iUniverse, Inc.
New York   Bloomington

iUniverse books may be ordered through booksellers or by contacting:

iUniverse
1663 Liberty Drive
Bloomington, IN 47403
www.iuniverse.com
1-800-Authors (1-800-288-4677)

ISBN: 978-1-4401-6517-7(sc)
ISBN: 978-1-4401-6516-0 (ebook)
ISBN: 978-1-4401-6515-3 (hc)

Printed in the United States of America

iUniverse rev. date: 10/01/2009

Dedication

To Steven and Christine

Table of Contents

Acknowledgments

Many people should be credited with my continued advancement as a human being, but it would be remiss of me not to acknowledge these few:

Joanie: Thank you for having the faith to believe that I could master my limited-writing skills and produce a finished manuscript which was at least as interesting as you said my endless stories were.

Aunt Emma and Aunt Mercy: Thank you for the countless times I returned home to find a box of food waiting on our front porch, or next to our door when Eddie, Tony and I were young. You sacrificed so very much so that our family could eat.

Grandma Mendoza: Thank you for rescuing me at those times in my life when I needed it most.

St. Catherine's Military Academy: Thank you for showing me there was a better way to live. It proved to be the start I needed.

The Los Angeles County Fire Department: Thank you for

your patience as I matured as a man. The countless acts of heroism, performed on a daily basis, seldom left your firefighting personnel unequal to their tasks. The memory of the years I spent as a firefighter and engineer will stay with me forever. I have never known a group of men and women who were as dedicated as the men and women in your charge.

Ed Murrieta and David Galindo: Thank you, as well as Virginia and Kathy, for believing in me.

Steve and Christine: Most of all, I want to thank "The Mick" and "The Bop" for not abandoning me. Your threat to disown me or lose you both forever proved to be exactly what I needed. I have now attempted to make the changes you asked of me so that we can forgive and forget then go on with our lives.

Introduction

The very thought of writing this manuscript has sometimes been overwhelming. Reliving those memories of the sorrowful, the hurtful and the unfair, as well as the pleasurable, the funny and enjoyable times I have experienced has sometimes left me totally exhausted. At other times I have ended a writing session with a feeling of contentment. I guess you could say that this contentment came from my finally finding and accepting the complete truth.

It's extremely important to me that my children know the story of my life. My story is not unique; I realize that everyone who has lived any length of time has a story to tell. But this is *my* story so I have chosen to record all that has happen in the only way I know. Maybe then Steven and Christine will have a clearer understanding of their father's life and those hurtful things which led to a bitter divorce then continued as I did things which a loving father would never consider doing.

Now in 2009, as I am attempting to write about the experiences which are so indelibly engraved in my memory, I find it difficult to sleep. I leave my computer in the sleep mode, instead of turning it off. My computer is located just a few feet from my bed, so I prefer to listen to the music stored in my computer, as I attempt to sooth myself, clear my mind and reach that relaxed state which allows sleep to come naturally.

But lately I've begun having flashbacks of certain events which I had forgotten to include, so I jump out bed, strike the *enter* key and have immediate access to three folders which are reserved for this writing: one for notes, one for the chapter I am writing and the other for completed chapters. But that didn't completely solve my problem because I would have flashbacks when I was driving to the market or doing various chores. Suddenly the answer hit me: why not buy an inexpensive voice recorder? So I stopped what I was doing then rushed out of my townhouse and went to Radio Shack.

There I found exactly what I wanted. My voice recorder is a simple piece of equipment: it's not one of those you can connect to your computer or anything like that. Now that problem was behind me because I carry my recorder everywhere I go. It was sometimes embarrassing when I would be having supper with a date. I would pull out my recorder and whisper a thought or two; but it worked, so that's what really mattered. I have become impatient. Time seems far-more important than it did last year; before I actually started writing this manuscript.

Now I have diabetes so I have begun to put my "House in Order." The fear of dying doesn't frighten me: long ago I lost my fear of death and accepted death as being natural, and therefore acceptable. What does frighten me, however, is abandoning this project before my health fades and I am too weak to continue. Now however, I have something so important to do; something that I must finish so that my children will have *my* version of the events which occurred along my journey.

The thought of ever having my story actually published was still a pipedream – one which I stored deep in the recesses of my mind. I almost abandoned the idea of having this work published because I am not a gifted writer. After drifting into melancholy, I suddenly had a thought which solved my dilemma: I realized that it was basically my job to only commit everything to paper; everything I had stored in my brain; everything that only I possessed the knowledge of, and therefore, the only person uniquely qualified to write this story.

One question remained: how was I to write the story of my life? The answer came to me as I was watching the film *My Life*. The story is about a man who learns he will soon die. So he decides to film himself while he tells his still-unborn child about those many problems the child may expect to encounter in life. It's a heartwarming story I have often watched in an attempt to capture the spirit of what was said. The way the father tells his story is exactly how I wanted to write this manuscript. In one of the final scenes the father is riding on a roller coaster with his hands held high, waiting for his final breath and his journey into the hereafter. I used that scene as the title of my manuscript because I felt as though my journey had always been a roller-coaster ride.

If this manuscript were to ever be successful it had to be written as I speak and feel deep in the recesses of my soul. Aunt Arlene told me that only by writing the manuscript in this way was I ever going to convey to Steven and Christine my deep sorrow for my past mistakes, so from that day on I never worried about punctuation or grammar. It was the job of an editor and other assorted, well-skilled people, who are in the publishing business to help me polish and refine what is written.

The idea of actually writing this account came to me from my cousin Joanie. She and her sister Sandy and their husbands Larry and Don had joined me for supper on one of those all-to-few occasions when our maternal family gathers to either celebrate a wedding or mourn the passing of a loved one. That evening was no different. My mother's last-surviving sister had passed away. After the services for our Aunt Mercy were completed, and we had said goodbye to all who had gathered to mourn, the five of us met at a Mexican restaurant and were reminiscing about all the events that had occurred in our lives which we thought were interesting. As usual I was holding court and telling them about the many different phases I had gone through during my journey. We were all laughing as the food and drink came and went, when suddenly Joanie looked at me and said, "Ralphie ...you really ought to write about your experiences; I think some people would find them very interesting."

Joanie's words planted the seed; as time went on the seed sprouted. I continued to think about writing the manuscript almost daily. Finally, I thought, "Why not...it might be fun!" The worst that can happen, I thought, is that I'll find another interesting thing to do now that I'm retired.

Many months would go by and I would do very-little writing, but would jot down thoughts and put them into a folder I have in my computer. I call the folder *Insightful Thoughts*. I use the folder to store various passages from literature and notes for this manuscript. Slowly my thoughts turned into sentences, paragraphs, and finally, chapters. Now that I have finished I am very happy that I wrote this manuscript.

There seems to be a healing process which occurs when you review all that has happened in your life then transfer those thoughts to words on paper. Most of the time we look at an incident from our perspective only, but as we become older and wiser, we begin to look at that same incident through other people's eyes, and begin to have a more in-depth understanding of events which happened along our journey; at least that's what happened for me.

This account begins from my earliest memories. You know:

those flashbacks that only give you a glimpse of an event but not the entire picture. I have now attempted to expand on those flashbacks and other events of which I retain a vivid memory.

My narrative has no orderly sequence of events. Often it skips large periods of time and jumps from place to place because that's the way my life seemed to go: skipping from time to time and place to place.

Here you will read the story of the life of a child as seen through his hazy and often unclear eyes. A child who somehow weathered his personal storms and came, in his later years to be thankful for *everything* he witnessed. Now, at sixty-six years of age, I firmly believe in the adage handed down from our forefathers which says that adversity is our best teacher, and Heaven knows I've known adversity in my life and so have you. But I've also had many wonderful moments which happen to everyone as we all-too-quickly pass from birth to death.

The earliest events in my memory are mainly of Mother and me and the extraordinary life we lived. Mother and I lived, for the most part, alone. In all, I enrolled in over fifty schools from the first grade through high school. Some of those schools I attended for as little as a week or two then Mother and I would move again. As a child, I almost never had lunch in school cafeterias, but instead mooched money from kids so I could eat; and I am certain I never took a lunch from home.

As my brothers entered our lives there is also some confusion because they would sometimes live with us or with others, or I would live with our mother or in another town or state. The memories of my brothers, especially those of Eddie and Tony are beautiful memories. Ramon, the youngest of us, was not born until I was in the military and stationed in Arkansas, so I have limited memories of him, although we did get to know each other during the last few years of our mother's life when they both lived in Ridgecrest, California. I would visit them often, and for a time I even lived there, so I came to know and admire Ramon very much.

Bookies and hoodlums have been close friends, and I've experience life in both the ghettos and gangs of East L.A. I've had the opportunity to meet and get to know truly-nice men and women while playing golf. Golf has been, and remains, a constant source of thrills and pleasure, while also being a source of frustration and heartache. I have flown on Air Force One and met President Lyndon B. Johnson and Secretary of State Dean Rusk. Most importantly, I was blessed with two children: Steven Mark, whom I tagged with the nickname "The Mick" and Christine Diane whom I saddled with the nickname "The Bop."

Attempting to recall all that is written here has been a difficult task. Recalling all the events as they occurred in my life was very challenging because there was constant change. Some people I knew briefly then they faded out of my life; others whom I knew well were also in and out of my life during different periods of my journey. Nothing remained constant. But at least I have attempted to accurately describe events as they actually occurred.

So, for better or worse, here is the story of personal roller-coaster journey. I hope you enjoy it.

My Obituary

Have you ever stopped and wondered what your obituary would read like after your death? Or have you ever thought how much fun it would be if *you* could actually write your own obituary? Well, I have and here it is.

I was exhausted after writing each day for three months. I didn't want to research my notes or do other tedious work which I needed to begin writing the next chapter. Instead I decided to take a brief break from serious writing and have some fun. But at the same time, I wanted to write at least something which would later be a part of my finished manuscript. Today is one of those days, so I decided this might be the perfect day to actually write my obituary.

Here it is how I would hope to have my obituary printed on July 14, 2043, in the *Las Vegas Journal*, *Las Vegas Sun*, the *Boulder City News*, or Boulder *City Magazine*.

Obituaries: July 14, 2043

1. **Ralph G. Mendoza passed away in his modest home in Boulder City. He died in his bed last night from natural**

causes; he was found by a woman who weekly cleans Mr. Mendoza's home. Yesterday was Mr. Mendoza's one-hundredth birthday. Mr. Mendoza moved to Henderson, Nevada, in 1996; eventually he settled in Boulder City, Nevada, in 2004. Mr. Mendoza is remembered for the one book he was ever to write. His book actually reached Number One on the *New York Times'* list of bestsellers for 2010. Mr. Mendoza's book is titled: *Life on a Roller Coaster.* The book is actually his autobiography; he had no desire to write another book.

Mr. Mendoza is survived by his son, Steven, and his daughter, Christine. We were informed that Mr. Mendoza died with a smile on his face. He will be missed.

Two thoughts come to mind as I read what is written. The first is: since 2043 is many years away, I still have many years ahead of me – years in which I will continue to enjoy living here in Boulder City. I hope to visit other parts of this fabulous planet on which many different and interesting people live and having the opportunity to view the many wonders of our planet. The second is: *Life on a Roller Coaster* will be published so people, other than Steven and Christine, may also read about my journey.

Chapter One

Awakening to Life

When you wake up each morning, thoughts aren't instantly clear to you, but are instead slowly becoming more apparent: like going from a misty fog into the sun's daylight. That's the way it was with my first recollections. With time my memories became focused; others were to become etched in my brain.

Almost all of my early memories are of life in Ramona Gardens which is located in East Los Angeles and which is considered a ghetto area. There were numerous buildings, each made of cement, which contained several units. Grandma Mendoza's unit was a two-story apartment, with two bedrooms and a bathroom upstairs and a small kitchen and living room downstairs. Several of my paternal cousins and I would stay there at Grandma's home until our mothers returned from work. Of all my cousins I liked Jo Jo best; even as a child he was funny. Jo Jo once broke his leg while doing back flips off of a high wall; the next day he was practicing jumping with one leg and continue doing back flips. Jo Jo and I were together each day during the week and would often spend the weekends together.

What I remember most about Grandma Mendoza's unit was the bedroom where all we children slept. The room had a stench when you opened the door because there were only urine-soaked mattresses on the cement floor. To this day I cannot forget how that room reeked of urine.

That is also the place where I first remember experiencing fear. In an effort to stop me from wetting my bed, Mother would dress me in a diaper and threaten to make me sit on the steps at the unit's front door. I would cry and beg her not to put me outside because that's where all the Garden kids played. I was sure they would tell everyone at Murchison Street School that they had seen Ralphie in a diaper.

When Mother and I were alone in our own unit, I was in constant fear of her having an attack. You see, Mother was an epileptic who had constant seizures so I was forced to endure each experience with her. What most-often happened was that Mother would experience an aura which she knew would always lead to a seizure. We would quickly move the furniture out of the middle of the room and she would lie down on a blanket and pillow so she wouldn't hurt herself. But when her seizure started I would be horrified and start to cry. I would place my rolled-up belt into her mouth and watch her jerk and bounce around until her seizure was over,

all the while I was yelling: "Mommy, Mommy and I'm sorry!"
Even though I was only five or six years old, I felt so helpless
and guilty: helpless because I could not do more and guilty
because I always felt that something I had done was the cause
of her seizures. Those are memories I wish I could forget
but even after all these years I can't. Guilt was something I
learned from my earliest memories; I would continue to feel
guilty about everything. I even felt guilty when I had nothing
to feel guilty about!

We never lived in one place very long because Mother could
not handle pressure of any kind, so instead of dealing with the
problem, we would move to another place. I was constantly
changing schools; I even attended the same schools three
or four times. I vividly remember the last time I enrolled at
Harrison Street School. I was probably in the second or third
grade at the time and no longer needed anyone to go with me
when I enrolled. When I walked into the office, a kind lady
who remembered me asked, "Ralphie...how long will you be
with us this time?" I guess I lasted there for a month or two
before we once again moved.

As time passed, Mother and I continued to live a helter-
skelter life; and, after living in several places and attending
many schools in Watts, Compton, South Gate and South Los
Angeles, we found a nice house on Second Street in East Los
Angeles. Our house was situated behind a large, wooden
house. Mother seemed to like our new home, so we stayed

there for over two years. Our yard was fenced so Mother allowed me have a little puppy that must have been abandoned by its owner so I kept him and named him Dog.

Dog and I would play in our yard after school and on the weekends; I was really enjoying life there. Mother seemed to enjoy it too; so she would often bake a chocolate cake with fudge frosting: it was so good when it was hot! I think I was beginning to feel secure for the first time in our little home on Second Street.

That's the way it remained until several things happened to alter our lives again. The first was when Mother met and became friends with a man named Ray. He was nice enough and took a special interest in me. After we had become friends, Ray asked Mother if he could take me to a drive-in movie. Drive-In movies were very popular at the time because you could pile the entire family into the car and bring your own food and drinks. After Ray had taken me to the movies several times, he began sitting me on his lap. That led to him placing my hand on his private parts. He never got violent but would always want me to do things I knew were sinful. When I refused to concede to his wishes he asked me not to tell my mother, so I agreed. Eventually I told Mother because, deep-down inside I felt what we were doing was an unforgivable sin. Mother immediately severed her friendship with Ray and told him never to return to our house again or she would report him to the police.

The second thing that happened was when Mother started dating a man named Roy. To look at Roy would scare anyone to death because he was covered with tattoos – even on his face! Roy had been in and out of jail for most of his life and had five or six children. But there was something very likeable about Roy. He idolized Mother and always called her La Reina because he thought of her as if she were a queen. Roy was the most-gentle man I had ever been around; which, up until that time, included my father. Although he smoked far-too much and was constantly drinking beer or wine, he still remained very gentle with both Mother and me. Mother and Roy would often drink and smoke the night away; but still we were happy. Roy was in and out of our lives almost as many times as he was in and out of jail during the time I knew him, but no matter what Mother would do to insult Roy, he would eventually return. Sometimes a year would go by, but one day, there would be Roy. How he found us after we moved is still a mystery to me. I suspect Mother would call Roy's mother and leave our new address and phone number; so I think that's how he would find us.

The last thing that happened when we lived on Second Street, and as it turned out, the first life-altering experience of my life, was when Mother asked me if I would like to go to a military school. She explained that it was expensive, so if I agreed, I would have to remain there for one year. At first I was frightened because I had never been away from Mother before, but after she explained that I would be living there as well as going to school there, and especially after she told me about the great, indoor-swimming pool which the children were allowed to swim in year around, I began to start to like the idea. But when I looked at her and said, "But, Mommy that means I won't see you for a year," Mother immediately sat me on her lap and replied, "No, no, no Ralphie, I'll come and visit you every weekend, and you can come home for Thanksgiving and Christmas vacation. Now that didn't seem so bad to me, and of course, there was that swimming pool!

So that summer we went on the streetcar to downtown Los Angeles and went to Desmond's. Desmond's is a specialty store that sold everything I'd need to attend St. Catherine's Military Academy. Mother took me to visit St. Catherine's about two weeks before classes were scheduled to begin and I instantly loved the academy! They had a dormitory for the young and another for the older boys and had a large bathroom that had several showers; everything was spotless! We were even invited to stay for supper. Wow! What great food we had; I even had two glasses of milk and a dessert. But the best part of our visit was when Sister showed us the swimming pool. I had never seen anything so large. It was hugh, with two diving boards and a rope separating the shallow from the deep end. That was all I thought of: I never wanted to go anywhere as much as I wanted to go to St. Catherine's.

The first night I attended St. Catherine's I wet the bed. The sister who was in charge spanked me and said I should have told her so she could have placed a mattress protector on my bed. Later she held me close and said, "I'll forgive you this time, but tonight I want you to go to the bathroom just before you go to bed...and be sure to put on clean pajamas!" Pajamas? I couldn't believe it: I had three pair! So that night, after changing into clean pajamas, I pulled back the blanket to discover that Sister had not only put a mattress protector on my mattress, but had even changed the sheets. I don't think Sister knew that I had rarely slept between sheets before; so I didn't say a word. I believe that the second night I slept at St. Catherine's was the last night I ever wet the bed again. Sister had been so loving after spanking me that I was beginning to feel a sense of security just being there.

Our school was very strict: no nonsense was allowed. When Sister spoke, we listened and we learned. Any funny business was always followed by her ruler! I hated that damned ruler and, if I close my eye, I can still see her ruler coming down and smacking me on my knuckles. After a while, I learned: don't piss off Sister! Saturdays were visiting days, so I would get excited because I knew Mother would arrive just after lunch and stay until just before supper. Sometimes she would check me out of the academy, at the front office, and we would have supper together. She would always take me, dressed in my uniform, to a quaint malt shop where I'd always order a cheeseburger, fries and strawberry malt.

Saturday night was always movie night so all the boys would

gather in the rec room. We always had great movies on Saturday night which were repeated on Sunday night. Sundays were, of course, church days. We had our own church on the grounds and were required to attend Mass every Sunday. After Mass, there was Catechism for the young, so we could prepare for our First Holy Communion and Confirmation classes for the older boys. After that we could play in the rec room or anywhere on the campus; always safely supervised. It was Heaven!

When it was time to celebrate our First Holy Communion all us kids were excited and would rehearse the prayers we had to recite. For me, it was special because my father and his second wife, Nellie, had agreed to join Mother and me in the ceremony and remain for the celebration supper which followed. Also invited that day were my sister Belinda and her sister Margo (from Nellie's previous marriage) and my Aunt Emma. I knew then, but I am even-more aware now, of the sacrifice Mother had to make to send me to St. Catherine's. She had spoken on the phone with Dad, but, from the start, he was against the idea and refused to assist Mother financially. Looking back, I find it ironic that he took such pride in his son that day, especially when he saw me in my dress uniform.

Father had definite opinions about things and he felt that the seventeen dollars and fifty cents the court had ordered him to pay every-other week was enough. Although, to his credit, he never missed a payment and continued to pay until my seventeenth birthday, which was the day I enlisted in the United States Air Force.

My year at St. Catherine's went by all-too quickly. I don't think I was ever so happy as I was during the year I spent there. I thrived and had become a good student. More importantly, I was starting to have some confidence in myself and, although I would always remain the class clown, I didn't feel the need to show off so people would notice me.

When a child transfers from one school to another as often as I had, he loses continuity. I would sometimes find that I was weeks behind the other children and didn't know anything about what they were studying; other times I was weeks ahead and became bored very easily. But the year spent at St. Catherine's was different: from the first day of classes until the school-year ended, there was a definite continuity.

I can't say anything bad about the year I spent at St. Catherine's other than to say that they sometimes ruled a bit-too harshly and relied on guilt as a tool for controlling the children. When something went wrong or I did something bad, Sister would always stress, "You'll never get to Heaven acting that way!" I had brought enough insecurity and guilt with me, so I didn't need someone in authority telling me I would never get to Heaven if I didn't obey!

Now, of course, I look back and laugh about it. I know of no other place I could have gone to that would have such a lasting impact on my future. St. Catherine's was aptly named because only a saint would have thought about providing an environment in which children could thrive, learn and grow as human beings.

Chapter Two

Learning about Life

When I left St. Catherine's and returned to Second Street I was very sad at first. I guess it was a natural response, after all, I had experienced things I never dreamed existed, and now I was back on familiar ground. Dog had run away, so that made me feel even worse; although I searched for him, too much time had gone by, so eventually I resigned myself to Dog being lost. What cheered me up most while I was passing away that summer was my Aunt Helen. Helen (as I called her) was the youngest of Mother's three sisters. Helen lived with us for about a month so she took care of me while Mother was at work. It wasn't necessary for anyone to take care of me because I could easily care for myself while Mother was at work; but having Helen with us was a lot of fun, especially for me. She taught me to swing dance and dance salsa style, which I would go on to dance for many years. So just about every day we were together, Helen would turn on our record player and we'd practice dancing hour after hour.

Helen had mastered the art of popping gum, so in her

nonchalant style, which she would display for the rest of her life, she would constantly pop her gum and pretended to look bored, while we practiced. One day, before Mother arrived from work, Helen was washing dishes as I snuck up behind her, pulled on her apron strings and ran away. She seemed preoccupied in thought, so she shouted, "Stop that…I'm busy!" I must have repeated that three or four times, when, as I was running, I suddenly felt something hit me on the head; immediately I fell to the floor and blacked out for a minute or two. When I awoke, there lying beside me was the cast-iron frying pan Helen had thrown at me; fortunately, it only glanced off of one side of my head. Helen was crying and asking if I was hurt. I said I was sorry and would not do that again, and assured her that I was okay. Helen was very loving, so I immediately forgave her; so when she asked me not to tell her sister, I agreed. Helen was just too kind to me to allow this little incident to disrupt their relationship. After Helen left I was very lonely for her. For that month we spent together I had really grown fond of her and was to experience many-more enjoyable times with her before she died of alcoholism many years later. The one thing I was sorry for was that Helen never taught me to pop gum as wonderfully as she could.

After Helen left, but before I returned to Rowan Avenue School, I experienced two things which were to forever remain in my memory. The first is the week my Aunt Emma and Uncle Chuck took me, along with my cousins Sandy, Joanie and Billy, to Pismo Beach. The second was the two weeks I spent living with my Aunt Mercy and Uncle John while Mother was on vacation.

Sometime in late July, Aunt Emma phoned her sister to ask if I could spend a week with them during the first week of Uncle Chuck's vacation. Mother agreed, so on the day they arrived to pick me up I was ready, and off we went. I had never spent an entire week at the ocean before, so I was really looking forward to the experience. We had so-much fun, romping in the ocean and chasing each other from morning until evening; but I especially remember the evenings. Uncle Chuck would start a fire and Aunt Emma would cook hot dogs or chicken or something; but everything she made always tasted good. Aunt Emma could really make a salsa which was mild yet tasted so good but never stung my mouth. What Aunt Emma and Uncle Chuck ate was a different recipe, which I soon was to learn to avoid at all costs. The first time I made the mistake and scooped out a large portion of the wrong salsa to put on my burger, I guess I jumped up and ran around the campfire as Sandy, Joanie and Billy just pointed a finger at me and laughed. They instantly knew what I had done; I guess they had done the same thing earlier in their lives. Joanie, who is five days older than I am, remains the closest maternal cousin I have. If we don't talk with each other for a year or so, it doesn't matter; we just pick up from where we left off. I try to always remember July 8th, because that's Joanie's birthday, so, I'll call and say something like, "Now I know what it's like to talk to a Really Old Lady!" The only thing I did to upset

Aunt Emma and Uncle Chuck that week was when I punched a kid in the stomach for being mean to Joanie. Aunt Emma grabbed me and said, "We don't do that in our family. You have to understand that if you want us to include you again!" Otherwise, that was the only thing that marred our wonderful week at Pismo Beach.

The two weeks I spent with Aunt Mercy and Uncle John were different because I lived in their home. Most of time I played alone or with Aunt Mercy. Uncle John was usually at work and two of my three cousins, Johnny and Lorraine, didn't want me tagging along with them as they visited their friends. Each was older than I, so I quickly got used to the idea. I don't remember if Louise had been born yet or not, but I do remember that I spent all day with Aunt Mercy. She always had her hair pinned and covered in a bandanna. She would work around the house and even had one of those old-fashioned washing machines which had a wringer attached to remove all the excess water before she would go outside to hang what was washed. Aunt Mercy had a way of looking at me that would make me quake in your shoes! She didn't say a word when I did something I shouldn't; she just gave that look that only she could give. I immediately would ask, "Aunt Mercy...did I do something wrong?" Her answer was always the same. After staring at me for a few seconds, she would say, "You'd better believe it!" Then she would immediately start laughing, so I knew all was forgiven. Two things stand out about the weeks I spent there. The first concerns organization:

Aunt Mercy and Uncle John were very organized. The weeks seemed to go normally enough, but on Friday night, after cashing his check, Uncle John would bring home his income and immediately they would leave and do all of the next week's shopping; then after they returned, while Aunt Mercy was placing all of the items in the cupboard, Uncle John would sit at the kitchen table and take care of the bills. Only after everything was completed did it officially become party time; and oh, how they could party! From late Friday night until Sunday morning Uncle John would entertain us kids with his dancing, his story telling or many of his antics. He would sometimes tell us stories of his youth that I found interesting because I had never heard them before. He always had a drink in one hand as he floated across the floor, so Aunt Mercy, who by this time had poured herself a glass of beer or something, would yell out, "Oh John...stop that!" We kids would just laugh and laugh because Aunt Mercy's giggle was so different than any we had ever heard, so we all laughed as she giggled. However, come Sunday morning, everything reverted back to normal: there was very-little drinking from Sunday morning until the next Friday night.

The second thing that was significant happened the following Saturday morning. Aunt Emma and Uncle Chuck, along with my cousins, came over for the day so most of my cousins and I were playing in the yard when we saw Uncle John and Uncle Chuck walking to Uncle Chuck's truck. We asked if we could come along; Uncle Chuck immediately responded,

"Well certainly...just hop in the back." So Joanie, Johnny, Billy and I jumped into the bed of the truck; I don't remember if any of my other cousins joined us, but they were definitely with me that day. As we were traveling down a busy street I was sitting on one side of the truck, but decided to go to the back and sit against the tailgate. I didn't know that the tailgate was unlocked but, since it was up, I assumed it was safe to sit there. But when I leaned back, the tailgate swung down and I immediately rolled out of the truck. The only thing I remember is the sound of screeching brakes as I tumbled to the asphalt, and the sound of my cousins screaming for Uncle Chuck to stop the truck. As I lay there on the asphalt, I remember that my eyes were closed. When I opened them, all I could see was the bottom-side of the engine and the front tires of the car which had swerved in an attempt to miss me; each tire had stopped less than two feet on either side of my head. Had this accident occurred even a few seconds later, we would have been traveling through a busy intersection and I'm certain I would have been crushed to death. Slowly I came out of my trance; all I could hear was the sound of my cousins screaming as they were running with both Uncle Chunk and Uncle John following closely behind. The driver jumped out just about then; that poor man couldn't apologize enough. But what he had done when he swerved to miss me had actually saved my life. Uncle Chuck, who had the ability to take control of any situation, immediately hugged the driver and sincerely thanked him. I don't remember much about what happened after returning to the truck.

I do remember, however, when we arrived at their home. Everyone was still shaken, but Uncle Chuck remained in control, so after recounting the story to all who had not been there, he finally relaxed. Both Aunt Emma and Aunt Mercy embraced me and a few tears were shed. All I can say, as I am writing this is thank God, Providence or just plain old Good Luck for smiling down on me that day.

After returning home and answering all of Mother's questions, things around our house resumed as before. I waited for school to begin and slowly adjusted. I felt I owed Mother for all she had done to make my life better, and I was especially thankful for those long bus rides she would take each week from East L.A. to Anaheim just to see me. I dug up this old shoeshine box we had stored and bough brushes and all the different colors of shine I would need to begin. Mother thought this was cute but I'm sure she didn't think it would last very long; but it did, and I liked it.

Each Saturday and Sunday morning, after making myself a bowl of corn flakes, I'd head to the corner of First Street and Rowan Avenue. I started there because there was a drug store on that corner so there were plenty of people going in and coming out, so I'd wait for a man to exit the drug store and I would ask, "Hey Mister, how about a shine?" I would charge fifteen cents, but I'd often get twenty-five cents, so I quickly learned to be charming and funny as I shined men's shoes so I could get that extra dime! I had stock answers for every question. I remember several men warning me, "Now be sure not to get shine on my socks." My stock answer would always be, "What, and waste my shine?" I found that the more I got the men to laugh, the more likely it would be that I'd receive a tip. A lot of my time was spent inside the many bars that, in those days, stretched from Rowan Avenue to just past Indiana Street. I especially remember the three bars that were located just past Indiana Street because those bars had prostitutes working from opening until closing, so there were always plenty of men to be found there.

The women who worked there were something to see. Each of them was Mexican and all were fat – too fat for their age. I don't think I ever saw a young or a pretty one in any of the bars where I hustled. One thing they had in common was that their faces all looked older and even I could see that they were all heavy drinkers. I know because I had known heavy drinker since my earliest recollections. I can clearly recall the smell of stale beer and tobacco as I entered those bars.

One of the first rules I learned was to never go to a corner table when a woman was on her knees because none of the three bars had back rooms which would allow privacy; instead I'd wait and return later to that table when the hooker was sitting next to the man and was persuading him to continue buying her drinks; I remember thinking, "I guess that's why they call them hookers!" I'd always ask the men who were sitting at a table with a prostitute on their lap first, because I knew they probably wanted to use the woman to satisfy themselves, and would try to impress them. While these prostitutes were sitting on their customer's lap and allowing all the men to fondle them, I would quickly give the man a shine and was often rewarded with a quarter or even a half dollar that was thrown into the air for me to catch. I'd always be sure to smile at the women and would often receive a wink. I spent a lot of time in some of those bars and soon people would begin to remember me, but I spent most of my time there for a purely selfish reason: money! Shining one man's shoes and receiving fifty cents was like shining two or three men's shoes while walking the streets, plus, some of the things that went on in those bars were new to me and very interesting. Several times a prostitute would raise her dress and give me a quick peek, then begin chuckling. That was the first time I had ever seen a woman's "private parts," so I remember thinking as I walked away, "Gee...her thing sure looks strange!" and I wondered, "do all people have hair down there?" Those women all thought I was cute and enjoyed teasing me. I seldom asked to shine the shoes of those men sitting at the bar. It seemed to me that they were sad and didn't want to be disturbed.

So I'd make my way from Rowan Avenue to the last bar just past Indiana Street, then I'd cross the street and work my way back. There is where I think I ever saw a fire engine I actually remember. There were three men riding on that particular fire engine and the truck had a large 1 painted on the door, so I would wave to them, and they would return my wave as they passed me.

On a good day I'd make over five dollars so I'd buy a candy bar and head home. I always gave Mother most of what I had earned, but kept one dollar for candy or comic books; I always made sure to keep enough left so I could take a dime to school each day during the week. Rowan Avenue was much different than I had remembered before leaving. I wasn't having the same kind of fun I remember having at St. Catherine's; I was bored most of the time. Now what was being taught didn't really register because at first, all I could think about was what the friends I had made at St. Catherine's were doing that day. The morning session always seemed to drag on, so I didn't like the morning session because that's when we had our daily dose of castor oil; but I somehow lasted through classes until morning nutrition. Morning nutrition was the one I liked best because the taste of castor oil seemed to linger in my mouth; so I would use my dime to buy a muffin, smothered with peanut butter, or a cup of hot chocolate. I sure hated the taste of that castor oil! Lunch was totally different: I just about never had money to buy an apple or something, so sometimes I'd play while the kids had lunch, or I'd mooch half a sandwich from those who had brought their lunches. I did basically the same at afternoon nutrition: sometimes I ate; sometimes I didn't. I had slowly begun to act as I had earlier in school and was considered disruptive. I was sent to the office several times and even had to take a few notes home to Mother, which she would have to sign before I returned the note. Sometimes I received a spanking; other time she would begin to cry and say, "I don't know what I'm going to do with you!" St. Catherine's would simply not allow any child to misbehave, and fighting was definitely not tolerated; so I quickly learned proper behavior for a year. But now I had returned to an environment which was much-more conducive to kids getting into trouble, so my bad habits slowly returned. I think the last report card I took home that year was the worst I had ever received.

Mother threatened to call my father and ask him to take me, but Dad now had two daughters whom he lived with along with his wife Nellie and Margo; so there was just no room for me. Secretly I felt that he just wanted me to live somewhere else. I thought Belinda, Laura and Nellie were more import to Dad, so I felt that all he wanted was to go one with his life with his new family and not worry about me. I saw very little of my father except when he would bring over the child-support money every-other Friday night. A few times he did pick me up and I would join him and Nellie for breakfast. We would go to Cookie's which was a fine restaurant that served authentic Mexican food. Nellie was always nice to me, so we got along well.

What I loved most was when Dad, Nellie and I would travel to the North Broadway section of Los Angeles because Grandma Mendoza owned a Mexican restaurant there. After we entered, she would always kneel down and give me a loving kiss and a great-big hug! I used to don an apron and, after finding a pencil and order slip, I would walk over to a table where people sat and were amused as I tried to take their orders. Grandma Mendoza always kept a close eye on me, so she would join me to be certain that the orders were taken correctly. I would do this until our order arrived, then return to Dad and Nellie's booth and sit and sip on my father's beer as we ate. Somehow, beer just tastes better when you ate a Mexican breakfast! Dad didn't seem to mind, but Grandma would always warn him, in Spanish, not to let me drink too-much beer.

One day my father drove over to our house on Second Street and honked the horn, so I quickly ran out and sat on the front seat with him. I was shocked when my father said he was planning to take his two daughters, Belinda and Laura, and Nellie and Margo to Sequoia National Park for their summer vacation. I was thrilled when he asked me if I would like to come along. I looked at him and immediately smiled and said that it would be great! After we said goodbye, I ran inside to tell Mother.

The day finally arrived. After sitting on the curb until dark I finally realized that Dad was not going to come. I remember sitting there; I couldn't stop sobbing. Mother came and took me by the hand and walked me in as I continued to cry. The next time I saw my father I immediate asked him why he didn't pick me up as he had promised. His answer was always the same one he would use many times until I became a man; his stock answer was always: "I didn't because I didn't...that's why!"

People say revenge is sweet; well I don't think so. Many years would pass before I grasped my opportunity for revenge. Uncle Ralph, who was my father's best friend and the man whom I am named after, died. That evening my father called to ask me why I hadn't attended Uncle Ralph's Mass or the burial services which followed. Dad said, "Son...what's wrong with you? Why didn't you come to say goodbye to your Uncle Ralph?" I took a breath and answered, "I didn't because I didn't...that's why!"

I hung up with a feeling of sadness instead of revenge. Uncle Ralph had been very loving to me all of my life; I was included with him and Dad when they went fishing. I knew about his death, but instead of attending his services, I chose to wait for my father to inquire. That was a mistake that still haunts me.

Chapter Three

Life in Yuma

That summer Mother, Roy and I traveled in his car that was not unlike any you would find in a junk yard. That thing was always breaking down! We were going to visit Grandma Navarro who lived in Yuma, Arizona. Roy's car couldn't travel more than fifty miles before the engine would start to overheat, so he always carried two of those expandable, fabric bags, filled with water. He would stop and cuss in Spanish as he removed the steaming cap from the radiator. Roy would wait until the engine had cooled down before pouring warm water into the radiator while Mother and I patiently waited and laughed at the way Roy looked. He was covered in sweat and never stopped cussing, but eventually we resumed our journey. It must have taken us over twelve hours to finally reach Yuma.

Grandma Navarro lived on Cemetery Avenue, which is located in the poverty area of Yuma. The house was old and in need of repair and paint. It was different from the other houses I had lived in because there was an outhouse out back. The only two things I liked about the house were that the front porch was completely enclosed, so there was always shade from the scorching sun, and the screens on the top half allowed us to see outside. The area had once been a burial ground for the Indians who had once lived there and Grandma's house was just at the base of one of the many hills that encompass the area.

After a day or two Mother said to Grandma that I was beginning to get into trouble again at Rowan Avenue School, and asked Grandma if I could live with her. Grandma didn't like the idea at first but reluctantly agreed. So I stayed in Yuma when Mother and Roy returned to East L.A.

Grandma Navarro was very hard to understand because she was so quiet and only spoke Spanish to me: either her entire sentence would be in Spanish or it would be a combination of Spanish and English. No one had ever spoken purely in Spanish to me other than Grandma Mendoza, so at first I didn't always understand Grandma Navarro. With time I learned to understand Spanish very well, but I didn't always use the correct words when I answered her. Grandma really enjoyed her solitude, so she would allow me to play all day with the other boys who lived just around the corner. When she wanted me to return she would stick her head out of the front door and holler RALPHIE in the most drawn-out way, with special emphasis on IE. Her shout would echo off the hills, and I'd come running: I soon learned not to keep Grandma Navarro waiting!

The first few days were spent getting to know the boys where I now lived. In all there were five boys I played with regularly; there was Raul Ochoa, and his two cousins, Richard and Pollieto Ochoa, who lived directly across the dirt road from Raul, and there were the Hernandez brothers whose names are Antonio and Fernando. We always called Antonio by the name he preferred, which was Tony. They were much different than those boys whom I had known in East L.A. What I liked most was the fact that there were no gangs to fear. Each dispute was always settled between the two boys with only their fists and feet as weapons. Each time I would return home dirty or with blood on my shirt, Grandma would immediately ask me in Spanish, "Ralphie, have you been fighting again?" Grandma simply would not allow me to fight. In a combination of Spanish and English she would always say, "If you fight, I spank you when you come home." The fighting between my new friends and me didn't continue much after that because Raul Ochoa, who we all called Boody, was much tougher and could definitely fight better than I could. I never really fought too much with the other boys, so I quickly learned not to mess with Boody. Plus, I'd have to face Grandma if I returned dirty or bloody.

The days were long and terribly hot for me that first summer in Yuma. My friends and I had plenty of time to play each day away. We would play a version of stickball all day on a patch of dirt in the middle of the desert. We used rocks as our bases and home plate, and swung a piece of wood at a rubber ball. Sometimes we would sit in a little shack which Boody's older brother Coco had built. In the shack we would read comic books over and over again. At night we would play hide & seek, kick the can or dodge ball and enjoy ourselves very much. Some nights we would invade the trucks that were stored at the packing sheds which were located just down a hill from where we lived. We'd climb on the trucks and place our arms as far under the tarps as we could, then steal all the grapefruit and oranges we could carry. Other nights, my friends and I would gather around the radio to listen to *The Squeaking Door*, or *The Whistler*, or any of those other radio programs that were so popular in the late forties and early fifties; my favorite was always *Amos & Andy*.

When I look back, what I laugh about most are the memories of those nights when we would quietly creep back into our little shack. There was no light, so we would always leave the door open after we entered. It was pitch-black inside our shack as we would tell far-fetched tales and horror stories. Each kid would try to top the story he had just been told. We would come up with some of the most hilarious stories we could think of. We were very competitive about everything; we even competed in farting contests! I think at the time, I held the record for the longest one. We would fall over laughing when one of us was able to rip off a long one of at least five seconds or longer. I think my best was one that lasted over eight seconds! We talked a lot about sex too. It's a normal thing all children do; and it was no different with our little group. We found ourselves asking questions like: what does it look like and what would it feel like the first time we actually had a sex with a real, live girl? I had seen several before when the prostitutes in the bars would give me a peek, so I told them what it looked like. I said that it looked much different than ours did, but confessed that I hadn't actually done "it" yet. Our hormones were literally bouncing around in our bodies which I guess is also normal for children our age. When we did what boys aren't supposed to do to themselves we would close the door because we were too afraid someone might catch us. I remember one night when Coco walked by; we could hear him giggling as he strolled past our shack because the door was closed. There's no doubt in my mind that Coco knew exactly what we were doing; I'm sure he had experienced the very-same phase during his childhood.

There was only one television station in Yuma and it only broadcasted at certain times, and on certain nights, but there were plenty of radio stations we could listen to. Grandma would always listen to Mexican music at night. She was a chain-smoker who smoked over two cartons of Lucky Strike cigarettes each week. I can recall her sitting in her chair and lighting her next cigarette from the one she was about to put out; she would do that all day and long into the night. What I recall most, and can still actually see if I close my eyes, is

Grandma sitting in her favorite chair listening to Mexican music. She always had a cigarette in one hand and a drink in the other. She would just sit there and suddenly rip off the longest and loudest farts I had ever heard. I had to hold my breath as I quietly tip-toed out. I used to have to go into my bedroom and muffle my mouth so I could just laugh my head off! Had I taken Grandma with me to our farting contests, she would have easily won!

Although Grandma had a television, it had stopped working shortly after I arrived. For some reason I started tinkering with the bulbs and wires inside the back of the TV and suddenly it started working again; I guess it must have been a loose wire or bulb. Grandma sure was happy about that and things were much better between us after that. Grandma really missed not being able to watch wrestling on Wednesday nights. She would become very animated each time Mr. Moto was advertised as being a contestant that evening because she hated Mr. Moto and loved to see him get beat. She would sit in her chair and jump and holler all during his matches!

I'll always remember awaking to the aroma of the tortillas Grandma made by hand each morning. I'd quickly dress and head for the kitchen. Grandma always drank coffee in the mornings so I'd pour myself a cup of fresh coffee and patiently wait while she rolled and twirled the dough into a very large tortilla. She would look at me and toss a hot, fresh tortilla on my plate where I quickly smothered it in butter and jam, or if we had a pot of beans left over, I'd ask Grandma to heat them up and enjoy Grandma's great beans with my tortillas. When Grandma made potato soup for supper I was really happy because Grandma made the best potato soup I had ever tasted. Those mornings are about the only fond memories for me because Grandma Navarro and I never really became close; instead, it seemed to me, that she had been forced to take me in and was now tolerating me; so I tried to be as quiet as possible all during the time I lived with her. Just after I had finished breakfast and completed a few chores, Grandma would tell me to go and play with my friends, but always warned me not to go too far in case she called for me.

There was one brief moment when Grandma Navarro and I seemed to bond, if only for a short period; here is what happened: Grandma and I had just finished breakfast when abruptly I asked her, "Grandma...why don't we go to church on Sunday mornings?" She gave me a look which said that somehow this was something so important, that she had better explain what she wanted to say so I could understand her completely. So she took me by the hand and said, *"Venga con migo,"* which means: come with me. She took me outside where we crossed the dirt road that led to the hills directly across the way. Grandma immediately pointed to a large rock and said, *"Siente abajo Ralphie."* I sat as she had directed and she said something that I didn't understand completely at the time, but have now come to believe that what she said to me that morning is one of the most-important things she ever taught me. In Spanish she said, *"No es necesario ir a la iglesia a obtener la inspiración del Dios. Si su corazón es puro, usted recibirá aún más inspiración que se sienta en esta roca."* What Grandma said was: "It is not necessary to go to church to obtain inspiration from God. If your heart is pure, you will receive even more inspiration sitting on this rock." I must have given her a look that said I didn't completely understand, so she finished by saying, again in Spanish, *"Cuál es la mayoría de la importación al Dios es que usted tiene un corazón bueno."* What Grandma was trying to teach me was, "What is most import to God is that you have a kind heart." It really is a shame that Grandma Navarro and I didn't have more exchanges like that one; it would really have meant a lot to me.

In September I enrolled at Mary Elizabeth Post Elementary School. What I remember most about the first time I attended that school was our English teacher. She was young and very attractive. It seemed to me that she was too pretty to be just a teacher! What was different about her, besides her obvious beauty, was that she always printed when she wrote things on the blackboard. I had never liked the way my writing looked when I was writing something in longhand, so I copied her and began printing everything. To this day I can only print when I write anything and even find it difficult to write in longhand when I sign my name. I remained at that school and continued to live with Grandma Navarro for about four or five months before returning to the Los Angeles area.

Now Mother was living in South L.A. so I finished the year attending yet another school.

When I finished elementary school I attended Stevenson Junior High School. Mother and I were once again living in East L.A. Now we were living in a small apartment that had once been the back portion of a large home on the corner of Rowan Avenue and Verona Street. What I liked most about living there was that there was a park directly across the street, so I'd go play in the park whenever my mother said it was okay. The firemen, who had their station just off of Verona Street, would come to the park each morning to run laps around the baseball diamond or exercise on the grass. I remember thinking how much fun it must be to be a fireman and get to ride on a shiny, red truck. Their truck had the number 2 painted on the truck's door.

I didn't like going to Stevenson because I was constantly being beat up and there was a lot of pressure put on me to join a gang. One Sunday, as I was entering the front door to Our Lady of Lourdes Catholic Church, I was stopped by three boys and pulled into the parking lot. I was told that I either had to give them all of my money, get beat up or join their gang. By this time I was tired of being beat up but didn't have any money, so I agreed to join The Little Valley Termites, which was their gang's name. Guess what? The initiation was to get whipped by the entire group! After they had each hit me a few times, they all patted me on the back and said that from that time forward I'd never have to worry about anything: if anyone messed with me, the gang would take care of the problem. That part was great but there were also things I didn't like about being a Termite. For one thing, everyone belonging to a gang had to do what the gang's leader wanted, and our leader liked ditching school all the time. Another thing that was bad about being in that gang was that we'd all enter a market as a group, and one of us was supposed to steal as much beer as he could carry while all the rest of the gang ran up and down the aisles or created a big commotion to distract the store's employees. I was really starting to get into a lot of trouble and my father even had to come over to warn me. Finally I had to choose between being expelled from Stevenson or leaving the Termites, so I told the gang I wanted out. That night at just about dusk, bullets shattered the windows of a car which was parked near our front gate and one even hit our front door. That was all Mother could take, so later that night I found myself on a Greyhound bus. Destination: Yuma!

Since I left in such haste Mother didn't have time to make arrangements for me on the phone. Grandma Navarro enjoyed her solitude too much to be forced to put up with me again so she declined. The only other immediate-family member I had who lived in Yuma was my Uncle Louie, the younger of my mother's two brothers. But I had lived with him in the past when we all lived in South Gate, so I told Mother that I didn't want to live with Uncle Louie again because he didn't like me.

I had known the Hernandez family who lived a little further down the hill from where the Ochoa boys lived, and I liked both Tony and Fernando, so I asked Mother if I could live with them. Since the Hernandez family didn't have a telephone, there was no way of confirming whether it would be okay to spend the summer with them. But Mother was desperate, so when I told her I was sure they'd take me in if she would send Mrs. Hernandez money every-other week, she finally agreed.

I arrived at the Yuma bus station just a little after dawn. The bus station was then located in the middle of old-town Yuma, so I picked up the one suitcase I had brought and started walking as the sun was rising. I walked past the train depot and began to walk on the railroad tracks that separate the Colorado River from where the Hernandez family lived. I remember it had already begun to get hot; even at that early hour. As I was approaching the Hernandez home, I was struck with the thought of how sad it must feel to live in a place like theirs.

There were three buildings on an open piece of desert: a dilapidated shack, a shower and an outhouse. The shack consisted of four walls enclosing two rooms, the sides and roof of which were constructed of corrugated metal. Inside there was a bedroom which had a dirt floor that had been swept so often that it seemed to be as slick as stone. There were four beds: one for Nana, one for Mrs. Hernandez, one for Marta and one for the boys, which would now include me. Other than that there was only a small dresser with a mirror on top, one chair and one light which dangled from the ceiling. The bedroom was separated from the kitchen by a long curtain, which was left open after we all woke up. In the kitchen there was a table with four chairs, which was also on dirt, a single, cold-water faucet which sat over the sink that had a pipe cut through the wall so the water would drain to the outside, an old-fashioned ice box and a wood-burning stove next to the only door the shack had. The kitchen was also lighted by a single bulb which hung from the metal roof.

The shower, which was just a few feet away, was also constructed of corrugated metal and had a drain that was attached to a pipe which went through the slats that were on top of the dirt and extended through the wall, so that this water would also flow down the hill; there was only a cold-water faucet attached to a wall and there wasn't even a light in that shower.

Finally, there was the outhouse. It was constructed of wood and rested on two, large wooden planks that extended across the hole that had been dug. When the hole would fill, the boys simply dug another hole, moved the outhouse and used the dirt to cover up the old hole. I quickly learned to hold my breath whenever I entered because the smell made me sick when I took another breath.

As I reached the final hill, a few of the dogs which roamed the area began to bark as I walked up that hill. I wasn't worried though, because I had played with these dogs each time I would go home with Tony or Fernando. I arrived just as Mrs. Hernandez was making tortillas and she met me with a wide smile, a "Ralphie!" and a hug. Mrs. Hernandez stood about 5' 1" tall and weighed over one-hundred fifty pounds, but she had a indefinable warmth about her that I really liked. I told her my problem but before I could complete what I was trying to say, she said, in Spanish, "Bien"; which meant that it was fine with her if I stayed with them. Marta (Tony and Fernando's older sister) entered the kitchen about that time, followed shortly thereafter by Fernando and Tony. We all exchanged greetings and the kids seemed happy that I'd be staying with them.

The Hernandez family was very poor and had no visible means of support, at least as far as I could tell. I told Mrs. Hernandez that my mother would be sending her money every-other week for my care, That pleased Mrs. Hernandez very much, but I actually think she would have still allowed me to stay; but the additional money would help, so she liked the idea.

Of all the people who lived in that shack, I remember Nana most. She was over one-hundred years of age and once told me that she had lived in that same place her entire life. The reason I single her out is that she remains one of the most-interesting human beings I've ever had the pleasure of knowing. After a breakfast which always included beans and freshly-made tortillas, we kids would help Nana outside the shack where she would sit all day in that blazing sun and fan her face to keep the flies from entering her mouth, nose or eyes. Somehow it didn't seem to bother Nana much when flies would enter her ears; but she would occasionally slap her ear so they would fly away. In the late evenings Nana would tell about the life she had led while growing up in Yuma. She would tell us about the soldiers who used to herd the Indians into this area they now call the Black Hills. She even had a tin box with a lid on it. She would tell one of us kids to fetch the box from under her bed, and she would show us many different arrow heads and quills. She had many other things in that box which included the claws of the birds she could name from memory, old bullets she had picked up as a child and young girl, and other assorted mementoes she had kept over the years. The neatest thing she had saved was the patch from a soldier's shirt. Her stories were endless and oh-so interesting. She even taught me a few Indians words, some of which were exactly like the Spanish words I had learned from Grandma Navarro.

I have forgotten his name, but there was a man who would come about every two weeks, so I assumed he was the children's father. He would show up some evening with a quart of whiskey or a bottle of wine, so he and Mrs. Hernandez would sit in the kitchen and just drink and talk until well after the rest of us had gone to bed. Several times I saw him reach into his pocket and remove some money from his wallet, then give the money to Mrs. Hernandez, so I assumed that this must be most of the money Mrs. Hernandez used to care for her family. One thing I'm positive of is that every Friday and/or Saturday night Mrs. Hernandez would put on a dress which had red flowers sewn on the front, and after applying lipstick and other makeup, she would walk to a bar where most of the other people, especially men, used to gather. I don't know much else except that she always returned drunk the next morning and had plenty of cash in her leather purse. That money, along with the money that man would give to her and the ten dollars Mother would send every-other week was all that Mrs. Hernandez had to support us.

Saturday or Sunday mornings were always a treat because Mrs. Hernandez would send Marta to the local store to buy lard, eggs, flour, beans and meat. Mrs. Hernandez would prepare this meat in a large pot and after adding onions and other spices she would smother the meat with hot chili and serve it over a bed of rice. That, along with the fresh biscuits she would make, were delicious! What was left of the meat she had prepared the day before was always served with eggs and fresh, hot tortillas the following morning. Just about each day, Tony, Fernando and I would cart their wheelbarrow down to the ice house and buy a ten-cent block of ice then gather all the pieces of wood we could find. Sometimes, when we had milk, we would buy a fifteen-cent block of ice because milk was precious and expensive, so Mrs. Hernandez wanted to be certain that it wouldn't spoil, especially on those hundred plus days when the metal roof made the kitchen feel like an oven.

Each day we kids would play in the Colorado River which was less than a mile from where we lived and sometimes Tony, Fernando and I were given a dime each so we could go to the public swimming pool which was located far from where we lived; but we kids didn't mind walking the distance because there were always plenty of girls in bathing suits swimming in that pool. On Sunday afternoon Mrs. Hernandez would sometimes give us money so we could walk into town and go to one of the two theaters in old-town Yuma. We never wore anything other than swim trunks that entire summer – not even shoes! But we were required to wear at least a T-shirt in order to enter the theater, so on those days we would also wear some sort of shirt. I remember feeling very strange with any kind of shirt on because by now I was used to wearing only my swim suit. I can also remember the heat that had been absorbed into the rails of the tracks we had to walk along in order to reach town. By now I was dark brown in color and my feet were as thick as leather, so it didn't hurt as much as it would hurt people who always wore shoes when we walked on those hot rails. We used to challenge each other to see who could stay on the rails the longest before jumping off – that's how hot those rails really were! Only when I would remove my trunks to shower would I see my natural color.

Life in Yuma was great for a kid who had only known ghettos. We were always safe and our families never worried about drive-by shootings, or that their child might suddenly be attacked by a gang. But, we kids did do one thing that filled me with terror. Sometimes we would hike to the All-American Canal; we did something there which probably remains one of the dumbest things I was ever to do. I don't think I was ever to be as anxious or panicky as I was that first time I "Shot the Bridge!" There is a power plant that is located next to the canal and, at the time I lived there, was fenced with a large "Keep Out" sign on the gate. Water was siphoned from the canal, and after it was used by the power plant the water shot out and under a long bridge. Sometimes, there was fencing under the bridge that was used to keep debris out. Later, when the debris began backing up, it was collected before removing the fencing. What made it so frightening was that we never knew if there was fencing under the bridge or not, so one of us would run to the far side of the bridge while the other boys climbed the fence surrounding the plant, then one of us would throw a large branch into the water, at the other end of the bridge where the water shot out of the power plant. If the branch didn't appear in a few seconds, the one at the far side of the bridge would signal us not to get into the water because the fencing was in place. Other times, when we knew the fencing was not in place, Tony and Fernando, and a few

41

other boys, would slip into the water and were quickly shot under the bridge.

At first I refused to do it, but finally, when Tony and Fernando double-dared me, I did try it. The first time was by far the most-frightening for me. I was shaking as I slowly slid into the water. Just before reaching the area where the water shot out of the plant, I almost turned back; but I had received a double-dare, so it was too late to back out now. Just as I was sucked into the flow, I took a deep breath and said a prayer. Instantly I was shot like a rocket into darkness. I was terrified, that first time, because it was pitch-black. The darkness remained that way for what seemed like eternity to me. My heart was pounding so hard that I could feel it as panic filled me. Then I began to see a speck of light, which got brighter and wider until I finally reached the far side of the bridge and swam to the bank. Those memories still haunt me when I think of what might have happened if the fencing was ever partially up.

Things went on like this until one day in about early September. Grandma Mendoza had always remained close friends with Grandma Navarro, so she had come with Mother and Roy to Yuma for a weekend visit. Grandma Navarro had moved from Cemetery Avenue by this time and was living on Orange Avenue in a duplex she shared with Uncle Louie and his wife Lydia. Actually, Grandma Navarro lived in an apartment on one side of the duplex with Helen, and my Uncle Louie and

Lydia lived in the other apartment, just across the hallway. After awhile Grandma Mendoza asked about me and said she wanted to see me, so she, Mother and Roy drove to where I was now living.

The moment Grandma Mendoza walked down the hill and saw me her face became distorted. She was sickened to see the conditions under which I was living. After hugging and kissing me, she turned to my mother and in the harshest words I'd ever heard her use, said, "Irene...you must have been crazy to send Ralphie to live in such a place." Nothing Mother could say would change her mind and Roy had the good sense to never say a word. Grandma Mendoza was unyielding: She wanted me out of there and she wanted out of there immediately! Mother started crying but that didn't matter to Grandma Mendoza, so we quickly gathered all my belongings, and, after saying goodbye to everyone, we returned to Roy's car.

When we arrived at Grandma Navarro's apartment, she was busy preparing supper; but she could tell instantly that something was wrong. Grandma Mendoza, who was still fuming, let out a barrage of words in Spanish that I'd never heard her use before. She said she didn't want to hear excuses for why I was living with the Hernandez family, and said that I could live with her if Mother or Grandma Navarro couldn't cope with me. Grandma Mendoza was emphatic: if I couldn't stay with Grandma Navarro, I wouldn't remain in

Yuma for even one-more day. Sobbing, while she sat in a chair with her hands covering her eyes, Grandma Mendoza said, if necessary, she and I would return to Los Angeles by bus that very same night.

Things were very tense from that point on. Even the next morning as we drove home in Roy's car, Grandma Mendoza would refuse to answer my mother when Mother would try to start a conversation. After dropping Grandma Mendoza off at her home, Mother, Roy and I went to where they were now living.

Mother had moved from East L.A. and now lived in an apartment building called The Brown's Apartments, which was located on 53rd Street, near the corner of Santa Fe Avenue. Immediately, I knew the reason both Mother and Roy liked living there so much. The reason was that there were two stores, each within one hundred yards: a liquor store on Santa Fe Avenue, just north of 53rd Street, and Tony's Delicatessen which was on 53rd Street, just down the block from The Brown's Apartments. It was very easy for either Mother or Roy to buy beer, wine and cigarettes there; and Tony's Deli featured great sandwiches as well as other assorted foods, and even sold everything in the store on credit to those whom the owner knew. We lived just down the block, so Mother always paid her bill on time. She could easily send me to Tony's Deli whenever she didn't feel like cooking or she just needed a pack of cigarettes.

I lived with Mother and Roy for awhile but eventually returned to Yuma. Mother called Grandma Mendoza to say that I was returning to Yuma, but would be living with Grandma Navarro again, so Grandma Mendoza finally accepted the thought that I would be safe living with Grandma Navarro. I think Grandma Mendoza would have preferred that I live with her. She had a modest, but well-kept home which had a extra, unused bedroom, and I remember thinking that living with Grandma Mendoza would be almost as nice as living at St. Catherine's. Grandma Mendoza truly loved me though I would sometimes do something that would irritate her. But she never spanked me, but instead, would patiently tell me I had to learn to behave so I would not upset people. To this day I'm sorry I didn't move in and live with Grandma Mendoza. I think if I had moved in with her, I would have gotten to know my father, Belinda, Laura, Nellie and Margo much sooner and better than I eventually did, because they lived on the next block, so Dad would come to visit his mother almost nightly.

Actually, what Mother told Grandma Mendoza was untrue. She had called Uncle Louie and asked if I could live with him but he too refused. Finally it was decided that I could live in the hallway between his and Grandma Navarro's apartment; so I was back on a Greyhound bus! The hallway I lived in contained only an old, fold-up army cot. That cot, along with my suitcase, a blanket and a pillow, were all that the hallway contained. That first night was probably the worst night I was to ever experience as a child or youngster. I just lay in my cot and sobbed under the pillow. I remember thinking, "I feel more alone tonight that I've ever felt in my life." Eventually I cried myself to sleep.

Mother had agreed to send Uncle Louie the same ten dollars she had been paying Mrs. Hernandez for my room and board. I was allowed to use Louie (which he preferred to be called) and Lydia's bathroom, but seldom was I included in their meal plans. Sometimes Lydia would bring me out a dish, so I would eat on my cot in the hallway and other times when Louie was not home she would invite me to join her. Lydia and I were great friends but the relationship between my uncle and me seemed strained so I think that is the only thing that kept us from becoming closer during that period of my life. Now, in 2009, Louie has passed away and Lydia has sixty children, grand children and great-grand children. She's known more than her share of sorrow too, so now I realize that others have suffered as I did during my youth. It's just the price we all must pay for living life I guess.

Grandma Navarro never seemed to care that I was living as I was, but she did include me for breakfast or supper on occasion when she cooked something special for Helen. By this time I had become an accomplished thief and would steal various lunch meats and other things from the markets in the area. I remember stealing cans of beer and drinking them behind our duplex; I did this until the manager of the supermarket began to suspect that I was the one doing the stealing. So I quit going to that market but continued stealing from other markets in the area. When it was time to start school again, I enrolled and went to Forth Avenue Junior High School, which is located just across the street from Mary Elizabeth Post Elementary School.

I finished the part of my schooling which I now call "My Yuma Days" by attending Yuma Union High School, then I finally returned to Huntington Park, where I completed my junior year at Huntington Park High School.

The only other thing that is noteworthy about the final time I was to live in Yuma was that it was the first time and place I ever had a sexual experience with a girl. Actually, to be truthful, it's the first time I ever had a sexual experience with someone other than myself!

What happened was that Mother and Roy had come again to visit Grandma Navarro and me. Grandma suggested that we go to visit her sister because neither Grandma Navarro nor Mother had seen Aunt Dora in quite-some time, so, Grandma, Helen, Mother, Roy and I all crammed ourselves into Roy's car and went to Aunt Dora's house. Since we hadn't been expected, Aunt Dora didn't have anything prepared but insisted we stay for supper. As usual, all the children were told to go outside to play or close the door to one of the bedrooms, so we wouldn't disturb the adults.

One of my female cousins had a girlfriend named Ruthie staying the weekend so we all played together until dusk. After supper, I decided to go into the bedroom and read a comic book, so I started to walk away from the table which had been set outside for us kids to eat on. When I turned around, Ruthie was following me. When I entered the bedroom I jumped on the bed and grabbed a comic book with one hand while my other hand rested on the bed. Just then Ruthie entered and when she climbed on the bed her butt landed on my hand. I was embarrassed and said something like, "Sorry!" Ruthie immediately answered with, "That okay…I like it there."

We were alone in that room and started playing that game all kids play at sometime in their lives: If you show me yours, I'll show you mine! When I saw what I had only seen in the bars during my shoe-shining days, I experienced a weird feeling that was a combination of fear and excitement!

Hers looked very different and had much-more hair than mine. Much later that night Ruthie and I snuck out of Aunt Dora's house and while lying on a blanket I was giving her a standing ovation so she took my virginity! What frightened me most about my first experience with a girl was not that I was finally going to lose my virginity – it was when Ruthie and I looked up to see my cousin covering her mouth so she wouldn't scream!

There remain periods of time that are still unclear to me.

Because I lived in so-many other places and went to so-many additional schools, which I have not included, I feel as though I have missed writing about additional events which readers might have found interesting. If you think it's difficult to understand about this period of my life – try living and then writing about it!

We actually lived in places for less than a week and then moved again. We even had boxes stuffed with clothing and other things that we hadn't unpacked yet. So the details are now too vague to allow me to write about them. This is, in no way, a complete account of that period of my life, and since almost every person I have written about has now died, there is no one with whom I can confirm actual facts and approximate dates.

However, there are certain things that remain clear in my memory, although the exact period of time in which they actually occurred, still remains unclear. I know Mother and I lived with Grandma Navarro, Louie and Helen in South Central L.A. and that we lived in the only home I was ever to live in that had a cellar. Helen and I would steal cigarettes out of Grandma's purse and go down to the cellar to smoke. On many occasions I would steal beer then Helen and I would go down into the cellar and drink it all before disposing the cans in the garbage. Other times I would go down to the cellar alone and do something I'm too embarrassed to write about; but sex was constantly on my mind, so I'm sure you can figure out exactly what I did down in that cellar! All I can say is: "Thank God for Ruthie!"

I also know Mother and I lived in South Gate as well Compton. What is memorable about the last time we lived in Compton are these two stories:

One night Roy brought another man to our apartment in Compton. There were only a few beers left, so Roy said he would go to the store and buy some more beer and wine, if the other man would pay for it. The other man agreed, but as soon as Roy left, the other man began to fondle Mother and place his fingers where they didn't belong, so Mother began to cry then ran into the bathroom. I did nothing other than to plead with the man to stop; so instead I waited. As soon as Roy opened the door, I ran to him and told him everything that had happened. Mother was in the bathroom so Roy calmly put the bag on a table then suddenly lunged at the man, grabbed him by the hair and yanked him out of the front door. He pounded that guy until he could do nothing but cry and beg Roy to stop. Roy even dropped to the ground and started chewing of the man's ear. When Roy was finally satisfied, he walked back into the house but I remained outside. There lay that man. He was only semi-conscious; half of his body was on the curb while his legs were in the street; and blood was trickling down his ear, as well as his mouth. The last thing I remember before entering our apartment was hearing that man moan. I was really proud of Roy that night. The second incident which occurred while we lived in Compton is this story:

Roy was back in jail so Mother was bored for a long time. Mother told me she was going on vacation and wanted to accompany two friends who were going to Kentucky or Tennessee. In all, she said, she would be gone for about twelve days, but wanted to know where I wanted to live during that time. Now that I look back, I realize it would have been the perfect time for me to stay with Grandma Mendoza, but that thought never entered our minds. Since school was still in session, we both thought it best that I remain at home. By this time I was completely self sufficient; at least I tried to outwardly look as if I was a confident kid. Inwardly, I was a wreck but managed to hide my feelings. A week later, her two friends arrived early Saturday morning. After placing her luggage in the car, Mother turned and hugged and kissed me and we both cried as we said goodbye.

The lonely feeling I felt now was completely different than the first night I slept in that hallway in Yuma. I guess it felt differently because now I was living at home, so there was very-little pain; instead I thought of all the neat things I could do for almost two weeks. I enjoyed sleeping in my own bed, so I slept well that first night.

The next morning, I was actually happy. Mother had left me enough money, so I knew I would be fine. I walked to the local market and bought milk and cereal then waited in line behind a man who was just about to leave. When I got to the cashier, he asked, "Do you know who that man is Sonny?" I didn't have any idea who the man was, so I said, "No sir...who is he?" He smiled at me then replied, "That's Duke Snider. He plays for the Dodgers!" Of course I knew who Duke Snider was; but I didn't recall seeing a picture of him. As I walked home that morning, I kept wondering just what Duke Snider was doing in Compton.

The two weeks passed quickly. I could easily take care of myself by now so nothing happened that was out of the ordinary except the following: I decided I wanted to go to see the Los Angeles Rams play a football game. Early Sunday morning I boarded a bus that led to downtown Los Angeles, but I got off and transferred to another bus, then got off in front of the Coliseum, where the Los Angeles Rams played. After watching the entire game while stuffing myself with hot dogs, popcorn, peanuts and pop, I returned home very happy.

When Mother returned I was overjoyed to see her. After saying goodbye to her friends, we sat in our apartment and I told her about what I had done while she was gone. When I told her about seeing Duke Snider, she immediately asked me, "Did you get his autograph?" My answer was, "Oh shit...I forgot!" Ordinarily I would have received a scolding or even a spanking but since Mother was so happy to see me she never said a word.

I know of another time, while living in South Central L.A., when I attended a different school. The reason this particular place remains in my memory is that I was the only Mexican boy who played flag football on an all-black team. I had a lot of fun going to school and playing with those boys. We used to "Wolf" on each other. For those of you who are not familiar with Wolfing, it is a response you give to someone who has embarrassed or insulted you. Here are just two examples: suppose Johnny has said something you don't like; a good response would be: "If You Mess with Me, You'd Better Run Fast, 'Cause Yo Mama's Got a Face Like a Bull-Dog's Ass!" Or, say someone has said something nice about Johnny, but you don't like Johnny; your response would be: "Johnny? Johnny's Tall...That All!"

Chapter Four

I Live with My Brothers

After leaving Yuma for the final time I returned to Huntington Park. Mother was still living at the Brown's Apartments in apartment 102. Roy had been caught doing something and was again in jail. During the time I covered in chapters two and three, my second brother, Eddie was born and was now a child living with his father whose name is Andrew. Mother and Andy were only married for a short period of time but when they divorced it was decided that Eddie would live with Andy's mother. Meanwhile our mother and Roy had a child. He was named Anthony, but we all called him Tony.

Now that I had returned to live with Mother, I wanted to experience living with Eddie and Tony, so after I enrolled at Huntington Park High School, I persuaded Mother to allow Eddie to live with us. After she discussed this with both Andy and Andy's mother the three agreed, so we drove to the North Broadway section of Los Angeles and picked up Eddie. We were now living in apartment 103 and would remain there until just before Roy was released from jail.

Mother was forced to work either the swing (4:00 p.m. to midnight) or the graveyard (12:00 a.m. to 8:00 a.m.) shift so I would be home each afternoon and evening to supervise Eddie and Tony. Mother worked at American Can Company where she had worked for many years. The company was located less than two miles from 53rd Street and the Brown's Apartments. Eventually she settled on the swing shift because I would arrive home just a few minutes after my last class and well before she had to clock in at work. In all, we lived in seven or eight apartments in that building, and after leaving the Brown's Apartments, we moved into a nearby apartment which resembled a courtyard but was also on 53rd Street. Finally, when I was sixteen, we moved to Pacific Boulevard which was within two blocks of 53rd Street. Mother and my three brothers would go on to live in many, many other places, but, I had decided to quit high school after my junior year and join the United States Air Force on July 13, 1960. It's impossible to forget that date because I was born on July 13, 1943.

Getting to know Eddie and Tony was a fabulous experience for me; we three bonded almost instantly. Eddie's left eye was injured when our mother took Eddie along with her to a party. Some man had accidently inserted a lit cigar into Eddie's left eye. There was no permanent ocular damage, but the nerves in the area of his left eye had suffered permanent damage. The disfigurement caused Eddie to squint from his left eye, so he was embarrassed about his looks at first, but that was about the only thing that kept Eddie from bonding with me sooner. Tony was still too young to notice, so Eddie's appearance never actually bothered him when he would play with Tony. Ramon was born after I joined the military, completed boot camp and was stationed in Little Rock, Arkansas, so I know very little about his early life.

Each school day after our mother left for work Eddie and I would play with Tony; but Tony was really a handful, so he was very hard to control. If you didn't watch Tony constantly, he would bolt out of our apartment and run up to the second or third floor before one of us would finally grab him. Once, he even climbed out onto the second-story fire escape, but before either Eddie or I could get to him he fell to the alley below. When Eddie and I reached him he was crying, but otherwise not seriously hurt. Still I had to call Mother at work to tell her about it and I definitely caught Hell when she returned that night.

I almost-always cooked our supper, but on those occasions when our mother left us some money we would buy our food. On other occasions Mother allowed us to charge for our food at Tony's Deli. Eddie would walk to Tony's Delicatessen and charge for a large sub sandwich or something. Both Tony's macaroni and potato salads were delicious, so on those days when Eddie did bring home food from Tony's Deli, he always included a salad. Tony (the owner) or one of his two sons was always there, so they knew Eddie well and liked him and had an agreement with our mother which allowed us to buy or charge everything. After eating, Eddie or I would give our Tony his bath. Each night, before going to bed, I ironed all of Eddie's and my clothing for school, but there was always plenty of time to play and watch TV before going to bed. Eddie and Tony went to bed at about 9:00 p.m. and I would follow after cleaning things up, so our mother wouldn't be upset with how we had left the apartment. I still can't understand why, because that whole building was infested with rats and roaches!

Have you ever been forced to eat a meal with roaches crawling all over the table or into your food, or seeing a rat run down the hall? Believe me, it is definitely not a pleasant experience; but was one which we just learned to live with. We continued with this routine for well over a year, so everything seemed pretty-much normal during that brief period: if you forget about the filth, rats and roaches, that is!

Without question, the most-shattering experience which once again altered our lives occurred one Saturday morning. On that particular Saturday morning we were still living in apartment 103, but were preparing to move into apartment 107 the following week. Mom and I were still asleep when Eddie suddenly ran into the apartment shouting, "Ralphie, Ralphie, a man is hurting Tony." I immediately threw on my pants and ran outside with Eddie following directly behind me. I couldn't see anything but I could hear Tony crying.

There was the back-seat door to a car open so I ran there because that's where Tony's cries seemed to be coming from. What I saw was sickening! A large man was on top of Tony and our brother was lying on his stomach with his pants pulled down. The man was attempting to sexually molest Tony just as Eddie and I arrived. Eddie and I began to pull the man off of Tony but it was obvious that he was much stronger than me or us.

I was fighting him off me when all of a sudden Eddie came running at the man with a board that had nails in it. Yikes! Eddie must have hit that man five times as I was biting the man on his thighs and legs; then the man took off running. He had blood all over the back of his shirt from the nails on that board. We fetched Tony and the three of us ran inside and calmed Tony down without ever saying a word to our mother.

Mother would pay me for watching my brothers, so when I had saved up enough I'd take Eddie and Tony to the movies. This one time I seemed to have enough money so I took my brothers on the streetcar to downtown Los Angeles. But, before I dared take Tony anywhere, I used to have to place a restraint on him that resembled what you might see on a dog; otherwise he would dart off in any direction.

People stared at us when we boarded that streetcar and later walked along the streets of downtown Los Angeles. There is a place there called Clifton's Cafeteria that had the greatest buffet. Of course it was the only buffet at which I had ever eaten, so I had nothing to compare it with, but looking back on the many buffets at which I've eaten, I still feel it was the finest. This place was so beautiful that Eddie and Tony just gawked at the water display that was located at the front entrance. Eddie and I were excited and Tony was acting wildly so I had to calm Tony down because we were beginning to attract the attention of the restaurant's manager. So we quietly got in line and filled our plates. Each of our hands was stamped when I paid for the three of us so we could return for second portions. Since we were allowed to have all the food we wanted, we returned several times and each time selected a different dessert. After eating 'till we were stuffed, I took them to the movies before returning home. Until I quit high school and joined the Air Force, Eddie, Tony and I had many such times together – just we three.

Another episode that remains in my memory is when Eddie was in a Christmas play. His class was doing *The Little Drummer Boy* and Eddie was the drummer boy. Everything was going normally, when suddenly Tony took off and ran on to the stage. Tony couldn't see anything because of the bright lights so he turned towards us and shouted, "Eddie, I have to go pee!" Our mother was furious and told me to go get Tony. I fell to my knees and crawled as I approached the stage, but Tony was running all over that stage and didn't stop until he found Eddie. Finally, I managed to pull Tony off the stage and brought him back to our seats. Needless to say, everyone was laughing and those poor children performing the play had completely lost sight of what they should be doing so it was a bit disorganized until their part of the play had ended. Stories like these – and I have many – always give me a warm feeling deep inside, because that period of time was the only period in which the three of us lived together.

Eddie, Tony, Ramon and I all had different fathers. Eddie is Edward Valles (pronounced Viyes), Tony is Anthony Reyes and Ramon is Ramon Rivas. Ramon's father is named Raul and I hated him! Even though Ramon now realizes that his father was not Roy, he still chooses to retain Roy's last name; so he calls himself Ramon Reyes. Roy was a completely different person from Andrew Valles (Eddie's father) or Raul Rivas (Ramon's father.) I definitely cared for Roy the most. I think Roy was the first man, other than my father, whom I truly loved.

A child always loves each of his parents and I definitely loved both my mother and father; but Dad was never around to give me guidance. Roy was; if even in his misguided way. Roy actually tried to teach me what I should be doing; not as he was doing. When Roy spoke to me, he always spoke in such a gentle way with his arm around my shoulder; so I tried to understand what he was trying to teach me. Roy said that I was really the man in our mother's family, so I was responsible for helping both Eddie and Tony, because, as he said many times in his broken English, "I won't always be around to help them with their problems; but you will!"

Eddie, Tony and I had many happy evenings with Roy while our mother was at work. Roy would chase us around our house and when Roy would catch me, we would always pretend to be in a boxing match; so when I'd throw a punch, Roy would fall to the floor and pretend he was injured. Or, when Roy would catch either Eddie or Tony, he would turn them upside down and blow air on their stomachs which sounded exactly like the sounds Grandma Navarro use to make when we lived on Cemetery Avenue. The only difference in the two was that the sounds Roy made didn't stink! All of us would sit and laugh at Roy as he told us tales that we knew were untrue; but we didn't care. I don't remember any of us three kids ever receiving a spanking from Roy; instead, in his butchered English, he would point his finger at us and say, "Some of these days...!"

When Roy was confined to a work camp, Uncle Louie, Mother and I went to visit him while my Aunt Mercy watched Eddie and Tony. Roy complained so much that he convinced Louie to help him escape. Roy had already devised a play that he was sure would work. So he asked Louie to be waiting for him that night when Roy climbed the barbed-wire fence which enclosed the work camp. Roy also convinced our mother that he missed her so much that he was going to crack up if she did not agree with his plan; so it was agreed that, exactly at midnight, Louie would be waiting in his car with the lights out, but the engine running. After returning to Watts to pick up Eddie and Tony, we all returned to our 53rd Street apartment and waited for night to fall. The work camp was located in Angeles National Forrest and was in the middle of nowhere, so, if you climbed the fence, you had to have someone waiting for you, otherwise you would have to hike all the way back to civilization and risk the chance of being caught and arrested again; which would mean that your sentence would be extended or even worse.

When the time came for Louie to leave, he asked me if I wanted to go along. Mother was reluctant at first, but between Louie and me, we persuaded her to allow me to go. Louie said there was no real danger to me: if caught only he and Roy would be arrested, and I would be returned to her; so she finally agreed. I was so excited I couldn't contain myself! When we arrived at our destination, Louie drove well past the work camp, turned off the lights, turned around and coasted to where he had agreed to meet Roy. A few minutes past midnight, by the lights of the compound, we could see Roy quietly, but quickly, climb that barbed-wire fence then sneak quietly to our car. Louie had the trunk unlocked, but open, so Roy immediately jumped into the trunk then Louie closed the lid. After jumping into the front seat, Louie coasted, with the lights out, for about a mile before he turned on the lights and shifted the car into gear. He didn't release Roy from the trunk until we were well clear of the area. Louie immediately found a liquor store and bought cigarettes, beer and wine. We had to stop again before arriving at Mom's apartment because we had already finished the beer! Finally, after a few more beers, Mother and I began to relax while Louie finished the beer and Roy drank that entire bottle of wine.

In a way we were ignorant because we didn't realize that the police could easily trace Roy's probable location, so a few nights later, the police arrived in full force. We were now living in apartment 107 and everyone had gone to bed. Eddie, Tony and I were in one bedroom, and Mom and Roy were in the other. The way the apartment was situated, the two bedroom windows were toward the back of the apartment and were located directly next to the alley. Suddenly there was a banging at the front door, and we could hear a police officer yell, "Police...open the door!" We kids all ran into Mom's bedroom to find Roy pulling up his pants and jumping into his shoes, but as soon as he raised the window shade, very-bright lights came on. There were several police officers waiting, with guns drawn, and the one in charge hollered, "Roy we know you're in there, open the window and climb out with your hands up, or I swear, you'll die tonight!" Roy didn't try to resist because he knew there was no way out. Roy climbed out and the police cuffed him and threw him into a police car.

When Roy was released from jail, Mom, Eddie, Tony and I were living on Pacific Boulevard. Around this time Roy and Mother got married. We all drove to Yuma for the ceremony and I was the best man. Later we had a great celebration at Grandma Navarro's apartment. Most of our relatives were there, even those who didn't like Roy, but Mom was happy so that's all we cared about. Roy managed to briefly stay out of trouble but he still never worked a day longer than it took for him to collect his unemployment compensation. So as soon as he became eligible, he stopped working. He would clean the house and do all the cooking while our mother worked. Roy and I were sitting out on the porch one night while Mom was at work and Eddie and Tony had gone to bed. I asked him what it was like to live in jails, prisons and work camps and about the men he had known. I had always felt that it was a rotten way to live but I was curious so I asked Roy to tell me all about his experiences. Roy said that I should live my life so that I would never have to experience a life like his, and then he told me about Raul. Roy said he had met an inmate named Raul who he liked at first, but as Roy said it, "Raul will take it up the ass without even putting up a fight." Roy said he had lost all respect for Raul and no longer wanted anything to do with him. I'm certain that if Roy had ever been confronted with that situation they would have had to kill him before he would have submitted.

Roy was a fearless fighter and a great thief. I have countless stories of the times I spent with Roy where we would steal anything. Once we stole tires and oil from one gas station, then sold them to another gas station a block or two away. Of course, we'd immediately head to a liquor store and even stole from them! All it took to make Roy happy was to have our mother close by, to have Eddie, Tony and me safe and to have a bottle of wine and a pack of cigarettes with him, and I seldom found Roy when he was not sitting next to Mom with a pack of cigarettes in his pocket and a glass of wine in his hand.

It was always a treat for Eddie, Tony and me when Roy and our mother would take us camping. We boys would sleep outdoors, while Mom and Roy slept in a small tent. We would all awake to hear Roy singing Mexican songs while making pancakes, bacon, eggs and coffee. On one such trip, we actually left Tony behind, but didn't realize it until we were far down the mountain. When we returned to our campground, there was Tony, playing some kids he had just met!

When Roy was back in jail he never knew that Raul had ever met any of us or had come to our apartment several times and was now having a relationship with our mother. Mother made us promise to never mention Raul's name in front of Roy. So while Roy was in jail Raul came to our apartment on Pacific Boulevard, under the guise of attempting to make up with our mother. I didn't like Raul from the first moment I met him and had grown to despise him! Raul was always trying to impress everyone with his manliness and told stories about being a Marine and a championship-caliber karate expert. He even lied to the extent that he said he was once a karate instructor. But Raul was a coward who only hit women and children!

He quickly charmed our mother into allowing him to live with us. Eddie, Tony and I slept in the only bedroom in the apartment while our mother and Raul slept in a large hallway between our bedroom and the kitchen. On a few occasions, when I had to go to the bathroom, I found Raul and our mother having sex and I didn't like it one bit! The smell of Raul's dirty feet and his stinky socks would permeate our entire house. On several occasions, when our mother was at work, Raul would punch me in the stomach and I'd bend over and attempt not to cry, but would finally run into our bedroom and sob. He would often hit Eddie for no apparent reason. Raul definitely disliked Tony, because Raul knew that Tony was Roy's child. I told our mother that we didn't like Raul because he was cruel. I am unable to forget her answer; she said, "Ralph, don't ask me to choose between Raul and you or your brothers. If you force me to make that choice, I'll choose Raul every time."

That's when I knew I had to get away. I wish Eddie would have been allowed to return to live with his Grandma Valles, where he was safe and happy. Just getting away from the life we were forced to endure may have altered Eddie's life. Now I'm sorry for persuading our mother to allow Eddie to live with us. There is not much I could have done about Tony. I know if Eddie had stayed where he was before, Tony would have still been forced to live with our mother; at least until he was older and could also escape. But, none of that ever happened, so Eddie and Tony would have to remain; but I finally did get away.

The greatest fight I ever witnessed was the day I saw Roy almost kill Raul in the most-brutal fight I was ever to witness. Here is how it happened:

Our mother was at home, but she immediately left when Roy called her to ask her to pick him up. She was going to a party in White Fence where Roy was briefly spending the afternoon now that he was again out of jail again. He couldn't drive to our house because our mother had Roy's car. White Fence is actually the name of a gang which controlled that area where the party was being held, so we just became used to calling the area White Fence. Our mother had left me to care for Eddie and Tony but had also left the phone number I could call in case she was needed.

About an hour after Mom left, Raul knocked on our front door. He asked me if our mother was at home and when I answered that she had left an hour ago he hit me again because he seemed frustrated. He just pushed me aside and walked in and went into the kitchen and grabbed a beer out of our refrigerator, then sat down at the table to read. Instantly I knew this was my chance for revenge. I quietly called the number our mother had left, and asked to speak with Roy. A minute or so later, Roy picked up the phone and I told him Raul was here at our apartment and was looking for Mom. In one second, I could hear the rage in Roy's tone. Roy asked me not to say a word to Raul; he just wanted me to lie and say that our mother wanted me to take Raul to the party and would be waiting. I ran into our room where Eddie and Tony were playing and told Eddie that he was in charge. I think I said our mother needed us, so Raul and I had to leave to help her. That was fine with Eddie, so I rushed into the kitchen and told Raul that our mother was excited to hear that he was back, and wanted me to drive him to the party. We jumped into Raul's car and I drove while Raul drank beer after beer.

When we arrived, Roy and Mom were sitting in the back seat of someone's car. I noticed Roy because he was getting out of the car even before I stopped. Immediately Raul's face took on a frightened expression as Roy continued to approach. Just after that I heard Mother say, "Roy, please don't!" I remember that my hands were sweating as I waited to see what would happen next. Roy stopped at a right angle to Raul; the only words Roy said, in Spanish, were that he was about to beat the shit out of Raul. Before Raul could respond, Roy threw a vicious right that landed squarely on Raul's left cheek. Down went Raul; he was now on his hands and knees, so Roy kicked Raul in his mouth so hard that teeth fell to the ground and blood gushed out of Raul's mouth. But Roy was not yet satisfied, so he kicked Raul five or six times before finally spreading Raul's legs and kicking him squarely in the nuts! Raul never threw a punch; he just lay on the ground writhing in pain. Other guys from the White Fence gang began to join in, and merciless continued to kick Raul in the head and body long after Raul was unconscious.

I don't actually know what injuries Raul sustained that day; I just know that someone had called the police and both an ambulance and two police cars arrived. Raul's limp body was being placed on a gurney as Roy was being handcuffed by two police officers. Roy never attempted to resist; instead he just kissed our mother and winked at me. I remember seeing Roy smile as he was once again being driven to jail.

I do know that before almost being killed by Roy, Raul stayed at our apartment on Pacific Boulevard long enough to get our mother pregnant again; this time she was pregnant with Ramon, but I had no way of knowing that at the time. If I had, I may have delayed joining the Air Force until after Ramon was born. Maybe that alone would have altered my future course as well as those of my three brothers.

I never saw Roy again after he was carted off to jail until Mom and Roy visited my wife and me at the second home our family lived in which was much later in time. We spent a nice afternoon together and Roy and I drank together for several hours. He said he was proud of me and thought I had come a long way from the way we used to live. I cried when I learned Roy had died from alcoholism in 1974. I will not attempt to judge Roy Reyes. Superficially he seemed to be a man no sane person would be willing to include in his or her life; but to me he was a very-special man. He taught me to treat others as they treated me and maybe if he had been raised in another time he would have become an entirely different human being. I will go to my grave thinking that he was a great man – a man I truly loved.

Eddie was a very-loving person to all whom me he cared for; but Eddie had a temper, so you had better have a good reason if you confronted him. That was never the case when it came to the relationship between Eddie and me. All of my brothers called me "Big Brother" or "Bro." Whenever I'd spank or scold him, he would begin to cry and say something like, "Hey, Big Brother, I'm sorry...so don't be mad at me!" I could never stay mad at Eddie for very long, and soon, all was forgotten. But that was not the case when other kids would hurt Eddie. I'll always remember the time when we were living on Pacific Boulevard. Our apartment was actually a small house which was located at the read of several apartments; probably seven units in all. Directly behind our house was an alley where Eddie and Tony would play. One evening, a kid, who was much larger than Eddie, was walking by and pushed Eddie to the ground. Eddie came up swinging, so as the larger kid was punching him, Eddie was biting and punching the kid in the stomach, when suddenly, that kid kicked Eddie in the scrotum. Eddie fell to the ground and lay there in deep pain and was crying. Our mother went out to see what had happened, so when she brought Eddie into the house she pulled his pants down. She could see that Eddie had been wounded in that area. Mom immediately rushed Eddie to the hospital. Eddie had one testicle which was swollen and red. Eddie stayed in the hospital that night, but after returning home, he stayed out of school for over a week. I remember Eddie saying, "Big Brother...I'm going to get that kid!"

I would have preferred to beat the crap out of that kid for picking on a smaller kid, but I was seldom home. I had a girlfriend at the time, so I'd spend a lot of time at her house because both of her parents worked the swing shift; so she and I were alone most afternoons and evenings. Eddie found this two-by-four and waited in the alley hidden behind a large garbage can. Finally, one night, Eddie saw that kid coming down the alley and waited for the kid to pass the garbage can. Like a spring, Eddie jumped out and hit that kid on his back with the two-by-four. He continued hitting that kid who remained on the ground; Eddie didn't stop until that kid got up and ran away. That kid never messed with Eddie again!

Eddie went on to become a cook in the Army. He spent much of his time in Viet Nam and was never the same when he returned. He was constantly in trouble and was shot in the chest in a bar fight. Eddie was a drunk who would fight anyone at the drop of a hat. I guess when Eddie was in Viet Nam, Marvin Gaye was very popular with the G.I.s over there because Eddie would call me at all hours of the night, always drunk, and would say, "Hey, Big Brother...what are you doing?" Of course I would answer with a sarcastic reply and say something like, "What the Hell do you think I'm doing? I'm sleeping!" But I couldn't stay mad at Eddie for long so he'd soon have me laughing. Each time he'd call it was always for one reason: to listen to my Marvin Gaye records. He'd say, "Hey, Big Brother, play *What's Goin' On* and *Mercy, Mercy Me* for me so I can fall asleep." So I would sit next to the record player and hold the phone next to the speaker while he listened to those two songs. It never failed: each time I'd play those songs he'd be fast asleep when I finished. Eddie was found dead on the side of a dirt road in 1997. He had a full military burial, complete with Taps being played, and is at rest in Johannesburg, California. Of my three brothers, I was closest to Eddie. He had a quality of warmth about him that was genuine. To this day I miss him dearly! I made a CD of Motown songs and sent copies to all of my friends: the first two songs on that CD are *What's Goin' On*, and, *Mercy, Mercy Me.*

Tony, on the other hand, had a sweetness which was real and possessed a fabulous personality, so he never got into many altercations in the period we lived together. Tony would say or do something that had the opponent instantly laughing. He had that knack that few people posses: Tony could make everyone laugh!

Many years would go by, but one day I received a package in the mail. Tony had sent me a gift so I opened it. Tony had learned that I was in love with the game of golf, so he sent me a book titled, *The Bathroom Golf Book*. I thought it was very nice of Tony to be so thoughtful, but I was busy at the time so I never got around to reading the book; eventually, I tucked it away with the other books I was beginning to collect, and forgot about it. Additional years would again pass before I noticed that book while I was dusting.

Tony was suffering from diabetes at the time so I thought it would be nice to read a few chapters from the book my brother had sent. When I opened the cover, there was a note which said, **"Hey Bro, don't spend too-much time in the head! Ha, ha, ha!** The note ended with, **"Love, Tony and Sabina."** Directly below there was printed, **"See back page."** So I quickly turned to the back of the book to find this written, **"When I saw this book I immediately thought of you. Sabina and myself** (sic) **are going to start learning how to play golf. This friend of ours at our church has offered to teach us how. Maybe by next year if you stop by I might let you win a game! Anyway, Happy Birthday. Love, Tony, Sabina, and Family."** Pasted to the back cover was a two-dollar bill. There was a final note that said, **"P.S. I was going to give you a dollar for each year, but I already sealed the package! God Bless, Brother! Love Ya, Tony."** I have both the book and the two-dollar bill safely stored away.

Eddie and Tony were totally different, but I loved them both; just in different ways. Each had several qualities I admired. Those few years we spent together will forever cause me to cry and laugh: cry for what we were forced to endure as children, and laugh at those precious, spontaneous moments that can never be rehearsed.

Tony never deserved his fate, but he never caught a break! Tony spent much of his life in jail or prison. He had inherited Roy's love of alcohol and much later in his life he did often get involved in situations, so he was forced to fight. Like Roy, when Tony fought there were no taboos! He was caught robbing several places, so long periods of time would go by before I would learn that Tony was in jail or prison again. Toward the end of his life Tony found religion and was a pain to be around because all he and our mother would do was to sit around and say "Praise Jesus!" every fifteen seconds...or so it seemed. You could say that religion drove Tony and me apart, as it had with our mother and me, so I wouldn't hear much from Tony for long periods of time. On those occasions when I did call to find no one at home, the recorded message was always the same: "Jesus loves you and so do we." I would always hang up before listening to the entire recording, because by this time, I had formed a different opinion about the difference between faith and religion. I don't really know how many children Tony had, but I know there were a few before he married Sabina, and later, Tony and Sabina would have three more. The last time I saw Tony was at our mother's funeral. Tony stood up and briefly told about his life in prison before Sabina sang a song. The last time I talked with Tony on the phone, he was scheduled to have open-heart surgery. This was after he had one foot amputated. Tony never recovered from the last surgery; he remained in a coma for over eight months before dying in 2007. He is now at rest in Phoenix, Arizona.

Life can be very cruel at times. Eddie and Tony should have had a life each truly deserved: one rich with happiness and filled with great memories! But that's the way the dice fell for them. Neither of them ever received the breaks I received, so I guess each was destined to live lives filled with pain and sorrow until their deaths.

Some readers may be wondering how I managed to avoid some of the pitfalls that led two of my brothers to lead such difficult lives then die much-too early. I've often wondered the same thing and I'm certain the answer is that I was exposed to some very-good things along with all the ugliness I witnesses during my journey. St. Catherine's Military Academy was a fabulous start. We were required to shower each night and brush our teeth; we actually slept in pajamas, between two, clean sheets and even ate three meals each day. We swam in our indoor, swimming pool; played football, basketball and baseball; always supervised, and always by the rules. Each weeknight, we all drifted into the rec room, where we could read, watch TV, or play checkers or several other games; and before returning to our dorm, we always had a treat such as cookies or brownies, and always with a glass of milk or chocolate.

I never knew children could live such a wonderful life. But, to some fortunate people, this is a normal life for a child: but it certainly had not been one for me. But more than anything, I was exposed to normalcy for the first time in my life and I liked it very much. I could sleep in my dorm and not worry about what might happen to me that night.

Later, the Air Force and, most of all, the Fire Department proved to me that I didn't have to continue living the life I was exposed to for so long a time as a child and youngster. I often thank God for all the blessings I've received over the years. Even being exposed to those horrible things I saw was a blessing because they taught me to see exactly how I didn't want my life to turn out! I'm happy to say that I pretty much came through everything during my youth with only a few bruises!

There is a passage in Daniel Defoe's novel, *Robinson Crusoe*, which deals with what I am writing about now. The passage reads:

"How mercifully can our Creator treat His creatures, even in those conditions in which they seemed to be overwhelmed in destruction? How can He sweeten the bitterest providences, and give us cause to praise Him for dungeons and prisons!"

I am not an overly-religious man although I do have a faith which is unshakeable, so I do thank our Creator daily for allowing me to pass through those most-difficult times when I felt totally alone in this world!

Now, as I am writing this manuscript, I am also watching the movie, *The Hurricane* on cable TV. Ruben "Hurricane" Carter endured a lot in his life: poverty-sure, prejudice-without a doubt, but mostly he suffered from never receiving a break in his world. Ruben never disputed being charged for his first crime; but under certain circumstances, any of us would probably have done the same thing. Ruben basically retaliated when he was attacked by a man who wanted to mistreat him. Ruben pulled out a knife and wounded the attacker in his shoulder. He was severely punished by a judge who saw meanness in Ruben; but never realized that Ruben was, to some extent, forced to be mean in order to survive. The judge chose punishment over understanding, for this very-young boy who thereafter was in and out of jail and prison. The judge sentenced Ruben to reform school. Later, Ruben escaped from reform school, but, years later, after being recaptured, Ruben spent additional time in prison for his original crime. At the age of twenty-two, Ruben was falsely convicted of the murders of three people and served many, many years in prison before his conviction was overturned. This time Ruben fought as hard as he could; he even wrote a book, and with the assistance of several people, he was set free.

In many ways I can completely understand what Mr. Carter had to endure. He, Eddie, Tony and I had it pretty tough for a period of years in our lives; but somehow, unlike Eddie and Tony, Mr. Carter and I were both set free. Mr. Carter was set free the day his conviction was overturned and I was set free the day I jointed the United States Air Force.

Chapter Five

The United States Air Force

Although my life would drastically change during the three years and nine months I was in the Air Force, this time was but a brief period; one in which I learned discipline for the first time in my life. In some ways it was like the period I lived while attending St. Catherine's Military Academy, but we were never treated cruelly at St. Catherine's. For the first ninety days of basic training we were treated like dogs; this was a completely-new experience for me. I never got used to the debasement airmen received from those who had a higher rank, but since I never intended to make the Air Force my career, at the end of my enlistment I was satisfied that I had accomplished what I set out to do.

Before actually enlisting I thought about which branch of the service might suit me best. The Army and Marines were definitely out because I couldn't see myself crawling through brush and being fired at for three years; plus, I had heard that their boot camps were very tough so I didn't want any part of that! The Navy or the Coast Guard seemed like the branches

I would enjoy most: the thought of traveling the world and seeing things I might not have the opportunity to ever see again was very appealing to me. But after reflecting on it for awhile, I realized that neither the Navy nor the Coast Guard was for me either, because in the past, I had always become seasick each time I was aboard any vessel. I wanted to spend three years vomiting each day even less than I wanted to crawl on my belly and risk being killed! That left only one branch of the service left: the Air Force. I liked the idea of probably traveling overseas and being stationed in some exotic country, or if I was lucky, I might even be stationed in great countries I had only heard about, such as England, France or Italy. Yeah… it was either the Air Force would I would return to finish out my senior year at Huntington Park High School.

I went to the local recruitment center in Huntington Park. After speaking with the Air Force recruitment sergeant, I learned two things that would help us decide what was best for me. At first, the sergeant thought I was too young and should probably return to high school and possibly enroll in a few classes at a junior college before making such a drastic move, and he reminded me that if I enlisted, I would be committing myself to a four-year pledge. I also learned that I would have to take a general-aptitude test to see in what areas of knowledge I was either weak or strong. After telling him my situation, he realized that basically I running from the life I had lived for sixteen years, so he altered his view somewhat and said that maybe it wasn't a bad idea to join the

Air Force after all. He said, "Ralph, the Air Force is a great place to acquire an education while you're seeing the world!" So I took the test. When he reviewed the results, he said that I had little-or-no mechanical skills, nor did I have any knowledge of the sciences, but there was one subject in which I did possess some knowledge: English. He said he thought I would be best suited working in some office doing clerical work of some sort.

That didn't sound bad to me. I could picture myself living in Hawaii or some-other fabulous place, looking out at a beautiful view as I pounded away on my typewriter; but here there was a small problem: I never learned to type! When I told the recruitment sergeant that I had never taken a typing class, he replied by saying I could easily correct that problem: I could learn to type while being housed, fed and paid by the Air Force.

So I decided that the Air Force was the place for me on the spot. He gave me the necessary consent form Mother would have to sign and it was agreed that I would enlist on July 13, 1960. I had no trouble getting Mom to sign the form. She knew how much I wanted to leave and now both Eddie and Tony were big enough, so they didn't need me to watch over them any longer.

Mom, Eddie, Tony and I gathered together and Mom said a little prayer as we had some cake on the night before I left.

The boys drank pop but I drank beer. I knew that this would probably be the last opportunity I would have to enjoy a few brews for quite a long time, so I polished off plenty of beer that night. The next morning I was up before the sun because I was restless to be on my way. Mom got up shortly after I did, so we had a cup of coffee together. I quietly picked up the few things I was taking which consisted of a few changes of clothing and a toiletry kit. The recruitment sergeant had told me I shouldn't take much else because as soon as I arrived everything I would need would be given to me; however, a few changes of clothing and a toiletry kit were a must. We quietly left Eddie and Tony sleeping and got into Roy's car. Roy was back in jail so Mother had the use of his car while he was gone.

We arrived in downtown Los Angeles very early. I think the induction center didn't open until seven or eight each weekday morning, but there was no where to park so we had our final kiss and, while tears were running down Mother's face, we said goodbye. She turned to me just before she drove off and said, "I love you, goodbye and Happy Birthday!" She drove off as I walked up and down the street and waited for the front door to open. When that door finally did open, I was the first to walk in.

Suddenly I realized that I had just walked into a new world. If you've ever seen the movie, *Heaven Can Wait*, then you will understand what my experience was like: it was similar to Warren Beatty's as he is walking through the clouds. However, mine was different because, in my mind, everything changed in one second! After asking a few questions, I finally arrived at the desk of a sergeant who informed me that I was early. I would have to wait for over an hour until those men who were scheduled to be inducted arrived. The sergeant explained that we would all participate in the official induction ceremony together. That hour seemed like a day, as I kept asking questions: was I doing the right thing, or would it be better to finish high school first. Did I really want to take an oath which would bind me to the Air Force for four years? Finally I thought of what I was escaping and was certain that I was making the smart choice.

Earlier in the week I had called my father to tell him that I would be joining the Air Force in a week; his answer was predictable, he said, "Oh yeah…fine. Write when you can." That was it; not even anything like "I Love You" or "Good Luck" was said that could help me as I began my new life. Dad was never in the military because he had a ruptured ear drum which prevented him from enlisting after Pearl Harbor was attacked; so I guess in some ways it may have been understandable; but not to a boy who yearned for his father's love and approval!

Soon the time came to take our oath. The officer in charge of administering our oath had a very-solemn look on his face. He asked each of us if we were totally aware of what we were about to do; and he asked if we were prepared to honor our commitment for four years. When we all said, "Yes, or, I do," only then did he stand at attention and while holding the official oath if front of his eyes he said, "Alright then, stand at attention, raise your right hand and repeat after me." That moment, as I was taking the oath, I realized that I was crossing a line I would never be forced to return to: my life of living in squalor, filth and hunger was over. I was now an Airman in the United States Air Force!

Immediately after we took our oath we were assigned to a sergeant who explained that we would soon be boarding a train to San Antonio, Texas; that is where Lackland Air Force Base is located and is still the base where recruits go to receive basic training. The sergeant called it Boot Camp, so that's the way I will always remember the three months I was to be station at Lackland Air Force Base.

Before boarding the train that would take us to Union Station, we had something to eat; I already had begun to notice the subtle difference in the way we were spoken to. It wasn't anything drastic; but it was definitely different than we were spoken to before we took our oath. After we finished, the sergeant said, "OK men, grab your gear and board the bus. It's waiting outside." After a short ride, we arrived at Union Station in downtown Los Angeles. The sergeant stepped out and said, "Fall out, single file and follow me." We all stood waiting while the sergeant spoke with someone, and after a few minutes we were led to an area where we were to wait until it was time to board our train. The sergeant warned us by saying, "I won't be joining you, but I expect all of you to behave properly. You now represent the United States Air Force; so behave like gentlemen at all times."

After boarding the train, a porter showed us where we would be sleeping and told us to store our luggage there; or if we had valuables, we could store them in another section of the train. Since I only had a few changes of clothing which were only a few pair of pants and a few shirts, socks and underwear, as well as my kit in my suitcase, I just found any empty berth and threw my suitcase on the bed. Some of the others stayed there and sat on their beds and began to know get acquainted while others made their way to the other areas of the train. I wanted to see what the dining car looked like, so I headed there. There were only a few people in the dining car, but I quickly noticed a very pretty, black woman seated at a table and I was glad to see that she was alone. So after waiting a few seconds, I finally felt composed, so I walked over and asked if I could join her. She looked up at me and smiled so that was encouraging. After giving her approval, I hastily took a seat directly opposite her so I could look at her face. I guessed her age to be about twenty-two or so, but I wouldn't have cared a bit if she been thirty-five! The hormones were beginning to stir inside me so her age really was not what I was concerned about; what I was concerned about was finding a way to somehow, later that night, separate her from her clothing!

She was naturally pretty, with short, black hair and large, black eyes. Her nose was tiny and her lips were full and had a delicate shade of pink lipstick. She looked beautiful just sitting there, and when she smiled, her teeth were even and very white. I wanted to get a look at her body, but after she caught me examining her I remembered thinking that she felt awkward or uneasy, so I only concentrated on looking into her eyes, and decided right then and there to change my tactics. What also concerned me was the dread I would feel if some man would suddenly show up and destroy all my hopes. I would have happily stayed the rest of the day and all that night with that angelic woman. We engaged in idle chit-chat for awhile before I asked her where she was going. I don't even remember what her answer was; I don't think I even cared where she was going. All I knew was that somehow I had to find a way to have reason to hope that I could charm her into her bed later that night.

What turned our conversation from awkward to friendly was when I asked her, "Are you traveling alone?" She looked at me and laughed, then answered, "Unfortunately, yes." She suddenly seemed to have a sad look on her face, so I asked, "What's wrong? Did anyone in your family die? Are you sad because you're going to a funeral?" Her reply was, "No, no, nothing as bad as that. It's just that today is my birthday, and I'm sad because I'm alone...that's all."

Instantly I found what I needed to strike, so I just shook my head and smiled when I said, "You probably won't believe this, but today is my birthday too! I'm probably worse off than you because I'm traveling to San Antonio with a bunch of guys whom I just met today!" I don't think she believed that it was actually my birthday because who in his right mind would choose to enlist on his birthday and travel with a bunch of strangers. But it really was my birthday, so I wanted her to know that I was at least being honest. Then I looked her in the eyes and gave her a smile which said I really wanted to flirt with her. I remember answering her by saying, "If you want me to prove it, I'll go to the sleeping car and bring you proof." Her reply was instant, "No, that's not necessary, I believe you." By this time she knew I was big-time flirting with her but since she was only mildly flirting back I thought I'd better back off.

Just then the recruits with whom I was traveling with began to filter into the dining car. I turned to her and said, "Those guys just enlisted too." Then I remember feeling crushed when she said, "Actually, I have a lot of things I should probably do before they start serving dinner, so I'd better be off." "Hell," I thought, "I had blown it!" But, like a gentleman, I rose when she did as she began to leave the table. "I hope to see you later," was all that I could think to say; but she turned to me and smiled. "Sure thing," was all she said before turning and walking away. Now was my chance to give her a complete examination, so I gazed at her butt, and thought, "If her breasts are anything like her butt, and if I can find a way to charm her, I might just hit a home run tonight!"

When I joined the guys who were now seated, one of them asked, "Who in the Hell was that? How do you know her?" I laughed while trying to think of a perfect answer, but could only think to say, "She's someone I just met a few minutes ago. I think she immediately realized how good-lookin' I am so she asked me to join her." Another guy jumped in and said, "Sure … and I guess those good looks kept her with you, huh?" We all started laughing and took some time to start to get to know each other.

When we all returned for supper, there she was again, but in a different dress. Her table was full so I sat and ate with our group. Our supper was great that night. There was a clean table cloth on our table, and everything had been arranged on the table perfectly. But all through supper I kept thinking about her and waiting for bed time to finally arrive. Her upper berth was located one car from the recruits' sleeping car; I know because later that night, when she got up to walk away, I discretely followed her.

Later, after everyone was asleep, I pulled out my driver's license showing that July 13th was really my birthday, as it was hers. I tiptoed to her berth. The curtain was drawn, but I knocked on the ladder, so she opened the curtain just enough so that I could see that she was between the sheets. Fine, that's where

I wanted to see her, and hoped to join her in a minute or two. I instantly said, "Hi, here is my license, showing that today is really my birthday." But, sadly, she was having none of it. She knew that we were only strangers who would never see each other again. Her final reply that night was, with a smile on her face and a look that said she knew exactly what my intentions were, "I believe you – good night."

Instead of a home run, I had struck out with the bases loaded in the bottom of the ninth inning! That woman knew that I was really just trying to have sex with her. I'm sure she was actually amused and possibly even flattered that a kid would go to such lengths just to sleep with her but realized that basically I was just playing a game. But, like all games: sometimes you win; sometimes you lose; and sometimes the game is stopped because of rain. She sure did rain on my game that night! The next morning I tried to locate her but never did. I guess she must have left the train at a stop along our way. "Oh well," I thought.

The only *major* event which happened on our trip which remains in my memory happened on our final night on the train ride from Los Angeles to San Antonio. We were all in our berths when suddenly, at about 4:00 a.m., we were jolted back to awareness. Without a warning the car we were in left the tracks and slid on its side adjacent to the tracks; we all found ourselves lying – one on top of the next or next to each other – in the aisle of our sleeping car. Everyone was groggy and no one knew what had happened; but none of us was injured. We slowly made our way from our car, past the other sleeping car, which also had a few passengers leading our way. When we staggered into the dining car we learned that it was the third car that had landed on its side before being automatically uncoupled. From the front of the dining car we were each able to push and pull everyone to safety.

Now we could see the whole picture: three cars had derailed and were lying of their sides. The engine and those other cars which were not derailed were slowly backing from where they had come to a stop. The conductor, as well as a few others, ran to where we were standing and immediately asked if anyone was hurt, and if there was anyone left inside those cars which were lying on their sides. The recruits knew of none who was missing, so one of them said, "None that we know of." The conductor told his two assistants to start a search of all three cars but he left and ran back to the engine or some other car in the front of the train. Well, thankfully, no one was seriously hurt; shaken, but, miraculously, otherwise unhurt. We all boarded those cars which had not been involved in the accident then continued our journey. When the accident occurred we were already in Texas, so we only had a few miles to go before reaching San Antonio so we did the best we could to stay as comfortable as possible.

When we arrived at the train depot in San Antonio shortly after dawn, there was a drill sergeant and a buss waiting. I think our drill sergeant's name was Sergeant James, Johnson or Johnstone; but I have decided to use Johnstone because our drill sergeant turned out to be as hard as a rock and before our ninety days were completed most of us would have gladly taken a dump on him! In a rather casual way, he said, "Good morning ladies...fall in." The next thing Sergeant Johnstone said, again in an almost casual manner, was to inform us that the bus would be taking us to Lackland Air Force Base where, he said, we would be spending the next three months of our lives learning to become basic airmen. His last command was, "Fall out and board the bus." So we all hurriedly climbed the steps and found a seat. I remembered that San Antonio was just about the same as Yuma: there was nothing other than desert as we traveled the short distance to Lackland AFB. After we turned toward the sentry's location, which is always outside any military installation, Sergeant Johnstone showed the sentry our authorization, so the sentry pulled the handle which lifted the bar that would allow us to proceed. When the bus finally stopped, we all knew instinctively that we had finally arrived.

Sergeant Johnstone's tone and demeanor completely changed after we were on the base; now we were not in the public's view and we belonged to him for the next ninety days. If you've ever seen the movies *Full Metal Jacket* or *An Officer and A* Gentleman, you will remember what any recruit in each branch of the military goes though. Both Gunnery Sergeant Hartman (Lee Ermey) and Gunnery Sergeant Foley (Louis

Gossett, Jr. – Gossett won the Academy Award for that film) begin to judge the character, or the lack of character, in each man who is assigned to him.

Sergeant Johnstone immediately assumed that role; so he stood up and yelled, "Fall out and form a line according to height from left to right!" All of us jumped, as one unit, and hustled outside where we took a few seconds to move, one way or another, and were now in place. From the moment Sergeant Johnstone stepped off the bus, he went on a tirade!

"I thought I'd seen everything in my twenty-four years of service, but I have never seen a group as fuckin' sorry-lookin' as you. You ran away from your mommy's and daddy's did you?" was the first thing out of Sergeant Johnstone's mouth. As Sergeant Johnstone walked from one end of the line and returned, he continued, "Well I'm sure not your mommy and I don't think I'm your daddy, but, I am *definitely* your God for the next ninety days." He stopped as a military jeep was approaching, then continued, "From this moment on, I only want to hear three words ever come out of that hole in your face you call a mouth when I'm talking to you; and you may as well know now: I absolutely *hate* repeating myself! Those words are: Sir, Yes Sir; Sir, No Sir; or Sir, No Excuse Sir, is that completely understood?"

We were all shaken, so we tried to reply in unison, "Sir, Yes Sir!" But Sergeant Johnstone just gave us a contemptuous look which said he wasn't happy with what he had just heard so, as his cheeks seemed to become red, he said, "What did you sacks of shit say? I couldn't hear you!" This time we shouted, "Sir, Yes Sir!" Again Sergeant Johnstone fired back with, "What did you bunch of vomit just say, I still didn't heeeeeeear you?" Again we screamed as loud as we could, "Sir, Yes Sir!" Just then an airman jumped out of the back of the jeep and joined Sergeant Johnstone. Sergeant Johnstone said, "This fine-lookin' airman is what I am going to make it my business to turn you into; his name is Airman Thomas. Airman Thomas will show you how the United States Air Force expects you to march!" With that said, he turned to Airman Thomas and said, "I can't take any more of this shit; take over." Sergeant Johnstone immediately turned then entered into a barracks we all assumed would be our home for the next ninety days.

Immediately after Sergeant Johnstone left, Airman Thomas, who was far-less forceful when he spoke said, "What we are about to learn are four basic maneuvers you are expected to learn because you will be doing these exactly as I am about to demonstrate for the next four years." He showed us the correct technique for a Right Face, Left Face, About Face and when given the order to, March, he showed us how we must always begin marching by first beginning by stepping out with our left foot. He looked really neat as he performed all these maneuvers. When he snapped to attention he looked authentic and each time he would execute those maneuvers, he would always end each with a snap of his heels. I looked down and noticed that even though his boots were spit-shined there was definitely a scuff mark on each boot which the shine could not completely hide.

For over an hour we drilled on those four maneuvers then we were marched to the mess hall. Our group was suddenly laughed at as the other men, who were all dressed in fatigues, realized that we were raw, first-day recruits who hadn't even had our hair cut or obtained our uniforms. We all formed a line as our meal was scooped into our trays, filled our glasses with milk or juice and finally sat down. I observed that it seemed like it was possible to gauge the time the other men who ate in the same hall had been there just by looking at the length of their hair. We hurriedly finished our chow, so after disposing of our trays, utensils and glasses, we all returned to where Airman Thomas was waiting for us.

After a quick "Attention...Right Face" we were marched to the area where we would pick up all of our bedding first, but we returned several times to collect such other things as clothing, boots, etc. After returning to our barracks we were assigned bunks, so Airman Thomas picked one bed to demonstrate what a proper military bed should look like when prepared correctly. That's where I first realized that, from this day forward, I would be expected to perform certain functions in a completely military manner.

Just then Sergeant Johnstone opened his door and yelled,

"Ten…Hut!" We all snapped to the front of our bunks where Airman Thomas had told us we were expected to stand whenever Sergeant Johnstone entered our area. When Sergeant Johnstone said, "At Ease," we relaxed a few minutes as he said that at least we had learned to prepare our beds properly; then he gave us some information about what we could expect for the next week of our training. The casual tone he used didn't last long, however, so suddenly he hollered, "Ten…Hut! You're about to receive your first military hair cut courtesy of the United States Air Force! Dismissed, Fall Out in front of the barracks where Airman Thomas will march you to the recruit barber shop."

The first four men in line disappeared into the barber shop then, about three minutes later, all four looked totally different so we laughed at how strange they looked. It didn't last long before it was my turn to enter that shop. The first thing I was told was, "Sit" so I jumped into the barber's chair and a minute or two later was told I was finished, so I joined those others who were waiting for the remaining men in our group to finally join us. I don't remember everything we did that first day, but I do remember that before lunch we collected much of our clothing, boots and a few other things. Each time we returned to our barracks, Airman Thomas would show us how to hang each item in our lockers and fold everything else in an exact way. He even showed us what a proper foot-locker should look like.

After our evening chow we were marched to our barracks and told to shower and shave, then hit the sack. I remember thinking how odd it looked to have ten or so commodes arranged about two feet apart where each of us was exposed. It was not uncommon for four or five men to be seated just next to each other while they eliminated waste. I never got used to either that or the showers where we would all gather. Some guys didn't mind it and would laugh and joke around, but I never did feel comfortable being totally exposed, so I remember taking quick showers then getting into my skivvies. The barracks lights were still glowing as Sergeant Johnstone suddenly entered the sleeping area and walked from one length of our barracks then turned and walked back. He only said, "Goodnight girls!" and turned out the lights. A few minutes later I heard what I was to hear for three months: Taps. I think I started to build a shell around me, something like a turtle's shell so no one could enter my private world and hurt me.

However, shell or no shell, it is impossible to forget what happened the next morning and would continue to happen each morning until the final two days of basic training. I suppose this is happening even today. At precisely 4:20 a.m. Sergeant Johnstone walked out of his office and began to rattle his baton in a large bucket and said "Good morning ladies!" Then, in a much-different tone, he continued, "Fall Out! You have exactly ten minutes to dress your bed, dress yourselves, hit the head then fall in outside the barracks in proper formation." Most of us were still groggy because of our sudden awakening; but we leaped out of bed and began what was to become our morning routine: some men hit the head first, others brushed their teeth and some dressed their beds first while others were jumping into their fatigues and lacing their boot. At exactly 4:30 a.m. Morning Revelry was played twice by a bugler then each flight was given the order, "Sound Off." Our flight was named Flight 788-89 so Sergeant Johnstone, who was stationed at the head of our flight, would respond when it was his turn, "Sir, Flight 788-89 all present or accounted for, Sir!"

I don't remember if we remained assembled and double-timed it to the chow hall first, or if we were dismissed to change into our work-out attire, so we could do calisthenics first; but I suspect we sometimes did the first and would alternate between each. Double-time marching caused havoc with my stomach, especially after gulping down a meal. We would rush outside and line up in formation, then immediately begin to double-time march everywhere we went. For the first few weeks all we did was run, run and run; march, march and march; calisthenics were easy by now and I really enjoyed our obstacle course. I especially liked the first part where each man grabbed a rope then attempted to leap a pond; several recruits fell into the water but that didn't matter to either Sergeant Johnstone or Airman Thomas. Each who had fallen in the pond would return until he successfully leaped the water. What I didn't like was when we had to climb a rope which had many knots in it. At first I could only pull myself up to the third knots then was unable to continue. Suddenly, Sergeant Johnstone would scream, "Jesus Christ, Mendoza, are you sure you have a set down there?" But more than anything, I could see the look on my father's face if I failed. After about a week I pulled myself up until I finally touched the top board; then immediately slid down the rope as fast as I could. Whatever we did, there was always the ubiquitous Sergeant Johnstone screaming in our ear. That was our morning routine. After chow in the afternoon we were double-timed to the dentist, ear doctor, eye doctor or received our shots.

The dentists were by far the worst. They didn't care if they were causing us pain. They often did not wait long enough for the Novocain to take effect before they would begin to drill; that was an experience I was glad not to repeat, because only one tooth required filling, so I was in and out in less than thirty minutes. Others were not as fortunate as I was, so if their X-ray showed that they required many teeth filled they stayed longer; those poor fellows who had to have extensive work done were to return several times before the work they needed was completed.

Those first few weeks flew by; but the weeks that still lay ahead were different. Each morning remained the same; but after our afternoon chow, those remaining weeks seemed to drag and drag. Our afternoons were different because now we were attending classes each day. Many of us would often doze off because we were so hot and tired. Summer in Texas is not really the best time when you're in a hot Quonset hut with only a fan to cool you. We used to have to take salt tablets each morning and afternoon to replenish our salt, or risk becoming sick. Those Quonset huts had us sweating as much as double-timing, so the heat made us feel constantly sleepy. Some classes made it even worse because we had to view old military films which covered subjects like: survival in the field, first aid and rescue and learning the Uniform Code of Military Justice. The UCMJ was by far the worst because the lights remained on so we were often caught sleeping. The sergeant in charge of those classes would have us stand while he meted out some humiliation or another. Those of us who were caught sleeping were required to stand at attention for the remainder of our class.

I'm sure some or all of us wanted to just throw in the towel but, that was something I was unwilling to do. Deep in my mind I could see my father shaking his head and thinking, "I knew Ralph didn't have what is required to stay the course." That thought alone sustained me when I felt like quitting no matter what the consequences of my actions would bring me. Some men didn't make it. I remember wondering what happened to those men whose bunks we would find undressed; with only a mattress where there had once been bedding. Fortunately, only two men washed out of our flight, but still that was a sad experience.

So this was how it remained for what remained of our ninety days. One day that sticks in my memory is the day we received our first pass; I think we received it just after our seventh week. Our pass was only good for the hours of 12:00 p.m. to 8:00 p.m. so we hurried to the bus stop and anxiously waited for the bus that would take us to San Antonio. A few of us gathered and decided to stay together that day. The first thing I remember was wanting to enjoy a good Mexican meal so I brought up the subject, and we all agreed that we would first eat, then see the sights and hope to meet girls. I suspected that there was some saltpeter in our salt tablets to numb the hormones which were flowing through all the young men. Sometimes we'd see someone go into the head so we knew what he was probably doing in there; I often did the same thing: at least it provided temporary relief so I could get some sleep.

We found a place that looked nice and clean, so we entered. After a few minutes, a waited tapped me on the shoulder and asked, "Did you notice the sign at the window?" I answered, "No sir, I didn't." He replied with a sarcastic remark, "Well, why don't you waltz outside and read that sign!" Sure enough, there was a sign which read: **NO DOGS OR MEXICANS ALLOWED!**

When I reentered the café and told the other recruits what was written on the sign, we all got up and walked out. I remember thinking how ironic it was to allow Mexican cooks and others of Mexican ancestry to work in the café, yet not allow Mexicans to eat there. This is actually the first time I was jolted into the reality of discrimination. Certainly I had heard about discrimination before; my father used to talk about it all the time. Dad would often say things about when he was growing up in the Zoot-Suit era of the early 30s.

But this was the first time I had ever come face-to-face with an actual problem; obviously, kids would say something once in a while, but remember that I had basically grown up with either brown or black people, so I was unsophisticated with the art of discriminatory treatment of others who were not white! We found another café which was not discriminatory, so we had a pleasant Mexican meal; then headed out to find chicks, and hope we got lucky enough to get laid. Well, none of us were lucky that day, so it was back to the head for some of us!

Another night which will forever remain in my memory is the night I was caught sleepwalking. About that time we were studying the UCMJ, Sergeant Johnstone came out of his room and shouted, "Ten...Hut!" He went from one recruit to the next and handed out some papers which were paper-clipped together in a folder he was carrying, Sergeant Johnstone passed out two or three sets of papers then suddenly stopped. In his now all-too-familiar style, he said, "Men, these are what is known as General Orders. Each of you will have to commit to memory each of these, and will recite, verbatim, exactly what is written on these pages I am now handing out." As he continued passing out our General-Orders sheets, he continued, "I don't want to hear a paraphrase, I will not accept an interpretation, what I want you to do is to recite each General Order exactly as it is written on the pages you are now holding. Am I making myself perfectly clear?" Immediately we answered with, "Sir, Yes Sir!" So for about three nights each recruit was given an hour to study our Ten Commandments, as we called them. Actually I believe there were eleven General Orders we were required to quickly learn.

On about the forth night after being given our General Orders, as we were entering our barracks, we noticed a table, lamp and chair which had not been there before. A few minutes later, Sergeant Johnstone slammed his private door and shouted, "Ten...Hut!" We quickly jumped into formation, directly in front of our bunks and awaited his next words. "Men, as of tonight, each of you will stand guard at the front door to this barracks. You see what has been set up next to my office? That is where each of you will assume the role of sentry and stand post. No one is ever to be allowed to enter or exit this barracks unless I personally approve it. Is that completely understood?" "Sir, Yes Sir" was our response. Sergeant Johnstone walked to the first bed and said to the man that was standing there, "You're first. Your watch will last exactly two hours then you will wake the man directly to your right, and after doing that you will return to your post. Never will you ever abandon your post until properly relieved, is that completely understood?" Again, "Sir, Yes Sir" echoed through our barracks.

About two weeks later, I must have gotten up while still asleep and placed my pith helmet on my head, then walked out of the barracks. Apparently, I had accidentally chosen that exact moment to leave the barracks as Bobby Davis, standing post, had briefly gone to the head; this is only what I assume happened. What I actually remember is waking to find Sergeant Johnstone's hand on my shoulder and turning me around. He was not mad at me, so he never uttered a word as he walked me up the steps and back to my bed. He only said, "Mendoza...go to bed." Then all Hell broke loose as he suddenly turned on the lights. He placed his face about an inch or two in front of the Airman Davis' face and his unexpected tirade woke everyone, so we all just sat in our bunks as he continued, "Airman Davis, exactly what does General Order Number 2 say?" Bobby, who was now shaking, replied, "Sir, General Order Number 2 states: I shall stand my post in a military manner, keeping always on the alert and observing everything that takes place within sight or hearing, Sir!" Sergeant Johnstone shouted, "Airman Davis, why did you do fail to obey General Order Number 2?" As Bobby began to answer, Sergeant Johnstone interrupted, "Airman Davis, what does General Order Number 5 say?" By this time poor Bobby was totally shaken, so he stammered," Sir, General Order Number 5 states: I shall quit my post only when properly relieved, Sir!" Sergeant Johnstone continued, "Airman Davis, did you fail to obey General Orders Numbers 2 and 5?" Bobby Davis' only answer was, "Sir, Yes Sir!" Now Sergeant Johnstone began to pace back and forth, then stopped and said to everyone, "Grunts ... apparently none of you heard or understood how import our General Orders are. By violating two specific General Orders, Airman Davis put us all at risk. Airman Mendoza was found outside the barracks sleepwalking. For those two violations, all passes for everyone are cancelled and will remain cancelled until I give further orders." With that said, Sergeant Johnstone stormed back into his room.

The barracks was as quiet as I ever remember it being. The next morning a few things were said to Bobby, but nothing serious, so the incident was forgotten. The night I first stood post, the sentry who wanted me to relieve him, shook my bed and whispered, "Mendoza, it's time for you to relieve me." I quickly jumped into uniform, hit the head and quietly relieved him. But you can bet your sweet ass that I read and reread each General Order that night!

About a week later, Sergeant Johnstone began calling each of us into his office. We all assumed he was going to drill us on our knowledge of the General Orders. When I heard, "Airman Mendoza, Ralph G. report to my office," I jumped out of bed then gave Sergeant Johnstone's office door one hard knock. When I opened his door, I snapped to attention and said, "Sir, Basic Airman Mendoza, Ralph G. reporting as ordered, Sir." Sergeant Johnstone was seated behind his desk so he looked up at me and asked, "Airmen Mendoza, how many buttons are on your fatigue jacket?" I had been caught flat-footed because none of the other recruits had mentioned being asked that question. I was suddenly confused, so I looked down at my fatigue jacket and began counting buttons, when Sergeant Johnstone screamed at me, "For Christ sake, Mendoza...what are you doing?" I snapped back to attention, then immediately replied, "Sir, I was counting my buttons, Sir." Sergeant Johnstone got up and stood directly in front of my face, then continued, "Mendoza ... you're the dumbest bastard I've ever met! What should your proper response have been?" I was trembling as I answered, "Sir, my proper response should have been, Sir, I don't know, Sir!" Sergeant Johnstone sneered at me, before replying, "Well, at least you *seem* to understand English! You're dismissed." When I left his office, I ran into the head, ripped my down my trousers and instantly had an attack of diarrhea!

As the week flew by we became seasoned recruits. We took pride when we marched and repeated a cadence which one member of our flight was assigned to lead. It went something like this: "I don't know but I've been told" which the man assigned to lead us in cadence would start to sing; this was followed by the flight repeating, "I don't know but I've been told." Then our leader would chant, "Air For life is getting old," after we repeated that, he'd ask, "Am I right or wrong" so we yelled in unison, "You're Right," that cadence was repeated again, then he's say, "Sound Off, Sound Off" and we would follow with, "One two, three four; one two...Three Four!" We had several different cadences we used and definitely enjoyed ourselves when we would pass first-day recruits.

The last two day we seemed to let our guard down because we all knew we had passed our first test. After returning from chow Sergeant Johnstone entered our area with a clip board and a folder in his hand. When he named a recruit, the recruit whose name was called would snap to attention then march to Sergeant Johnstone. When Bobby Davis' name was called he snapped to attention in front of Sergeant Johnstone and said, "Sir, Basic Airman Davis, Robert B. reporting as ordered, Sir!" Sergeant Johnstone didn't even look at Bobby – he didn't even smile or congratulate him – as he handed Bobby his assignment paper. I guess he had never forgiven Bobby for the sleepwalking incident. Sergeant Johnstone would then open his folder and pull out a paper which showed where other recruits would next be assigned. Sergeant Johnstone would say something like, "Congratulations Airman Shultz. I see your next assignment is as a mechanic so you'll be attending a mechanical school in New Jersey before your next assignment." We were all envious when we learned that a recruit in our flight was going to Scotland for his first assignment. He was the only one in our flight to immediately go overseas for his first assignment. I was informed that I would not be attending any technical school, but would report directly to Little Rock Air Force Base in Jacksonville, Arkansas.

Only after Sergeant Johnstone dismissed us did we become more casual and relaxed as we packed our gear into our duffel bags. That night is the only night I remember spending our time as leisurely as many of those evenings depicted in *Biloxi Blues*. We did have a few nights where we had a few minutes to exchange jokes and such as we prepared for Lights Out; but these were much fewer and shorter. We never lounged around every night to exchange stories like Eugene Morris Jerome (Mathew Broderick), Arnold Epstein (Corey Parker) and Joseph Wykowski (Matt Mulhern) did, as they kicked back and exchanged stories. Sergeant Johnstone was definitely not as easy as Sergeant Toomey (Christopher Walken) was during that movie about World War Two training.

On the last morning we said our goodbyes to the few friends we had and I made it a point to thank Airman Thomas for all his consideration and help. After our last breakfast together, we parted. As I was walking to the bus with my duffel bag slung over my shoulder, I stopped and suddenly started to laugh. There was Sergeant Johnstone was going through his ritualized debasement of his new, first-day recruits! It was exactly like the scene where Zack Mayo (Richard Gere) had just completed Officer Candidate School and sat for a moment to watch Gunnery Sergeant Foley (Louis Gossett, Jr.) chew out yet another class!

Some men chose to take the accumulated leave they had earned, but I chose to save my time and use the additional time I would accrue, so I could take my first leave around the Holidays. So, after boarding the bus to San Antonio and reaching the bus station, I waited for the bus which would take me to Little Rock, Arkansas.

As I wrote earlier, I had never planned on making the Air Force my career, so after serving less than a year at Little Rock Air Force Base and three years at March Air Force Base, I was satisfied with my military experience. It's true that I never served a day overseas, but I did learn to type, received my GED (which is the equivalent to a high-school diploma) and took a creative-writing class. So I have chosen to only highlight what I feel are experiences which changed my life during my remaining enlistment.

My first assignment after completing basic training was as a clerk at Little Rock Air Force Base in Jacksonville, Arkansas. I really enjoyed my time in Little Rock because it was much different than the desert of Yuma and was quaint in a way I had never experienced. When I first entered Arkansas I began to notice a change in the landscape; gradually I saw the rolling hills and all the different hues of the many different-type trees along our way. The sight was breathtaking because I had never seen so-many different colors on the trees back home. There were shades of brown, red, and crimson, yellow, blue and green on the trees we passed that day. I really enjoyed that first experience.

I was assigned to the office of the Base Locator; which was easy, even for someone with little or no education. There I worked at locating military personnel who were assigned to the base and helped people find their family or friends. Since I served in an administrative capacity we were housed in a separate building from the others. Our quarters were not barracks but resembled motels. Each room had two airmen assigned and two rooms shared a common bathroom. Gone were the days of latrines and having to expose myself to all the men assigned to Flight 788-89.

I'll never forget the day I met my roommate. When I opened the door there was another airman sitting at our table. "Hi," he said, as I entered, "my name is Richard Embrey but most people call me Rich." We shook hands and I said my name was Ralph, but I liked answering to Ralphie or Rafael best. Rich said that life here was not as it was at boot camp. Little Rock AFB was totally different, he said, especially for those of us who were assigned to the administrative section. I began to really enjoy our room. He went on to tell me that he was from Alabama. I knew he was from the South because of the twang in his voice.

I liked Rich instantly so we talked as I began removing articles from my duffel bag and hanging everything on my side of the closet. I asked him to explain things I ought to know, as I removed my cigarettes from my pocked he said, "Let's start there. Smoking is prohibited in any bedroom," then continued, "some guys smoke in their rooms, but I hope you won't, because smoke really bothers me and I can smell cigarette smoke on my uniforms." "No problem Rich" was my only answer. We remained together the rest of the evening. That night, as I lay in bed, Rich was writing a letter at the table, but I didn't care; I was happy and peacefully feel asleep.

We were treated like human beings but there was also a subtle difference. We conducted ourselves according to the disposition of those who held a higher rank. With officers we maintained military decorum at all times but with enlisted personnel we were much-more free to be ourselves. Unfortunately there are some enlisted personnel who are willing to destroy anyone under their control in order to climb the ladder so they can be promoted to a higher rank. Fortunately, I was not to experience that until my next assignment.

You can best describe Little Rock as girls, girls and more girls! Everywhere you looked there seemed to be several blond, blue-eyed girls; most in their late teens or early twenties. Since Little Rock is the capitol of Arkansas, many girls, fresh out of high school, would exercise their independence for the first time and move away from home. Herds of them flocked to Little Rock to find jobs in all those offices of every imaginable type which are typical of any city which also is the capitol of a state. Most of the girls rented apartments and had roommates so it was common to find two, three or even four girls sharing an apartment. Many times I got lucky and would wake up next to one of these beautiful girls and immediately dress, so I could catch the first bus back to the base.

In 1960, the thought of dining with a black man was something a white woman was unwilling to consider but somehow Mexicans were treated normally. There were far-fewer Mexicans living in Little Rock than say, El Paso, Texas. The changes I was exposed to – the difference in the way human beings were treated– was the most difficult problem I was to ever to deal with from then until today.

In 1960-61 discrimination is another word which some people could use to label Little Rock – Little Rock is a Southern city with Old South traditions and values. Hidden from the public there remained, at least in 1960-61, the stigma associated with being black – the difference between the two races was never discussed with strangers. But actions speak louder than words so I always felt that prejudice and bigotry were always hidden from view yet festered in the hearts of both races.

Those months I was stationed at Little Rock AFB and spent most of my off-duty time in Little Rock were my first experiences in learning about discrimination and the subtle ways in which it was applied. The four things that remain in my memory are: jobs, buses, shopping and the Catholic Church.

Blacks were hard to notice when you got off the bus: only those men, women and children who happened to be walking were visible. Blacks tended to have jobs which were out of public view. I remember stopping at one of the shoeshine parlor which seemed disproportionate for a small city like Little Rock. There seemed to be a shoeshine parlor on every block or two. I would pick one and enter to find rows of black men eager to shine my shoes. Black adults and young boys stood in line until I chose the one I wanted then I jumped onto one of the six to eight stands which were located where the light was adequate for us to read the paper while my shoes were shined. I was not allowed to pay the employee directly; instead he would walk up to the counter, directly behind me, and the owner would hand him a token. We weren't even allowed to tip directly; instead we gave the owner extra money which was meant to be giving to his underpaid worker as a tip. Whether the money was ever paid, remains unknown to me.

On those days in which I would take a ride around Little Rock to explore the sites, black men would always sit at the back of the bus; although each of them was required to pay the exact fare everyone else was charged. What's worse, however, was when the bus became crowded some white man would say something like, "Hey Boy, get up so this lady can sit down!" I'm sure that those men who would rise from their seats already knew the custom very well but had not risen quickly enough to suit this particular chivalrous, Southern gentleman. That really irritated me!

On those days when I went shopping I always found it ironic that black families were required to use separate toilet facilities and drink out of separate drinking fountains; however, their money was always placed into the same cash register as the money white people gave the attendant!

Churches bothered me most because a church represents, to me, a place where God's spirit resides. No one, even to this day, has ever proven to me that God is White; so therefore, I could not reason why Blacks were required to only sit in the balcony in a house of worship!

But I knew there was nothing I could do to change the conditions which existed in Little Rock in 1960-61. But I was determined to forever treat a human being as I wanted to be treated – regardless of ethnicity. None of these practices ever existed on the base; so I felt free to associate with whomever I chose; and I did.

Below, is a speech by President John F Kennedy. Although he would not make this speech until 1963, I found it many years later and saved it in my *Insightful Thoughts* folder in my computer. Discrimination was something which I learned to be fact as I struggled with understanding why some Americans were treated so differently in Little Rock in 1960-61. This, I thought, was the exact place to insert what I copied exactly as

President Kennedy spoke it that day in 1963. What follows is only a paragraph of President Kennedy's speech:

"The Heart of the question is whether all Americans are to be afforded equal rights and equal opportunities, whether we are going to treat our fellow Americans as we want to be treated. If an American, because his skin is dark, cannot eat lunch in a restaurant open to the public, if he can not send his children to the best public school available, if he cannot vote for public officials who represent him, if, in short, he cannot enjoy the full and free life which all of us want, then who among us would be content to have the color of his skin changed and stand in his place? Who among us would be content with the counsels of patience and delay?"

I took my first leave during the Christmas holidays but when I returned to Huntington Park I found things to be even worse than before I left. Eddie was no longer living with our mother so I was unable to spend any time with him, but we talked on the phone. He said he was happy to be back with his Grandma Valles but missed me. I missed him too and promise that we would spend some time together on m next leave. I did spend one afternoon with Dad and Nellie; for one afternoon I thoroughly enjoyed the time we spent together. Dad seemed impressed when he saw me with one stripe on my uniform and said he was pleased that I had been promoted so quickly. I finished the day by having supper with Grandma Mendoza.

I really missed her and the way she was always concerned for my welfare. Aunt Mercy and Uncle John came to visit just before I was ready to leave. Uncle John was the same jovial man he would remain for the rest of his life and Aunt Mercy could still make me laugh each time she chuckled.

When I returned to Little Rock I met a girl from a little town in Arkansas. She was a typist in one of the many offices which seemed to be everywhere in Little Rock. After spending a few nights together, she gave me a key to her apartment so I was free to come and go as I pleased. Her name is Laurie; she was one of the most beautiful girls I ever met, and yes, she had blond hair and blue eyes! We would remain lovers for the rest of the time I was stationed at Little Rock AFB; but things became a bit strained when she began talking about us getting married. She was looking for a husband but I hadn't sowed enough wild oaks yet so marriage was something I was unwilling to consider. All the girls I met in Little Rock seemed to want to marry and Laurie was no different. When I received my orders to report to my next assignment, Laurie and I broke up. I missed her but I was still too young to marry her and take her with me so we parted with me angry and her crying.

From the day I received my orders, I didn't do much in the way of doing additional work. When the day came for me to leave, I said goodbye to all those who were so nice to me. Rich and I went to dinner in town so we shared my last meal.

After I left the base, I returned to Dallas by bus. From there I flew back to Los Angeles. On the flight I couldn't stop thinking about what life was like living in another part of America. The injustice I witness gave me a thirst for knowledge. Now I have countless books that deal with that topic, so I'll forever be thankful for the brief time I spent in Little Rock.

On May 1, 1961, at about six-thirty in the morning, my father drove me to March Air Force Base's front gate and wished me well and actually got out of the car and gave me a hug. I waved goodbye as I picked up my duffel bag and a suitcase, then walked to the sentry's shack.

From the moment I stepped off the jeep which happened to be going by I felt as if I had been transported back to Schofield Barracks. If you've ever seen the movie, *From Here to Eternity*, you will quickly understand exactly what I felt as I gazed around the area in front of the 22nd Operations and Maintenance Squadron (22nd OMS). What struck me first is that this building was different from the administration building where I had been assigned to the office of the Base Locator. I later learned that I was now in a barracks of mechanics; some of whom flew each day on B-47 and KC- 135 aircraft. Administrative personnel who worked in the several offices contained in that building were also housed there.

The only difference in our building which was different from the Schofield Barracks is that instead of having a three-story barracks as seen in that great movie, our barracks was only two-story. I lit a cigarette and looked out over the parade ground, which was just opposite the Base Exchange and theater. All were within a close distance of where I stood so I finished my cigarette and walked to the orderly room. After opening the screen door and hearing it slam behind me, I met two men who were to become important in my life because I would work with them daily for three years. The first man who came to the counter was Staff Sergeant Broadus F. Cox. He introduced me to our squadron's First Sergeant whose name is Master Sergeant Frederick J. Quinby, Sergeant Quinby welcomed me and informed me that I would be working directly under Sergeant Cox, then pointed to a desk and said, "That's the desk you'll be assigned to; but first, Sergeant Cox will show you where to pick up your bedding and show you where you will be sleeping." Sergeant Cox immediately said, "Follow me, Airman"; so we walked out. Sergeant Cox showed me the mail room where I would sometimes be working. From there, he pointed to the office where I was to later collect my bedding then he took me to the second floor in the main section of the building. He showed me my bunk, then turned and said, "That is all for now Airman; take the rest of the morning, then report to the orderly room at 1300 hours promptly," so I spent much of the morning storing my personal items and adjusting to my new home.

By 1100 hours I had completed unpacking and spent a few minutes viewing the head, showers and most of my barrack;

as well as other offices which were housed in that building. As I walked outside I asked an airman who happened to be passing, "What way to the mess hall?" He pointed his finger and said, "That way … it's not very far." I thanked him and smoked a cigarette as I headed to the mess hall. Nothing was as modern as Little Rock AFB: this was a base which had a long and rich history. When I entered the mess hall, however, I felt at home because everything was arranged about the same, and there was that same relaxed attitude. I picked up my tray and utensils and filled my plate. One thing I heard before entering the military was that the Air Force served the best food of all the branches. As far as I was concerned, the food was great!

At 1300 hours I reported to the orderly room where Sergeant Cox and I sat at his desk. He explained that at first, I would basically be typing daily, weekly and monthly reports; then I would be assigned additional duties as mail-room clerk, as well as other assorted jobs. Finally he said, "After you have proven to me that you are competent, I will assign you to another administrative office." I later learned that the other office was on the flight line, where both he and Sergeant Quinby had a second office; there, he said, I would be assigned other duties. A few months later I was promoted to Airman Second Class.

My job was easy at first, so I quickly learned the reports I would have to type each day, as well as updating files. That was easy too because I just had to find a file, then remove certain pages, then insert new pages which had current information. Soon I was spending less time in the orderly room and more time in the mail room. I made it my business to keep separate the mail we received: for those men who were still on base, I would place their mail in a small cubicle which had the name of each man assigned to 22nd OMS. For those whom I knew were flying, and were unable to collect their mail until the following day, I would go through the barracks and place each man's mail under his pillow. Soon it got around what I was doing with the mail, so a few men would stop me and say thank you.

One day, as I was walking to the mess hall, I noticed a guy sitting with his back against a building. He waved at me to come over, so I walked to where he was sitting. He said, "Look in those windows!" When I turned, I saw the female enlisted women's quarters. It was hot that day, so a few curtains and windows were open. Just then I noticed a girl walk by with only her bra on. We both kept watching to see what else we could see, so I knew that we both spent far too much time being absorbed with the ladies.

His name is Ruben O. Cabrera; Ruben, or just plain Rube. He was also from Los Angeles, so we sat and looked into those windows for awhile. Ruben remains the first person I would ever call a friend. We still write to each other by email and speak on the phone. He joined me as we walked to the mess hall so I learned that he was assigned to the 22nd Field Maintenance Squadron, (22nd FMS). Ruben's job was to fuel aircraft while in flight. He was the one who extended a long wand which was then inserted into a receptacle of the aircraft requiring fuel. Ruben's barracks was just next to mine so Rube and I did almost everything together. The first weekend I traveled with him to Los Angeles, Rube introduced me to his mother, father, his brother Bobby and sister Diane. From the moment I met them I felt instantly at home. Mrs. Cabrera seemed to run the house, but Mr. Cabrera seemed to remain quiet that first day; Bobby was likeable enough, but we never became close.

Diane, however, was completely different: from the moment I met her, I think I lost my heart for the first time in my life. Rube and I sat together as I started to light a cigarette; immediately Rube called me outside, then said, "Ralph, my mother doesn't approve of people smoking in our home; so please smoke outside, okay?" My answer was, "Sure thing Rube" so nothing was ever mentioned again. We sat together for about an hour before Rube drove me to Huntington Park. We promised to meet during the week, so before leaving I said goodbye to his family and gave Diane a special smile.

I had arranged to have another friend pick me up Sunday night so we could return to March AFB together. I would go on to return to Huntington Park on Wednesday evenings, two times each month, but would always ride with Gary Killeen, who lived in South Gate. Gary also worked in 22nd FMS, but it was much easier for me to ride with him because Ruben's home was a much-further drive; where Gary's parents lived less than five miles away.

When we were at the base, I would use any excuse I could think of to get Ruben to call home. There was an office, where after 7:00 p.m., we were allowed to call just about any place; so I would talk Ruben into calling home. Soon I would take the phone and talk with Diane for as long as possible. Rube would become bored and ask me to hang up but I would still linger on the phone with Diane. Whenever I was at the Cabrera home, Diane would charge me a quarter to iron each piece of my clothing, as I sat and listened to some of her jazz albums. Sometimes we would dance in the living room and I'd hold her close. A few times Mrs. Cabrera allowed me to take Diane to a dance if Ruben was also going.

One night we went to a dance in Huntington Park so Diane and I sat with Ruben and Gloria then we danced together all night. Finally, on our way home, we stopped to get a burger, so as we were waiting, I leaned over and tried to kiss Diane but she pulled away. When I dropped her at her home, I shut off the engine and walked her to the back door. Again I leaned over but again Diane backed away. We only said good night that night. As I was driving home, I felt badly but had not given up hope...yet.

I had been approached by an officer who was looking for qualified clerical personnel to be assigned overseas for one year, but, if I accepted the offer, I would be returning to March AFB at the completion of the year. That sounded very appealing to me; especially when I was told that we would not be living on base, but would be paid per diem to live off base, and would work at the American Embassy as clerical personnel in London, Paris, Berlin and Saigon for three months each, before returning to our old assignments. For a few nights, as I lay in bed, I kept thinking that this was great, because I was sure, with time, I would show Diane how much I cared for her.

Mrs. Cabrera would not allow me to date Diane on a regular basis. Mrs. Cabrera though Diane was too young to date anyone other than to go out on a casual basis; then only when Ruben or Bobby was along. But I was sure Mrs. Cabrera would not mind if Diane and I exchanged letters. I started fantasizing as if I were Walter Mitty about how I would send Diane a porcelain doll from each country and hoped that after a year Diane's feelings would change. In addition, I thought that after another year, Mrs. Cabrera would be more likely to allow us to date as boyfriend and girlfriend. So that was my plan; now I only needed the right time to approach Diane with the idea. My opportunity didn't take as long as I thought it would.

For those of you who are unfamiliar with Walter Mitty: he is a fictitious character whom James Thurber wrote about in a short story. Mr. Thurber's short story first appeared in *The New Yorker* in 1939. His story was later made into a comical movie starring Danny Kaye.

One night when Diane and I were on the phone she asked me if I would help her learn to drive a stick-shift car. Her parents would not allow her to drive their car because she had not-yet learned to drive a car which had a standard transmission. I thought: here is my chance! I borrowed my father's '51 Ford which had a stick-shift and went to pick up Diane. We drove to a parking lot that was empty, then, changed positions. At first, Dad's car would surge then stop, as the engine would die. We worked at it for over an hour before I said, "Diane, that's enough for today; let's go for a drive." She said that it was fine with her, so I drove up to the Hollywood hills and parked. We both got out and were enjoying the view, when suddenly I asked Diane, "Would you mind if I kiss you?" Her answer was, "Ralph...I don't want to be asked to be kissed!" I looked at her so she could see the hurt in my eyes, so she continued, "I want you to show that you care for me and that I'm not just another floozy to you, but I also have to care for you before we can share a kiss and I'm not sure if I care that much for you yet." All my plans turned to ashes. I refused to tell her about my offer to go overseas, so we drove back to her home, she got out, and I sped away.

I had met a girl named Eileen and we began going out on the

weekends. But we seemed to attend the same parties, so it was impossible for Diane and me not to meet. I especially remember one party where many of my new friends were gathered; I had asked Eileen to accompany me so we were also there. I was now only dating Eileen, but Sergio, who was later to become my daughter's godfather, was her friend too, so I left Eileen and Sergio talking outside as I walked into the kitchen to get another beer. I saw Diane waiting in the hallway as she was in line to use the bathroom. I guess I had just enough beer in me to summon the courage to confront her, so as I walked up to her, I said, "Don't you know how crazy I am about you?" Before Diane could answer, I pulled her into my arms and gave her a very-gentle kiss. She just looked at me and said, "Ralph! You're with Eileen!" I didn't care who I was with, I just wanted to take her into a private room and tell her how much I cared for her. But when I grasped her hand she again backed away.

From that time on I refused to allow any thought of Diane to enter my mind. I would show her: I would marry Eileen, who liked me and wanted me in her life; then maybe Diane would be sorry for rejecting me!

There were three functions where Diane, Eileen and I were together. The first was when Ruben married Gloria; the second was when Diane married David; the last was when Diane invited Eileen and me to attend a party at their new apartment.

That last occasion was memorable because Diane and I entered their bathroom at the same time. We both felt awkward but neither of us moved. We were only standing a few feet apart, but we seemed to be inching closer. I felt my knees shaking as we just looked into each other's eyes. I wanted to say that I still cared for her so maybe we would kiss. I even thought of saying, "You owe me a kiss because I never kissed you on your wedding day." But I couldn't do it. Finally, I said, "You were here first," so I just backed out of the bathroom. Diane was one of the few girls who could really get to me!

On an impulse I decided to take a "Hop" on a KC-135 which was taking a training flight to Hawaii. I asked Eileen to drive me, so Mother, Eileen and I drove back to March AFB. As we flew, I had to make a decision: would I continue to pursue Diane, or would I remain with Eileen. In some ways, I now think I should have done neither. Maybe all would have turned out for the better if I had chosen to take the temporary-duty assignment and just leave. But I finally decided to remain with Eileen.

My work in the flight-line office was very interesting. The job I enjoyed doing most was assigning the forth man to a flight crew. Each forth man was a mechanic who was assigned to 22nd OMS. Each of them had to accumulate twelve hours of flight time so he could receive monthly-flight pay. When the fellows learned that I was now the one doing the assignments they asked me for flights which lasted just under seven hours;

that way they would only have to fly twice to be eligible for flight pay. So I would assign the forth man to a flight which was returning within eight hours to my friends. Some flights lasted twenty-four hours, so I would assign those flights to men I didn't like.

Although I still did normal, clerical work I enjoyed my job in the mail room and my assignment work the best. One incident I will never forget is one which happened in about 1963. I had assigned Tech Sergeant Pete Gutierrez to a morning flight which was due to return after six hours. Pete was a man who enjoyed chasing the ladies and drinking the night away so we became instant friends. We would often stay up until late in the night in the parade grounds across from the Base Exchange. Pete always brought the beer so we'd just sit there and exchange stories about girls. The flight I had assigned Pete to went down as it was about to lift off and all aboard that flight were killed. That was the only aircraft to crash while I was assigned to March AFB. I suddenly felt sick as I stood outside our office and saw the smoke and flames from that B-47. I was sure Pete was on that aircraft so I felt even worse. A few hours later, Pete came into our office and signaled me to come with him. When I did, Pete asked, "When is my next flight scheduled?" I answered, "Didn't you get the messages I left for you?" "What messages?" was all Pete asked. I told him I thought he was *dead* because I had scheduled him to be aboard the B-47 that had crashed. Pete just shook his head and then said, "Thank God!" Apparently Pete never received my messages and for that I am thankful. But Pete just wasn't lucky: he was killed in an automobile crash a few months later.

Before Pete died he was involved in a dispute with First Sergeant Quinby. Apparently each began shouting at the other then Pete asked Sergeant Quinby to step outside so they could settle their problem "Man-to-Man." Sergeant Quinby had the good sense not to take Pete up on his offer because I am sure Pete would have cleaned Sergeant Quiby's clock in any fight!

I began disliking Sergeant Quinby when I rode into Riverside with him. We were driving on a freeway when a German shepherd was trying to cross the crowded lanes. Sergeant Quinby never even attempted to avoid the dog; instead, the dog glanced off Sergeant Quinby's bumper then the dog just lay in the next lane while car after car ran over him.

I hated Sergeant Cox because he was so obsequious. We would be having a normal afternoon in our flight-line office when Sergeant Quinby would enter. Sergeant Cox would suddenly stand and begin to chastise us for even the smallest of mistakes.

But, apparently I pleased both Sergeant Cox and Sergeant Quinby, because I was promoted to Airman First Class at the first possible date after I became eligible.

Just after 1964, Sergeant Quinby informed me that I had an appointment with an officer whose job it was to ask airmen to reenlist for an additional four years. I knew there was no way I would ever do that! I had seen far-to-many men who were double-timed to the mess hall. One man in particular caught my attention: he was wearing a fatigue jacket which plainly showed six trips missing from his worn-out jacket. I was *never* going to allow anyone to have that much control over me!

I kept that appointment but told the officer I was not interested in enlisting again. He tried to stress that I would certainly be promoted to Staff Sergeant and possible be able to choose an overseas assignment but even that didn't dissuade me so our talk was rather short. I was honorably discharged from the Air Force shortly after that conversation.

Chapter Six

Married Life

Now we come to the hardest chapter I knew I would ever have to write if I were going to be truthful and tell the complete story of my journey. I have to accept that both Steven and Christine will one day read what is written here and I will be judged by the words I use and the way I use them. Only Eileen and I know the complete story of the time we spent together, but I'm sure that she will agree that there are words that are better left unsaid. I have attempted to write this chapter in a way that won't be too hurtful to my children, yet be as honest as I possibly can be. So I pray that I have chosen my words wisely.

No one really knows what causes a marriage to fail. Even after a thorough examination of all the facts there still remains a certain amount of doubt: was I to blame or was she at fault, or were there circumstances beyond either of our control which led to what followed? I realize that those questions will never be answered so I have to accept the fact that, in the end, my wife and I didn't have any desire to continue with the life we had shared for over seventeen years. As for me, I now believe the cause of our divorce was mainly my fault. My insecurity or, more probably, my immaturity led me to do things that are not accepted in a healthy marriage.

If a percentage can be assigned then I must admit that sixty percent of the blame was mine and twenty percent of the blame was Eileen's, while the remaining twenty percent was caused by others who were the source of festered wounds which never healed.

Eileen was no saint, but she entered our marriage with the hope that we would remain together for life. Basically that's what she had seen all her life, so I'm sure she hoped our marriage would be no different; but it was. Our backgrounds were so different: she came from a healthy, loving environment, while my life had been filled with chaos. Eileen and I would go through some tumultuous times during our marriage; but in the end, we were not able to salvage what was left.

Between my mother and father, they were married nine times. To me, after my divorce, getting married again was unthinkable. In contrast, Mother often told me: "If your marriage with Eileen doesn't work out, you can always go to Tijuana, Mexico, and get a quick divorce." That is how cavalier Mother felt about marriage. Likewise, my father would often tell me: "If this marriage doesn't work out for me, I'll just get a divorce then I'll find someone else!" Thinking like that made me realize, when we finally divorced, that I would try to not make that same mistake again. If I did marry sometime in the future it would be for life without equivocation. Maybe that accounts for my being married only once and continuing to run away when later relationships seemed to be leading to a possible marriage. Some of the women I began a relationship with and later discarded were some of the nicest women I have known; but eventually the talk of marriage would come up; that's when I'd start looking for a way out. Now, I have remained single for about thirty-two years; I just couldn't accept the pain I associated with the failure of another marriage.

I'm not writing this so that someday Steven or Christine will say, "I knew it. It was Dad's fault!" These are merely the facts, as I see them *today*. Maybe by reading this Steven and Christine will realize that life is, in some ways, a journey where a person – even their father – evolves into what he will later become.

Toward the end of our marriage Eileen would spend a lot of time on the phone with her friends telling them – while the children would listen – what I had done to cause her to decide to divorce me. When children hear only one side of an issue – especially when they hear their mother repeating over and over again the facts as *she* perceives them – the children naturally accept her version as the truth. Now I will attempt to tell, as honestly as I am able, *my* version of the facts.

Eileen and I even disagree on the day we actually met. She thinks we met many-months earlier, but that is not the way I recall the event. So I'll start this painful chapter on the day I believe we first met.

The day was my eighteenth birthday so Ruben, Sergio and I had agreed to really make it special. The three of us had decided to go to two parties that weekend so I brought two sets of clothing suitable for nightwear, but had only brought one pair of dress shoes. I was staying at another home on 53rd Street where Mom, Roy, Eddie, Tony and Ramon had moved.

When Ruben and Sergio picked me up they just honked the horn; so I quickly hurried out. I already had a few beers in me from the toasts both Mother and Roy had made. We were headed to our first party which was being held in Central Los Angeles, near the Coliseum where the L.A. Rams used to play. After parking, we entered a crowded room, when suddenly the lights went out. The only thing visible was the back yard; apparently, the street lights had remained on but it was hard to see clearly. Just after opening the sliding-door, I took a few steps then fell into a swimming pool! By the time I got out everyone was laughing at me and laughed even louder when the lights came on. I grabbed Ruben by the arm and pleaded, "Rube, let's get out of here!" Less than an hour later we were back at Mom's home on 53rd Street.

Mother asked, "Back already?" Sergio and Rube started laughing and told everyone of how silly I looked when I fell into the pool. I wasn't in good humor so I asked Mother to dry my shoes as best she could while I changed into the other sports-jacket and slacks I had brought. Mom was laughing while she stuffed both shoes with paper and placed them into the oven to dry. After changing, and impatiently waiting, I finally said, "Mom...that's OK. Come on', let's party!" So I put on my still-wet shoes then, after gulping down our beer, the three of us left again. Serg said, "Well what do we do now?" Ruben was still dating Gloria at the time, so Rube cut in and said, "Gloria's at a house party tonight in South L.A. She invited us to drop by." So that's where we headed.

When we entered, we saw Gloria and Eileen standing and talking with a few people so Rube led the way with Sergio and me closely following. Gloria and I had been friends since I first met Ruben so she introduced Sergio and me to Eileen. I remember feeling uncomfortable because everywhere I walked I left prints from my still-wet shoes. Eileen asked me to dance and instantly began to kid me because each time I moved we could hear a squish-squish. She ribbed me that entire night so I decided to ask her for a date the following weekend; when she agreed, I thought, "Great!"

From that point on, I only dated Eileen if I exclude a few times when I'd sneak away. Eileen and I had not become intimate yet; so, when I had the urge for sex, there was always Denise

"The Piece" and several other girls I knew who would gladly exchange sex for an evening out. When the time came to propose marriage Eileen accepted. We agreed to go to Las Vegas so we could save all the money we would spend on a normal wedding. We wanted to save all we could to buy our first home. So on the morning of our marriage, Mary Ellen (the woman Eileen called Mother) joined us. Several times along the trip I wanted to say, "I'm sorry Eileen but I'm just not over Diane yet, so maybe we should postpone or cancel the wedding," But I didn't have the guts to say that so later that afternoon we picked a wedding chapel and in a few, brief minutes, we were married. Eileen looked lovely that afternoon; I just wore the sports jacket my father had bought me; he also gave me fifty dollars. Mary Ellen, on the other hand, gave us five hundred dollars which was far more than she could afford.

That night we went to see Bobby Darin at the old International Hotel & Casino. I had never known that there was such artistry available for normal people to see. His performance that night left me with a desire to continue seeing live shows from that day to this. Mary had insisted on paying for our first show, but when the waitress came over to take our order she used our table as a serving block for all the other tables in her area. After the show the waitress presented me with the bill but Mary grabbed it from me and said, "I told you both that this is my gift, so I'll pick up the check." When the waitress returned there was the money on her copy of the bill and there were two pennies off to the side. Mary just looked at the waitress and said, "Thank you so much for your service. This tip is my way of saying thank you." The waitress gave Mary a look which said that she was unhappy with her tip, so Mary said, "I love leaving tips to show my appreciation so those two pennies are my way of showing you how much I thought of your service!" I was embarrassed but had learned another rule to guide me: always treat others the way you want to be treated. Roy Reyes and Mary Ellen McCarthy would never be considered equal as human beings because each was different. In their own way each had values I will forever admire.

We returned the following day to Mary's home on 117th Street in South Los Angeles, where we lived for many months before Eileen and I moved to Riverside, California. Mary seemed to enjoy having both of us with her because she used to serve us brunches and suppers in her dining room as opposed to her kitchen. Mary was a fine cook and would sit and talk with us. Her Irish brogue was new to me and was always charming. Sometimes she would dance some of the dances she learned as a young girl in Ireland; she still remembered all the steps, even after all those years. Mary's sister, Anna, lived on the next block and her husband, whom Eileen and I used to call Uncle Jimmy. He was a sports fan, but he especially loved boxing. On several occasions Uncle Jimmy and I would go the Olympic Auditorium in downtown Los Angeles. Sometimes my father met us there because he too was a boxing fan. We saw Joe Frasier when he was not-yet famous, among others; so my father and Uncle Jimmy would talk about the all the boxers they had followed during the Depression. Sometimes Dad would look at me and ask, "What did he say?" Uncle Jimmy had a brogue that was so thick that even I couldn't understand him when he talked fast. Sometimes Mary, Eileen and I would walk over to spend the evenings with them. I really enjoyed those days we lived with Mary and I actually cried when Uncle Jimmy died.

Eileen and I had our ups and downs, like most couples do when they first marry, but I guess you could say we were happy. The first major fight, which almost caused us to separate for the first time, was the day President John F. Kennedy was murdered in Dallas. I was at a repair garage on that day: November 22, 1963; which is a date I will never forget. It was about 3:30 p.m. when I arrived, but the mechanic said he would fit me in. When we heard the news he and I just sat there and could not believe what we heard on the radio. As soon as he finished his work I drove straight over to Mary's home because that's where Eileen was waiting for me. When I entered the living room there were Mary and Eileen sitting and listening to the radio. You can imagine how sad they both were because both had been born in Ireland, and JFK was a witty man whose heritage was Irish.

All three of us embraced and Mary cried because she admired President Kennedy very much. Eileen suddenly said, "I have to run, or I'll miss my appointment at the beauty parlor." I looked at her in disbelief and asked, "What? You can't be serious!" Eileen gave me that "Irish" look which said she was about to fire a barrage at me, then said, "Yes! I'm serious!" Before she could continue, I fired back, "You've gotta be kiddin' me! Don't you realize we just lost the President of the United States today?" We started arguing so loudly that Mary started crying and had her hands over her face. Eileen finally took my keys and rushed to our car. I just could not stay there for a second longer so I walked out the door as Mary was pleading with me to stay. I don't remember a word she said because all I could think of was how insensitive Eileen had been; I was fuming so badly that I wanted to kick something! So I started walking and thinking about John F. Kennedy's *Profiles in* Courage: his Pulitzer-Prize winning book, and later began thinking about *The Making of the President 1960*. That book is Mr. White's first-hand record which chronicled the presidential election of 1960. I first read the book as an assignment in a class I was taking, but after rereading it in 2005, I now consider that book to be the finest book written by Mr. White. I had bought, and still have, those two fabulous books. I also thought about that speech by President Kennedy; a portion of which I have included earlier. Without realizing it, I had become interested in politics for the first time. Eileen and I often talked about JFK so I couldn't understand what caused her to behave as she had.

I walked all the way from 117th Street, across about five miles until I reached Santa Fe Avenue then headed north to 53rd Street to our mother's house. I turned the TV on and was watching Walter Cronkite's report which included a scene aboard Air Force One where Lyndon Baines Johnson was taking the oath of office with Jacqueline Kennedy at his side. You could see the grief on her face! As I watched I called Gary Killeen and asked him to pick me up there when he was ready to return to March AFB. Things remained tense with Eileen and me for several weeks; I think that was the beginning of our actually realizing that we both had made a mistake by getting married at the age of eighteen.

We only remained in our Riverside apartment for about two months before moving to Sunnymead, California, which is only a few miles away from March AFB. We both seemed to enjoy our apartment which was a duplex, but she would often scold me when I was in the bathroom. Our toilet was in the same location as the toilet in the other unit; so I'd blow air into my arm which made obnoxious sounds, so we could hear the other tenants laughing. Eileen would be lying on our bed and suddenly had to place the pillow over her mouth to keep her laughing quiet. Whenever we saw the other couple, we both avoided eye contact and would just say, "Hi!"

Work at March AFB was now easy. I had been assigned to the 22nd OMS office on the flight line. There I worked under Sergeant Cox and Sergeant Quinby; but either one or both of them was often gone in the morning hours and would only arrive at our office late in the day. So I worked all day in our flight-line office then did my work in the mail room. Whenever someone in our squadron had a death in his family, I would pass the hat, to collect as much money as I could and place it in an envelope with a card signed by all who had donated. Usually I would collect between twenty-five to forty dollars.

Four things were to happen during those years I was stationed at March AFB which I will never forget. The first was when I was approached for the second time by an officer of the base's assignment division and asked if, this time, I would be interested in joining a group of clerical personnel who would be assigned on temporary-duty status for a three-month period at each American Embassy in London, Paris, Berlin and Saigon; he went on to say that after completing that one year I would return to March AFB. I remember thinking, "Timing is everything!" Now I was a married man who had moved his wife away from her secure home. Maybe Eileen would have gone on to meet someone else while I was spending a year seeing all those places I had hoped to visit. Again I declined. As I wrote earlier, the first time this assignment was offered to me was when I was interested in Diane.

The second thing that happened was that on October 1, 1963, I was promoted to the rank of Airman First Class. I remember this event because my father had told me how proud he was when Nellie's family received a telegram from Nellie's nephew;

I believe his name is Tony. Dad was excitedly when he was telling Belinda, Laura and me how thrilling it must be to be promoted three times in less than four years. When I received my official notification, I immediately called Dad. When I told him my great news, his reply was only, "So?" Again I had allowed my father to wound me! I didn't even bother to mention that attaining that rank was the highest rank anyone could receive in four years, unless he agreed to reenlist. I just said something lame like, "Gotta run Dad...Bye."

The third thing that happened was when President Lyndon Baines Johnson was scheduled to meet President Adolfo Lopez Mateos of Mexico. Their meeting was to take place on February 21-22, 1964. I was told that March AFB had been contacted and asked to supply personnel to assist so I requested to be considered for that assignment. So on February 20, 1964, a group of forty-two of us rode on the short trip to Palm Springs, California. I had originally thought I'd be working as an interpreter but when our assignments came out I learned that I had been assigned as Pierre Salinger's chauffer. The next day I met Mr. Salinger. He didn't sit in the back seat as I had expected, but chose to sit in the front next to me. I liked him immediately and drove him everywhere. On the first evening I drove him to the Racket Club; there he sat at a table with Charlie Farrell (the actor and owner), Bob Six, who was the CEO for Continental Airlines, Jane Meadows and a few others. I spent the evening sitting at the front entrance. One time, I was thrilled when Jane Meadows walked over to me and asked if I needed anything. Later that entire group went to a private, luxurious home; there I remained seated in the kitchen. There were so-many dishes prepared, so I feasted on them as I waited. Both Jane Meadows and Pierre Salinger entered the kitchen and Ms. Meadows again asked me if there was anything I wanted; I answered, "No thank you; I'm fine." Mr. Salinger said he wouldn't need me for the rest of the evening, but asked me to pick him up at 7:00 a.m. so I answered, "Yes sir."

The next morning I was up at five and had breakfast, but was at his front door fifteen minutes before he had requested. He looked out the door and saw me, then said, "I'll be with you in a minute." Mr. Salinger said he had to attend a briefing and conduct a press conference, then told me what time I should be waiting. He asked me a few questions about my family as we drove, so I told him that I was married and lived in Los Angeles. I mentioned that Eileen was pregnant and was staying with her mother while I was on temporary duty. He didn't say anything at the time, other than to ask me to run an errand for him. He handed me eight one-hundred-dollar bills and a twenty. Mr. Salinger said, "I lost this last night playing poker, so I want you to go to a bank and get exactly eight-hundred and one one-dollar bills and have them put them in two or three canvas bags; you can keep the rest." So later that morning, after completing the errand, I was waiting where he had asked. When Mr. Salinger returned I drove him back to where the party had been held the night before. I followed him in to the home, then he and the owner laughed as they walked outside to the swimming pool. Mr. Salinger looked at the lady and said, "I'm a man who always pays his debts!" Then he turned to me and said, "Ralph, I want you to dump all eight-hundred and one one-dollar bills into the pool." They both really enjoyed seeing most of the money floating on the top of the water, while other bills were flying through the air and drifting like feathers over the woman's back wall. Mr. Salinger told me to wait outside for awhile, which I did.

When Mr. Salinger returned to the car he said, "Now we're going to join a motorcade which will take the President, to the airport. We will be flying to Los Angeles, so I've made arrangements for you to come along, if you want to." I almost fainted from the sudden rush of blood then said, "That's wonderful Mr. Salinger; I'd love to go along but I'd like to call my wife first so she can meet me at the airport." Mr. Salinger reached into his suit jacket and pulled out a pass. He said, "Be sure to keep this visible at all times because the Secret Service will want to see your permission card before you will be allowed to board Air Force One." "Great!" I thought; "what a wonderful experience, I may even see the President in person!"

On the back of the pass there contained a report with information about our flight. I still have that pass in a safe-deposit box along with a few other mementoes from that flight. I also called my father to invite him to join us; but once again he said he was too busy to attend, so I slammed the receiver, then thought, "This is one time I won't allow Dad to spoil my day!"

When I began to walk a short distance behind Mr. Salinger a Secret Service agent came out and tried to stop me. When I handed him my pass the agent looked at Mr. Salinger who nodded his approval.

The flight only took about twenty minutes and I was one of the last to exit Air Force One. The aircraft was in a secluded portion of the airport, but as I walked down the ramp I immediately saw Eileen and Mary waving at me. We were to remain together for about three hours, so I told them how exciting it was to meet famous people and said how wonderfully Jane Meadows and Pierre Salinger had treated me. When the motorcade began to return we said our goodbyes and I promised to call Eileen later that evening. As I approached the aircraft, the same Secret Service agent nodded to me, so I boarded Air Force One without any questions. I took the same seat I was in the first time and a few minutes later Air Force One began to taxi. I could feel the thrust of the engines as we sped along. After we were airborne I felt someone tap on my shoulder; it was Mr. Salinger. He leaned over and asked, "Ralph, would you like to meet the President of The United States?" No words can adequately express the emotions which began flowing inside of me as I answered, "Oh yes Mr. Salinger!" He said, "Follow me." As we were approaching the President's private-residence section of the aircraft, Mr. Salinger said, "Wait here Ralph." He knocked on the door and entered. My heart was racing and I felt my palms sweating, so I wiped them on my trousers. In less than a minute, Mr. Salinger opened the door and gestured for me to enter. As soon as I walked in, there was President Johnson seated at a table across from Secretary of State, Dean Rusk. Across the room, seated at a sofa, were Mrs. Johnson and Mrs. Rusk. Just then Mr. Salinger said, "Mr. President I would like to introduce Airman Ralph Mendoza." President Johnson extended his hand, but as I was trying to return his gesture I felt my hand shaking, but we did shake hands for a moment. I remember thinking, "I just shook hands with the President of the United States!" The President's hand was twice the size of mine, in fact, he was much larger than I remember him being when I saw him on TV. Then President Johnson said, "I understand you have been traveling with us because your wife is expecting your first child." I stammered something like, "Yes Sir, Mr. President, she is." After he released my hand he said, "Meet Secretary of State, Mr. Rusk and Lady Bird and Mrs. Rusk." I quickly shook hands with Mr. Rusk and bowed to the ladies, then turned to the President and said. "Mr. President, this is the greatest honor of my life!" Everyone smiled as I began backing out of his quarters. I felt queasy as I returned to my seat. Mr. Salinger smiled at me as he walked by. I sat and had a feeling of honor I had never experienced in my life.

After Mr. Salinger returned to his car, I thanked him over and over again. He simply smiled and didn't say a word. I drove him to his residence then I placed his luggage into the trunk as he walked out; then I drove him back to the office where I had met him that morning. As I was removing his luggage he reached out and we shook hand for what I thought was the final time. As he was walking into the building, I began to feel tears beginning to well in my eyes. What an experience!

I was to meet Pierre Salinger again in 1964, when he was campaigning for election to the U.S. Senate seat he had been appointed to by California Governor Pat Brown. We met at one of his campaign stops in East L.A. I was surprised he remembered me; we briefly shook hands and he asked me how I was doing. I told him that we were doing well and that Eileen was expecting a child. We only spoke for a few minutes because he was late for his next campaign stop so we shook hands for the final time. For the next few days I couldn't stop thinking how kind Mr. Salinger had been to an ordinary twenty-year old kid. After all, he had been the press secretary to both President Kennedy and President Johnson and lived a life I only dreamed of, yet he had taken the time to pull some strings so that I could fly on Air Force One and meet President Johnson. Mr. Salinger was to be a news correspondent for ABC News and was Robert F. Kennedy's campaign manager. His death in 1964 affected me very much because he had been so kind to me.

Later that night, as all the temporary-duty staff got onto the bus, a few men were patting on my back while others were hollering. One guy said, "Man, we couldn't believe it when we saw you on TV! How were you picked to fly on Air Force One?" I answered, "That was the President of the United States! If he can't spot quality when he sees it, no one can!" Just then a few of them starting throwing wadded paper at me and I smiled. It was well after 1:00 a.m. when I called Eileen from our apartment. We talked for over an hour as I told her about the greatest experience of my life. I have often wondered if she fell asleep feeling proud of her husband that night.

The final event I remember as though it were yesterday, was the day Eileen went into labor. Mary had come to stay with us during the final two weeks, so Mary took care of everything and we waited. Each evening the three of us sat and tried to decide what to name our child if he were a boy or girl. "No way will I ever saddle my son with the name of Ralph or some other goofy name," I said. We finally decided on the name Michael Phillip if the baby were a boy and Mary if the baby were a girl. I loved the names because they rhymed so well. Mike or Mary Mendoza...yeah...that sounded great to me! On afternoon, Mary called me and excitedly said, "Eileen just broke her water so we called a cab." I said, "Great Mary I'll meet you at the base hospital." I asked permission to leave, then jogged and ran to the hospital. Mary was waiting for me but Eileen wasn't there when I arrived. Eventually, we entered the deliver area where a few other women were screaming, cussing and raising a commotion. Eileen only moaned as her contractions came and went. Finally Eileen was rolled into another room so Mary and I returned to the lobby. We had some coffee and we both spent hours outside just smoking one cigarette after another. The doctor came out much later. He said that Eileen was doing fine and we now had a son, but there were tests he wanted to run so he had placed our son in an incubator. He said he would allow us to see Eileen for a few minutes; but before leaving, he said he would call me at home when he knew more. Eileen was weak and tired during the ten minutes we sat with her; then a nurse said we should leave. Both Mary and I kissed Eileen then I drove us back to our duplex. Late in the night the doctor called and said we should return immediately so Mary and I quickly dressed and jumped into my car. I think we both felt a bit uneasy but neither of us said a word. A few minutes after we entered the hospital the doctor came in and said, "I'm so sorry...but we were not able to save your son: he died just a few minutes ago." The doctor and I both thought Mary was about to faint because her face turned very pale so the doctor and I helped her to sit down, then I thanked the doctor as he left. We learned later that Michael had underdeveloped lungs. The name of the disease our son had is Hyaline Membrane Disease which is curable now but was not in 1964; at least to those infants who were prematurely born. Patrick Bouvier Kennedy also died of Hyaline Membrane Disease but that was on August 9, 1963. He was the son of the man I have grown to admire more than any-other President, with the possible exception of Thomas Jefferson.

Mary and I went to see Eileen as soon as Mary recovered. Eileen was unable to speak; she only sat in her bed, as tear after tear fell to her gown. She felt that she had done something which had caused Michael to be born prematurely, but no matter what Mary or I said, we couldn't change her mind. She remained in a constant depression for several weeks.

I was very touched when the men of the 22nd OMS contributed almost one-hundred dollars for us to use to bury Michael.

In the mean time I had requested an early discharge. I used the excuse that I wanted to return to Los Angeles and enroll in college; so in May, 1964, I received an honorable discharge.

Eileen, Mary and I returned to 117th Street. Eileen and I seemed to become united during the first year after Michael's death. I began to view her as a wonderful girl whom I was starting to love. After I left the Air Force, I got a go-nowhere job as a timer repairman then I left to work for the U.S. Postal Service in Inglewood.

Steven was born on June 15, 1965; he was a healthy baby boy. I think the day our son was born and Eileen realized he was a healthy baby was the first time she began to relax since Michael's death. Steve was born at Centinela Hospital Medical Center in Inglewood. I remember praying and asking for guidance for this innocent baby we were blessed with. I asked God to help me to remember my childhood and asked His help so that Steve would have a normal, healthy childhood. I repeated that prayer when Christine was born on January 5, 1967. I guess I didn't pray hard enough because I was to go on to commit some terrible errors in the years that followed. The only thing I did which may be considered normal was to provide a safe environment for Eileen, Steve and Tina. But I did show our children all the love I had; so I guess that, at least, is something.

After about eleven months I took a job with the Southern California Gas Company. I attended a two-week course in repairing gas ranges, refrigerators, water heaters and furnaces. I liked the job because I was beginning to learn mechanical stills for the first time. After completing training I was assigned to the Hawthorne base, and remained there for over a year. I enjoyed the job, but most of all, I enjoyed meeting and becoming friends with John Ramirez. Eileen and I became friends with both John and his wife, Anita. Johnny and I played golf on the weekends and Anita always had fine Mexican dishes prepared for us when Eileen and I arrived. After our divorce we lost touch with Johnny and Anita but they remain both Eileen's and my dearest friends even after all these years.

I transferred for a brief period to the Los Angeles office of the gas company, but because Diane also worked there, I only remained for about a month. Finally I transferred to the Belvedere base where Ruben worked. We worked together at schools where we would calibrate all the ovens in the school's kitchens and service all of the gas-burning equipment. We would stop and go to a park for lunch, then return to what we had been doing. About this time we bought our first home on See Drive, in Pico Rivera. Ruben and Gloria lived four houses away so either of us would drive to work, then later in the evenings Ruben and Gloria would visit us, or we would visit them.

But in the back of my mind there was still one thing I wanted more than anything: to become a fireman for the Los Angeles County Fire Department. When I failed the 1967 Los Angeles City exam, I volunteered to work one night a week at the East Los Angeles Service Center. I passed out material for students and sat and explained what little I knew about some subjects. But I also absorbed a lot of what I had never learned before so I enjoyed the work. Later I did some assistant teaching to a class on how to pass civil-service examinations. I was determined to be as ready for the 1969 exams as I could be. Thing began to change during that period. My father also lived in Pico Rivera, so he would come over about twice a month and see the children; so slowly we started to enjoy being together. When Eileen decided we needed to paint our kitchen, all three of us did the work in one day then sat on our back porch and drank for hours. Mary had sold her home on 117th Street and moved one block away; so either Steve or Tina, or sometimes both would spend the night with Mary. Nonnie was the name our children called Mary. I fondly remember that brief period as one when we were happy together. The children were enjoying having their grandmother and grandfather around so this was an enjoyable time for all of us.

After work I would go to Rio Hondo Junior College in Whittier and jog five miles around their track, then I would finish by running up and down the seven-story stairwell of their library building; I ran that stairwell four or five times until I was totally exhausted.

When 1969 arrived I passed the L.A. City written exam. L.A. City sent me a notice stating that I could now go to the second phase of their total exam but I declined because I had also passed the L.A. County written, physical, oral and medical exams. Then about two weeks later I received a notice stating that I had finished number nine on L.A. County's list of eligible men who would be hired. Eileen and I were thrilled because we had read in the *Los Angeles Times* that there had been over five-thousand five-hundred men who took L.A. County's written examination.

I was nervous because I had been offered a job in the sales division of the gas company; so I didn't know what to do. I was filled with anxiety because I knew I was about to burn a bridge I might never be able to cross again. I attempted to leave the gas company on good terms, so I could return, in case I washed out of recruit training; but my supervisor, who had approved my promotion to sales, became hostile. The day I gave him my two-week notice, my supervisor said, "Ralph, as far as I'm concerned, you can walk out the door today and never return." I didn't want to end my job that way, so I said, "Mr. Montgomery, I really appreciate your backing. I have enjoyed working with you, but being a fireman has always been a dream; but I will remain working for you for two weeks because I think that is the least I can do to say thank you."

In the back of my mind I was haunted with the thought of washing out and not having a job to support my family, our new home and new car. The strain began to show on Eileen and me and our marriage was definitely headed toward divorce. During the time I was assigned to the county's fire-training facility, I was on duty for twenty-four hours, but off duty for the following forty-eight hours. I was required to study many things before returning for another twenty-four hour shift. I began to notice times where Eileen and I would become ill-at-ease or even hostile with each other. Those times led to many quarrels, so both Steve and Tina would take refuge from our constant bickering by staying a few nights with Mary.

Eileen was beginning to associate with people I didn't know; she even took a job with some company without discussing it with me first. One evening after I returned from a day of studying at Mary's apartment, I found Eileen dressed in what I thought was inappropriate for a married woman to wear so I blew my top. Mary decided it would be best if she took the children to her apartment. After Mary left, I went into a hysterical rampage. I asked Eileen where she was planning to go dress as she was. Eileen began to verbally attack me as I was attacking her, then she said, "I'm going out with a friend; we'll be having a few drinks, but I won't be late." When I asked her where she was going she would not answer. I waited until about 3:00 a.m. then, when Eileen returned, I tore into her once again. I said, "I knew I should never have married you. I should have waited and married Diane." Eileen was livid and I could see the hate on her face when she retaliated by asking, "Is that why you wanted to name our daughter Diane Marie?" There was no way to stop Eileen after what I had just said. She went on, "If you never were able to get over Diane, why did you ever marry me?" I had no answer: there was no possible excuse for blurting out such hurtful words. Eileen stormed into our bedroom, so I slept on the sofa. I was up very early because I had to report for training again that morning.

Two weeks were to go by before Eileen and I finally resumed a civil, if not loving, relationship. After I graduated from the tower, I was assigned to Fire Station 47 in Temple City. We began a habit which would last until we divorced: we would buy either a new car, a different home, or take a trip; we even had a swimming pool built in one of our back yards. In short, we did everything to avoid the obvious fact that we would finally, one day, divorce. But we were basically throwing money at a problem that needed to be corrected if our marriage was to continue.

We began shopping for a home which was closer to Temple City. We finally found a modest home on Danbury Street which all four of us liked so we bought it. For a few months things did improve but eventually, things returned to what they had been. I was unhappy because now I had to work overtime to pay for the constant upgrades we were making and Eileen was no-longer working. We must have bought three new cars within the first four years of our marriage. I transferred from Fire Station 47 when I realized that there weren't enough fires. I wanted all the experience I could get in fires and rescues so I chose Fire Station 164 because, as a youngster, I had seen the Huntington Park engine responding to fires almost daily. The only time Eileen and I talked on the phone was when either Steve or Tina misbehaved. I would get on the phone and speak with them and warn them that I would deal with their misbehavior harshly when I returned home. To this day, I have never spanked Steven or Christine; it really wasn't necessary because they had the guidance of their mother and especially Mary so they never got into trouble. Mary had rented a house in Temple City, so she was again within a block of our home.

I began a ritual I probably performed every time either of our children misbehaved. I would arrive at home and sit in my favorite chair then I would call the culprit and ask the one who had misbehaved to come and sit with me. I would say, "You know why your mother had to call me last night...don't you?" He or she would immediately begin to cry and say, "I'm sorry Daddy; I promise I won't do it again!" I always answered with the same words, "You leave me no choice! I want you to go into our bedroom closet and pick out the belt you want me to spank you with." When the offender returned, I would tell the one whom Eileen had been complaining of, "Now drop your pants and lay yourself over my lap." I would slowly take the belt and say, "Before I spank you, you have to tell me exactly what you did." You've never heard such begging! Steve or Tina would say, "Dad, if you don't spank me, I promise I will behave from now on and do everything Mom wants me to do!" So I would then say: "Okay, I'll believe you this *one time only*!" So Steve or Tina would pull up his or her pants, then immediately run into their rooms.

On those evenings when Eileen and I would fight, the children would call Mary. A few minutes later, there would be Mary in our kitchen, asking if she could take the children to her house to spend the night. We never declined, so after they left I would walk to the local liquor store and buy a six-pack of beer and would return to find Eileen gone.

Mary would even begin to take Steve and Tina for the weekends. Once she asked me to drive her and the kids to Magic Mountain; I agreed so when the gates opened I dropped them off then headed to Montebello golf course. I would stay at the golf course or in a bar until it was time to pick up Mary and the children then return them to Mary's apartment.

Steve and Tina had begun playing with a few kids from Rio Hondo Preparatory School so when I got back from playing golf, they would always be at that school in the afternoon, and would often return after supper. The school was well supervised so neither Eileen nor I worried very much.

In an attempt to patch things up, we had a swimming pool built in our back yard. I liked the idea because when I would work five consecutive twenty-four hour shifts, I didn't have to return home and do as much yard work as I had done before. Our back yard was a little smaller than our front yard, so instead of spending time working in the back yard, Steve Tina and I would swim together. Eileen only joined us a few times because she said that this was her time to be alone. I totally agreed that she needed her private time, but Eileen had many nights to be alone when I was at on duty and the children were with their grandmother. She no longer accounted to me for her actions and I had stopped accounting to her for mine.

One night Eileen began to talk about her family who were still living in Ireland. That was a subject Mary and Eileen would attempt to avoid so eventually Eileen told me the whole story:

She had been born Cork, Ireland, and had left her mother, father and many brothers and sisters when she left Ireland as a small girl to live with Mary and Mary's husband, Ned. She said she really hoped to one day visit her natural parents, but never did because Mary would become sensitive whenever Eileen occasionally received a card from home. I asked a few questions then I had an idea. I said, "Eileen, we're having a tough time being happy so why don't I shuffle my time so we can go to Ireland for a month?" She didn't answer for a moment, but then shouted, "Really!" I could feel the mood change for the rest of the night. I answered that it was something we could probably afford if we saved some money and I worked all the overtime I could. In those days L.A. County had a rule which said that no fireman was allowed to work more than five additional twenty-four hour shifts per month; I was already working about three additional shifts, so it was not unrealistic to work an additional two shifts, if I only did it for a year, so I said, "Sure! If we stop buying all these useless toys and save, I'm sure we can swing it."

We fell to sleep that night making plans. Eileen would first have to tell Mary then write to her family back in Cork. While she was waiting for a reply, we obtained our travel documents. I had never had a passport before, and Eileen's papers had long ago been lost, so the following week we began to organize everything. Mary said she would be happy to live in our home and take care of The Mick, The Bop, and our new dog whose name was Ruff McDivot. I chose that name because I was always in the rough when playing golf and I was known to take divots when hitting a golf ball, so it was only natural to call him that because he was an Irish setter.

We chose to join a club and take the discounted fare on a chartered aircraft. So, a few months later, all was set. We were terribly disappointed when at 6:00 a.m., we received a phone call from the airline company saying that our flight had been delayed until 10:00 p.m. We decided not to mention the delay to our children, but instead just leave as originally planned. We called Anita Ramirez and asked if we could spend a few hours with them that evening while we waited for the time to board our aircraft. Anita said she and John would be happy to have us over for supper that evening, so she would prepare everything. We made a date to be at their home at 6:00 p.m. We left our home about noon but didn't know what to do for the afternoon. I asked Eileen if she felt like spending the day at Hollywood Park so we could pass the time while enjoying watching the thoroughbred's race. She was in a great mood so we went. What a day we had! Eileen didn't know one horse from the others; she just picked winner after winter. Soon people would ask her what horse she liked in the following races. I whispered into her ear asking, "What are you doing?" She whispered back, "I don't know. I just like a horse's name or I close my eyes and just pick one!" She never missed but once in all the eight races we saw that day. We made a pile of money even placing small bets; but greed took over so I started upping our bets as we continued to win. I went from betting two dollars to betting five dollar and ten-dollar bets so we cleaned up when she picked a long-shot winner. All the while we were downing several beers so we were high when we arrived at John and Anita's home. We had a wonderful, if only a spur-of-the-moment, visit that evening. I was definitely feeling no pain when we boarded the airplane. I fell asleep and didn't wake up until we arrived in Bangor, Maine. We refueled there so we didn't have to change planes, but in less than an hour we were on our way to Shannon Airport.

We arrived at midmorning, Ireland time. As we were approaching the airport I could see how truly beautiful Ireland was. There were uncountable patches of different shades of green, as the airplane's landing gear came down. After landing, Eileen suddenly became very nervous when we looked out the window to see a group of people waiting. She almost fainted so I grabbed her as she was walking down the steps; we waited until the color returned to her face, then we continued.

If Uncle Jimmy had a brogue, it was nothing to compare with Eileen's father's brogue. I didn't understand a word he said, as everyone hugged and kissed Eileen. They had failed to be notified that our flight had been delayed, so they spent the day playing miniature golf and resting in one of the local pubs which seemed to be on every corner. Eileen and I got into a car with Jerry Fox (Eileen's father) and Maggie Mae (Eileen's mother) then we all returned to Cork. The streets were narrow and seemed to constantly twist along our journey. Eileen said,

"Look how their driving. They're driving on the wrong side of the road!" Jerry Fox turned to Eileen, but before he could say anything, I said, "Eileen...they aren't driving on the wrong side of the road – their driving on the opposite side of the road!" Jerry Fox just smiled at me and even I could understand him when he said, "Well said lad."

We had a great time while we were driving to Cork. When we arrived we found that her parents lived in a townhouse-type building, with rows and rows of townhouses which reminded me of Ramona Gardens back home. The interior of their home was well decorated although the rooms were rather small. I thought their TV was comical because they used to have to insert a shilling into the set to get it to turn on. Then after about an hour the TV would abruptly shut off. Everyone gathered in the kitchen, so it was difficult to understand who asked what. In that kitchen were Maggie Mae, Jerry Fox, Eileen and me, in addition to Eileen's brothers, Finbar and Joe. One of the twin sisters was seated with her arm around Eileen as we rested and talked. Later, after tea, we all joined arm-and-arm and walked down to the family's favorite pub. We all got totally intoxicated that first night.

Learning about Ireland for the first time was a wonderful experience for me. I really enjoyed the landscape and the culture, but most of all I enjoyed the people and the way they seemed at peace with their lives. Eileen could not remember much about her childhood, so it was a new experience for her too. I remember that it stayed light until well past 10:30 p.m. I would step outside and marvel at the children sitting on the sidewalk. They enjoyed just sitting on the curb and singing song after song. Eileen and I were divided most of the time because she was off with Fin on his motor bike or was with her oldest sister Margaret. I spent most of my days with Jerry Fox. We roamed the hills and he showed me where his dogs raced. The family's living room was filled with trophies which told me just how much they enjoyed competing in dog races. Each afternoon Jerry Fox and I would walk down to the pub. I guess I stood out because of my dark skin and the clothes I was wearing. He introduced me to many of his friends who would go to the pub for a pint or two while they read the paper, made phone calls or watched free TV. Once in a while someone would break out in a song, so soon everyone joined in and began singing. That experience, I thought, was exactly as ones depicted in *The Quiet Man*. All their beer was served warm and had a very thick and bitter taste, so I asked Jerry Fox about it on our way home to tea. I was embarrassed when I asked him to speak more slowly, so I could understand him. Jerry Fox said that the reason their beer was served warm was that winters in Ireland were severe so there was nothing like a nice, warm drink when they got off work.

Each pub was actually two pubs: one was reserved for gentlemen only; the other was for escorted women. Several times I heard a knock on the window then realized that it was a woman who wanted to be escorted into the women's area.

Men were free to come and go, but women were restricted to that one side. "Just another form of discrimination," I thought. These pubs were known as "Sing-Song" pubs because everyone took turns singing a song, then others would join in and finish the song. Eileen absolutely refused to even get up on the stage, and there was no way she was ever going to sing any song. I always enjoyed being in the spotlight so I would jump on stage, where I would always sing my favorite song: *Smile.*

Jerry Fox took me to the main firehouse in Cork so I got to meet the fellows who were working that day. I still don't remember a thing anyone asked because they all tended to talk too quickly and several men were asking questions at the same time, so I did my best to answer questions about life in the "States." Jerry Fox took me one afternoon to Little Island golf course. The courses I played in Cork all tended to be empty, except for Wednesday afternoons, when all the priests played. Jerry Fox grabbed one of my rented clubs and took a few swings at a ball on the first tee; each time he swung he missed the ball completely, so I started to laugh when he said, "Lad…the game's a bit harder than it looks!" The weather was unpredictable because one minute the sun was shining brightly then rain was pouring down on us a few minutes later. The rain never lasted too long so we would just sit under a protective shed on Little Island golf course. A few minutes later the sun was visible because all the clouds had disappeared. The air was so think that it felt better when I took a deep breath. Smog was never even heard of so I liked taking a breath of clean, fresh air; it was much better than the air back home.

Meanwhile, Eileen was spending the day getting to know her mother, so she sat in the kitchen while Maggie Mae cooked supper. I don't think I ever saw Eileen as happy as she was that month we spent in Cork. She would be gone for an entire day with her twin sisters or with her brothers, Eddie, Finbar, Joe and one or two others. One evening we were scheduled to go to a nightclub, so I asked for some hot water so I could take a bath. Everyone looked at me strangely because it was their custom to only sponge-bathe themselves nightly. So Maggie Mae removed everything from the stove and placed a large pail on two burners, then added water. I felt badly asking to take a bath, but I couldn't stand myself. Having body odor was considered normal: it was a sign that someone had been working hard that day. Later that evening we went to the nightclub with Finbar and his wife. I was dressed in a light-colored sports jacket with matching slacks. People looked at me and stared because it was also the custom for men to wear black, blue or gray attire; so I stood out with my dark skin. I kind of liked being looked at by all those freckled-faced, red headed girls. Eileen just poked me in my side and say, "Hey... watch it fella!"

All-too-soon our trip was over but we did get to enjoy a few days with Michel, Eileen's oldest brother who flew in from Manchester, England. I never drew a sober breath for the entire time Mike was there. Later we took a trip so Eileen and I could kiss the Blarney Stone and visit several places with Jerry Fox and Maggie Mae.

When the day of our departure arrived, the entire family joined Eileen and me as we returned to Shannon Airport. When we had to board the airplane, Eileen and I experienced one of the most emotional moments of our lives. Everyone was crying; including me. Eileen and I just ran to the door, turned and waved goodbye.

On our flight back to Los Angeles, I just couldn't get over our experience. Eileen asked if we might return some time in the future. I answered that it would be a wonderful experience for Steve and Tina, so before we even landed we agreed to return the following year and would include the children on our trip.

Life was hectic during the year that followed. I was busy paying back days others had worked for me while we were on the first trip; now, in addition to working five days of overtime, I was also working additional shifts so I could store them up for next year's trip. I was often gone for five days, then I would be off duty for only one day, before returning for an additional two to five days. The children were doing well because, when things got bad, they could always stay with Mary. Eileen would become irritated when I chose to play golf on my one day off so we bickered almost nightly on the phone. Our yard was so large that there were fifty-four sprinklers which needed tending as well as the other gardening I would have to do. I know about the number of sprinklers because I actually counted each one, as I trimmed a circle around each of them after returning from a day of golf.

I think we didn't get a divorce about that time because we only saw each other a few times each month. Eileen was resentful when I would scold the children about something I didn't like, so Eileen would jump in and say, "I don't want you teaching Steve and Tina something that I want them to do differently; you're never around, so let me deal with them." Well, I'm sorry, but I totally disagreed: if I didn't have a right to correct Steven and Christine, what the Hell was I doing living there? Was I just a paycheck who was tolerated on those days I was home?

Now Steve and Tina would spend all of their free time away from their regular school and would play at Rio Hondo Prep. In an effort to make a change, I bought a used trailer, so we could spend some time together as a family. But by now the kids were so involved with activities at Rio Hondo Prep that is was impossible for them to find time to get away. Each day they left early and returned late and often spent the night with Mary. Finally, I decided to move out of our home, but first I had to keep that promise I had made to take Eileen and the children back to Ireland.

Both Steve and Tina had a wonderful time. Steve spent almost every day with Jerry Fox just walking the dogs over those beautiful hills. Tina was also busy. She spent many days just getting to know her cousins, whom she had just met. Eileen and I were noticeably different on our second visit, so no one was surprised when I said I wanted to cut our visit by a week. I cancelled our return flight, and instead, we flew to London. Then we remained there for about five hours and flew non-stop back to Los Angeles.

We did attempt to seek help from a marriage counselor. For some reason Eileen wanted to see one in Hollywood, so she made the appointment. On our first session, we each had our turn telling him our version of the problems for which we were seeking help. Within forty-five minutes the counselor had made his judgment. He said Eileen was entirely correct, and in his opinion, I was probably suicidal. When we left I kept asking myself, "How in Heaven's name can this educated man make such a judgment after only seeing us for less than an hour?" I can just imagine him closing the door then thinking: **"How very, very interesting. I think Ralph belongs in some asylum!"**

One night Eileen and I confessed our prior sins. I had a memory filled with things I had done wrong in our marriage, so I felt that this was the right time to rid myself of all the guilt I had inside for having been such an unfaithful husband, so I told Eileen about all those one-night-stands I had with other women. I wanted to finally clear my soul and begin again with a clean slate, so I tried to tell Eileen everything. Eileen said she too had done a few things she was ashamed of but would not elaborate. How I allowed things to go this far is a question I can't answer. But we had both committed some major mistakes so I felt that this was the time to forgive and forget so we could get on with our lives. I still wanted to remain married, although some of my actions may lead readers to think otherwise. Being with Steven and Christine was more important to me than any sins Eileen or I committed in our past so I stayed. We finished our night holding each other and promising to forgive our prior sins.

From Danbury Street we moved to Arcadia and bought a much-more expensive home on Woodruff Avenue. The children transferred from Rio Hondo Elementary School to Longley Way Elementary School. Steve then went to First Avenue Junior High School for one semester. By this time Steve and Tina wanted to attend Rio Hondo Preparatory School, which was the private school they loved so much. So I made a deal with Steve: if he would bring home his next report card with only As on it, we would allow them to transfer to Rio Hondo Prep. That's exactly what Steve did; so the next semester each of them enrolled at RHP. Once they started attending RHP, they seemed *too involved* as far as I was concerned. We only used our trailer once because they had chores to do at school almost every afternoon after classes; sometimes they would return after supper so I felt like I never saw them on the days

I was off duty. The weekends were worse because I would almost never see them since they now had so much work to do or were involved in so-many different activities at their new school.

Steve had begun taking summer trips with RHP when we were still living on Danbury Streeet. The group was gone from ten to twelve weeks that summer, then, the next summer Tina joined the girls for an eight to ten-week trip. The reason I'm uncertain about the length of their trips is that they continued to take trips each summer until each graduated, so their itinerary changed yearly. There trips went from California to Florida one year, then they would alter their route, but each trip included a visit to Washington D.C. The kids had the opportunity to visit the Smithsonian Institute several times and perform plays in the Pentagon.

Steve wrote to me about once a week. I still have all his letters in a box inside a trunk with my collection of picture that I saved in Dad's garage. One is special because after Steve closes with, **Love, Steve M. Mendoza, he continues with aka: Best friend to James Worthy, acquaintance of Harrison Ford, agent for Eric Dickerson, best buddy of Peter Ueberroth, personal advisor to Ronald Reagan, batting-practice pitcher for Pedro Guerrero, head mechanic for Bill Elliott, one-time caddy for Tom Watson, financial advisor for Magic Johnson, beat reporter for the *L.A. Times*, special consultant to Casper Weinberger**; then his letter says to turn the page over so I turned the page. Steve finished with: **and son of Ralph Mendoza.** You can bet I have that letter saved in a special place!

I now realize I had no right to complain. After all, I had attended over fifty schools but Steve only attended four schools and Tina only three. I guess I was jealous because Eileen and Mary would see them every night, while I was only with them eight to ten times a month and on those days when I was home they were gone most of the time and often slept at Mary's apartment. I also felt the coaches were taking my place to some extent. In short, I felt useless.

The final home I shared with my family was a beautiful home on Crescent Drive, in Monrovia. During the last five years of our marriage, I moved in and out several times. One day Steve called me at the apartment where I was living in San Gabriel. After we spoke for a few minutes, I asked, "Mick what do you think about your mother and me giving it one last try?" He immediately answered, "Dad...please don't. When you're together everyone is unhappy. We like it better this way."

Now Steve was not only touring with the boys, he also toured with the girls. Steven was now an assistant who helped erect the stage the group used to perform plays on where ever they went. Steve was also elected Student Body President in his senior year, so he had additional duties.

Eileen and I finally had to face the fact that we were never going to salvage our marriage. We made a deal which was mutually agreeable and we made certain that Steven and Christine could finish their education at RHP before going to college. She gave a little and so did I. On the day we were to appear at the Los Angeles Superior Courthouse, Eileen chose not to go, so when the judge read our agreement, he asked, "Are you certain Mr. Mendoza you are willing to abide by what you and your wife have agreed to?" I answered, "Yes, Your Honor, I am." With that the judge dropped the gavel then said, "So ordered."

Our chaotic marriage was finally over. On my way back to my apartment, I thought how sad it was that Eileen and I could never find a solution to our problems. A deep depression was to stay with me as I adjusted to being alone. During that period I increased my dosage of Xanax to rid myself of the panic attacks I was beginning to experience.

Over the years I continued to raise my dosage and drank so much that I had blackouts. When I was up to eight times my original dosage, I suffered a minor stroke which, to me, was a warning sign that I had to alter my life. You will read about that terrible period of my journey later. Now I have finally accepted divorce as I accept death. That's what divorce really is, you know: Divorce is the death of a marriage.

Chapter Seven

The Los Angeles County Fire Department

In 1967 I took the Los Angeles City Fire Department exam. About two-weeks later, I received an official notice in the mail which said that I had failed to attain the minimum score needed to advance to the next phase of the examination. Also in that notice was written that, if I chose, I had a three-day period in which to review my written exam and speak with someone to discuss my failure. The first day of review was scheduled for the following week so I took a day off from the gas company and was waiting at the specified time. After a few minutes I heard my name called, so I stood up and waited. A captain opened the door which led to offices and invited me in. He introduced himself and we briefly shook hands before he asked me to take a seat. He opened a folder on his desk and asked me if I wanted to see my actual test. I answered, "No thank you, sir. What I want to know is what I can do to better prepare myself for the next exam." He replied, "Ralph, I'll give it to you straight: you lack the basic knowledge which most firemen have attained before taking our exam." He went on to explain that, if I was serious, I needed to start from

173

scratch to learn more about tools and their proper use, I also needed to learn much more about math and at least a few of the sciences but ended by saying that the only part I had done better that most was in English. He suggested that I enroll in night classes and maybe take a class or two in auto repair, basic electricity, or a few others. So now I knew what I would have to do during the next two years, because he mentioned that the next exam was scheduled to be given in 1969.

One afternoon, about a week later, as I was driving my gas company vehicle, I had to stop because there were red-lights flashing just ahead of me. Engine 1 was backing into their firehouse. I remember thinking how ironic it was to once again see a fire truck with a 1 on the door. I thought about those days when I was shining shoes as Engine 1 would pass, and how the firemen would always return my wave.

So I decided that this would be a good time to learn more about the job I hoped to have as my career. So I parked my truck and crossed the street to Fire Station 1 and rang the door bell. Captain Eladio Carrillo, Engineer Vince Canales and Fireman Andy Waroff were on duty that day. Captain Carrillo answered and invited me in. We introduced ourselves as we shook hands. I briefly explained the facts, so when he asked, "What are you prepared to do?" I quickly answered, "Whatever it takes, sir." He asked me to sit down so I did. From that moment until he retired and even after he was to remain the one person who made it his business to guide me.

Vince, or, Vinnie, as I would later call him, and Andy both called Captain Carrillo "El Oso Negro" because, in a way, he did resemble a large black bear. Years later, Eladio would often call me "Worms" in front of all the other firemen; so I'd sit there and fume! He gave me that nickname because I was always anxious. I never could find it in me to fire back at him because he was one of the reasons I was sitting there.

That first day I met them they wouldn't let me leave. I explained that I was working, so I had to document my time. Finally, Captain Carrillo allowed me to leave, but not before I agreed to go to Fire Station 2 so I could meet Captain Harold McCann. A few days later Captain McCann answered the door. When I introduced myself, he was very cordial and invited me in, so, in his office, I again explained the facts. Captain McCann said he would help me if I showed the willingness to learn. I answered that I would do whatever he thought was best. I continued to visit both Fire Stations 1 and 2 when I knew either Captain Carrillo or Captain McCann was scheduled to work.

After our first meeting I started attending night classes at Rio Hondo Junior College in Whittier. Both Eladio and Harold invited Eileen and me to their homes where Eileen and I had supper with them. We got to know Jane (Eladio's wife) as well as Mona (Harold's wife.) Mona McCann was a very gracious woman who happened to also be of Mexican ancestry, so we began speaking in Spanish. What I didn't know at first was that Harold had long ago mastered Spanish, so there were a few embarrassing moments. Whenever Harold and Mona invited us over, Harold and I always ended the evening in their den; there we would discuss my problems in understanding mathematics. He had a photographic memory and was a whiz at math, algebra and geometry and Harold had a way of answering all my questions which allowed me to understand the subject much better. Eladio, on the other hand, would have private talks with me, both at Station 1 or in his home. He concentrated on the problems I might encounter and taught me many things that later proved to be very useful. Captain Carrillo also took one day to discuss racial problems I would often face during my future career. He said, "Ralph, you will find that veteran firemen will test your from the first moment you meet them." Then he went on to explain what I should do when I found myself in those-type situations. He was especially helpful when he explained what I might expect in my private life. He said, "Try to keep your personal affairs private and try to separate your personal friends from the friends you will make once you become a fireman. There have been many cases I know of where men on this job have become too friendly with men who also work on our department." The last piece of advice he gave me was, "Ralph, you will find that it's very tempting to spend more than you can afford, so remember not to count on overtime to pay your bills."

Andy was very animated when he would tell me about many of the situations he had encountered in his career. He seemed to dwell on what I should remember to do if I was even caught in a building with all the air in my breathing apparatus depleted. Andy had that exact thing happen to him, so I listened intently when he said, "I'll never forget when I ran out of air the first time; I was panic stricken, so if that happens to you, remember: *Don't* Panic!" He would say, "Now Ralph, don't do this or don't do that," as he paced back and forth. I would smile as Andy would ramble on and on in the kitchen at Station 1. Andy taught me so many common-sense solutions to problems that I would have had to learn on my own. Another time Andy said, "Now Ralph, remember to count your steps when you enter a smoke-filled room, and never, never take your hands off your water hose because that's always the way you'll find your way out." Andy is one of those firemen you find impossible to forget.

So that the way it went for the next two years: I went to Rio Hondo Junior College to learn what I should have learned in high school, got myself in the best condition I had ever been in and continued to spend time with Eladio Carrillo, Harold McCann and Andy Waroff.

On the week before our class was scheduled to begin, Eileen and I attended an orientation meeting for all those who were scheduled to begin training; our wives or girlfriends were also encouraged to attend. Captain Thomas gave an informative talk and emphasized what wives and girlfriends could expect to encounter when their husbands or boyfriends didn't return as they normally did. He said, "Just be patient because you may later learn that he was called out in the middle of the night, and is now in Malibu fighting a brush fire." Another thing Captain Thomas stressed was that the ladies would find they now lived two separate lives: one with their man and one when their man was away for long periods of time. He said, "It's not always easy to find a phone booth somewhere out in the wilderness. So if he's gone longer than you expect and doesn't call just phone the fire station or battalion headquarters. They will have all the information you have been waiting for." I looked at Eileen after Captain Thomas said, "You will find that your life will change because you may develop your own interests, and make new friends, which don't include him. So be especially careful about that." Eileen smiled back at me, but I don't think she understood how important it was to learn what was just said. Captain Thomas gave us all plenty of information we would later find useful because he covered several out-of-the-ordinary situations most of us would encounter during our careers.

On November 10, 1969, I was one of ninety men who began their careers. Our class was the largest the fire department had ever hired. The ninety men who were hired that day were divided into three groups and were assigned to either the "A," the "B" or the "C" shift. I was assigned to the "C" shift and given the number nineteen to wear on my helmet. We worked twenty-four hours then we were off duty for forty-eight hours for three months.

Our on-duty days went like this: Our day began at 8:00 a.m. where we would run two miles and do calisthenics until 10:00 a.m. before being divided into groups. While one group of recruits was practicing hose lays, other groups were raising ladders or climbing an aerial ladder to the top of our tower, then either running down the fire escape or the interior of the cement building. Still others were practicing repelling off of another section of our tower or practicing jumping into a rescue net one floor below. Our training captains wanted us to be finely honed so we would be prepared to execute any assignment on the day we graduated.

I really enjoyed the mornings because, to me, it was fun and exciting. Our afternoon sessions were the same, except that we didn't do calisthenics. At 5:00 p.m. we were allowed to leave the tower in groups, so we would eat supper where ever we liked. At 7:00 p.m. our class-room sessions began, and would often last until midnight or 1:00 a.m. Then we were allowed to shower and all thirty of us would drag ourselves to bed. Don Murray was one of the first men I got to know and like; he slept in one of the thirty beds which had been set up in what was to become our dormitory. Bob Martin was another great guy who kept men like me loose because he was always goofin' off and telling jokes. Bob was a seasoned fireman who had resigned from another department to begin to work for L.A. County. Bob's bed was directly next to mine, so a few of us laughed ourselves to sleep because he would never cease telling jokes and old, war-stories about life as a fireman.

On many occasions we were awaken in the middle of the night by our training captains. The lights would come on and suddenly we were ordered to report to our tower on the double. The tower had been primed while we were asleep, so we would see smoke coming out of the open windows of the higher floors. We were ordered to don our breathing apparatus, then, as a group, three or four of us would team up and search for a manikin which might be hidden anywhere in the tower. The first team was assigned to search the basement, while other teams ascended to higher floors. Our captains wanted to be certain that each of us was able to enter a smoke-filled environment, then, complete our assigned task without becoming disorientated and panic. Once or twice I used up most the air in my tank; I knew because when there remained only five minutes of air, a bell would begin to ring. I instantly thought about what Andy had said so I would grab someone on our team, then shout, "I'm out of air; let's get out of here!" We would leave as a team, change air bottles, and then reinter the tower. Other men were assigned to extend ladders, and then search other floors. It was scary; but in a way, it was also exhilarating! The adrenalin which was flowing through me would not allow me to sleep but Bobby's incessant chatter did!

We were given so much homework that we needed a place where we would be undisturbed so Mary volunteered to vacate her apartment on our off-duty days so Don Murray and I could do our work without any distractions. Don and I would leave the tower, then stop and have breakfast at some restaurant, before going to Mary's apartment. Mary always had something for us to munch on, so she would leave after spending a few minutes with us; then she would walk over to spend the day with Eileen and the children.

Don and I drew diagrams of ladders and hose lays showing what each man on a four-man engine was required to do; we even strung ropes all over Mary's apartment as we practiced all the knots and hitches we were required to be proficient in, if we were to graduate.

When graduation day arrived, I learned that I was to be assigned to Fire Station 47 in Temple City. I still don't know if Captain Carrillo had used some influence to have me assigned there because I felt it was more than just coincidental that Eladio and Jane lived only a few blocks away. I had been assigned to the "B" shift, and the "B" shift was on duty that day; so after the ceremonies were concluded, I dropped Eileen off at home and headed straight to Temple City.

When I rang the door bell, Captain Munger answered. We shook hands, then he said the men were about to eat lunch, so he invited me to join them. We walked past the apparatus floor and opened the swinging doors which led to the rec room. There were four men seated at a table eating lunch. Captain Munger said to find a plate and fill up; but when I looked there were only five places to sit; the other seat was

obviously Captain Munger's, so I asked, "Sir, where do I sit?"
All the guys looked up and one pointed to a table in front of
the chalk board where there was a small table with one chair.
He said, "That's your table." Immediately I thought about
what Eladio had warned be about. On the chalk board was a
poster showing a black woman holding her daughter's hand
and there was mucus running down the child's nose. So I
filled my plate and then walked to my table. As I was sitting
down I asked, "Where did you guys get that picture of my wife
and daughter; I love it and I'd like to take it home!" Everyone
started laughing; so I knew I had passed my first test.

Later Captain Munger took me back to his office. He asked
me to sit down then he said, "Ralph, you have just successfully
completed three months in the tower; but you still have six
months of probation remaining. It will be my job to observe
you to see if you will become a permanent fireman with Los
Angeles County." He would go on to explain that I would
be expected to draw a map of station 47's district. On that
map, I would have to include the names of each street, the
hydrant locations and indicate where any "Target Hazards"
were located. A Target Hazard is an especially hazardous
building or area which may store any number of chemicals
or explosives, etc.

He also said that during those six months I would not be
allowed to lounge in the rec room or watch TV, but I would
be expected to study each night for at least three hours

before going to bed. So after we completed our conversation I went into the locker room and stowed all of my clothing and personal items in a vacant locker. When it came time for supper, I sat at the table with all the rest of the guys, as if nothing had happened. I enjoyed myself but when it came time to clean up, I assumed that I would have to wash the dished and mop the floor. Our engineer, whose name I have forgotten, stopped me. He said that it was the custom to play cards and that the loser would do the entire cleanup. After not losing at cards that night I took our district map and went into our dorm, then sat at a desk to begin to learn as much as I could about our district. Engine 47 didn't have any calls that evening but Squad 47 did. I learned that I would be assigned to Engine 47 for at least two months before being allowed to work on Squad 47.

I went home the next morning after meeting the members of the "C" shift. That was fun because the captain was Doy Cahoon, who had been one of my training captains, was on duty that day.

I spent the morning telling Eileen and the children about my first day as a fireman. I even took my "Turnout" clothing, then went into our bedroom and came out chasing the children. Steve and Tina started running from me, so I caught them and we fell to the floor laughing.

I successfully passed my probation, but before I did, I had to prove to Captain Munger just how much I wanted the job. Each shift I would arrive at 6:30 a.m. and move the engine and squad out onto the ramp. I would wash the engine first, and inventory every storage compartment. I had to memorize where each item was located and also had to restock anything that had been used on the previous shift. After doing that, the men who were on our shift would begin arriving so I would get help. Cooking wasn't a problem either because Eileen and Mary gave me several recipes, and I practiced at home before cooking for my new friends. I had no problem learning 47's area, so when it came time, I drew a map which included everything I was told should be shown. Captain Munger was pleased so that part was over for me. When the time came to return to the tower, I passed every exam with little problem. Now I was an official fireman! The pressure to succeed was gone. Station 47 was nice enough but it was basically a station where men went who were waiting to retire. I was new and wanted *action*, so I eventually left to begin work at Station 164 in Huntington Park.

About the only thing I enjoyed during my time at Station 47 was that I was allowed to be the aide to Battalion Twelve's Chief Ed Spruill. I was able to spend several twenty-four hour shifts with him so he too could evaluate me. We responded to any incident in battalion twelve. I got to see and participate in fighting large fires for that period and I liked it very much. We would also visit each station assigned to battalion twelve. That's where I first met guys I would continue to work with my entire career. John Laur was one of those guys I would work overtime with when he was a captain at Fire Station 164 and later a captain at Fire Station 3. John and I would go on to have some fierce matches against each other when we both played with the Los Angeles County Fire Department Golf Association. John now runs a tournament he calls "The Inferno" because it's held in Palm Springs in late June. Anyone who has played golf in Palm Springs knows that it is an inferno in late June because it's impossible to escape the heat. But still, he gathers about one-hundred twenty of his pals and we enjoy three days of great golf, with a little night-life thrown in for extra fun. John also joins a group of about twenty of us who travel to Baja each year to play golf at three fine golf courses. I can't say that John beat me every time; but that's the way it seemed.

I was to work as a fireman at Fire Stations 47, Fire Station164 then Fire Station 1. When I was promoted to engineer I returned to Fire Station 164 then transferred to Fire Station 22 where I remained for over 13 years; I did leave for about a year because Station 22 was being remodeled so I transferred to Fire Station 3 but I again returned to Fire Station 22 when the remodeling was completed. Fire Station 40 was the final station I worked. I transferred there because my father lived only a few blocks away. I was working at Station 40 when I became disabled, so for the last few years, I would work for a few months then was on disability for several months. I'll explain more about that later. So much of my private life is intertwined with the department and the men whom I worked with that I think this is the best way to approach this chapter.

On January 1, 1971, I reported for duty on the 'C" shift at Station 164. Most of the men who formally worked there had been transferred, except for six Huntington Park engineers who remained. Two were assigned to each shift and were experienced with Engine and Truck 164 as well as their district. Los Angeles County had officially included Huntington Park under their umbrella of cities they protected in addition to the unincorporated areas of Los Angeles County. As of 2009, the number of cities is currently fifty-four.

One of the first firefighter I worked with was Vern King. Vern was a little younger than I, but had a definite set of principles from which he refused to deviate. On our first shift, our new captain had a drill where he had the engineer on Truck 164 extend the ladder straight up, in the parking-lot section of the station. The ladder was made of wood and had no side rails, so I felt uneasy when our captain told me to climb the ladder, touch the top rung and then come down; I did it but it frightened me when the ladder began to sway. When the captain told Vern to climb it, he refused. I don't remember that captain's name, but he really got mad. He was an old smoke-eater who believed that a captain's word was law. He asked Vern, "Are you refusing my direct order?" Vern didn't hesitate when he answered, "I sure am!" Vern's father was a chief on our department, but knowing Vern that didn't matter in the least. Everyone was uneasy as we worked that first shift. We remained busy the entire day doing various chores, and then when we had supper, the captain said he would make immediate changes. "On my shift the engine will no longer respond to rescues in our district," was the first thing he said. That meant that only one man would handle all our rescues while the other four men stayed in the station. After supper, he had us rearrange the captain's office to suite himself.

When we returned a few days later, we found the captain's office back in its original configuration. The other captains had heard about the "C" shift sending only one engineer to our rescues, so they were unhappy. Our captain didn't remain long; he was immediately transferred. That old truck was replaced by a better piece of equipment and we returned to having Engine 164 respond to each rescue in our district. It remained this way until Squad 164 was assigned to our station. We had many, many fires during the year I was at Fire Station 164, but I left a little after one year. By this time I had a respect for Vern King that would last my entire career. He later was to become a captain at Fire Stations 1 and 3 and was loved by all who worked with him. Vern was promoted to battalion chief shortly before I retired, but I'm sure he was as fair-minded then as he was as a recruit.

When I returned to Fire Station 164 as a newly-promoted engineer, things were now as I knew stations should be. Again

I was assigned to the "C" shift and worked with Captain Doug Warr, Engineer Jim Hannum, Firefighters Paul Neal and James Howe. I believe Rosie Banks and Fred "Digger" Graves were the two men assigned to the squad, but I'm not certain. I am still confused because I don't remember who worked on the squad when I was first a fireman, then later an engineer.

This time we had a great crew who played practical jokes on each other daily and we sure had a lot of fires during the time I worked with these men. Now we were no longer called firemen: women had begun to join our department so it was too awkward to call them fireladies or firewomen, so we all became firefighters.

Two men died in the line of duty during my time on the job. Jim Michili was the first. I knew Jim briefly but he was so-well thought of that our annual golf event in El Cajon is name after Jim: it's called The Michili Invitational Golf Tournament. We gather for four days and play golf from dawn 'till dusk, so it's an event all us golfers look forward to enjoying.

The second was James Howe. For me, as for most of those who worked with Jimmy, or heard about this *living-legend*, who was simply know as "Taz" or "The Tasmanian Devil" or several other nicknames, he was unforgettable. Taz will continue to be loved as long as there remains one man on active duty to continue telling endless stories about Jimmy.

Even though he cracked my nose while we were playing

basketball, and I walked around with "Owl's Eyes" for a few weeks Taz would just rub my hair then smile the same smile for which he will always be fondly remembered.

Another time Jimmy and I were on the apparatus floor when I asked Taz what he had done in the military; his answer was that he was a MP. So I assumed a wrestler's position and said, "Well, show me what you've got Big Shot!" He smiled that famous smile of his and replied, "Well, come and get me!" In the next two minutes Jimmy threw me onto the apparatus floor four times. I pretended to wave a white flag and said, "OK...you win; now help me up." Howe just grasped me by the arm and lifted me to my feet. He was deceptively strong for a man of his size. Jimmy just rubbed my hair and put his arm around me as we walked upstairs to the kitchen.

A priceless event was the time we were having Sunday brunch together. Seated next to me was Battalion Chief Robert Messall, but we all called him "The AC/DC BC" because that's what he called himself. Messall kept putting his left hand under the table and rubbing my thigh. I was very uncomfortable so I asked Jimmy to change places with me. Taz knew what was coming, so he waited until the chief tried the same thing with him, then Taz filled his mouth with scrambled eggs, stood up and snapped Chief Messall's head toward him, then began to kiss the chief on the mouth while scrambled eggs were oozing out of Taz's mouth. We thought Chief Messall was going to puke right there and then. Several of us had to walk out of the kitchen and laughed 'till it hurt!

The last story I'll tell about Taz is one where Paul Neal and I were standing and resting. We were exhausted from tossing smoldering tires off a large heap, in an outdoor area in Station 9's district. Paul just looked at me and said, "Look at Taz...he just won't quit!" In fact, every firefighter other than Jimmy, quit for twenty-minute intervals before returning to what was an exhaustive task. Jimmy just kept tossing tires with each arm, and would smile that "Taz" smile then stick his tongue out whenever he saw us staring at him. Taz continued tossing tires for over three hours that day!

Jimmy Howe was one of the nicest human being I ever knew during over twenty-six years of living the life of a firefighter. He had a finger ripped off while fighting a fire but that didn't keep Taz from returning to work within a few months.

Before Squad 164 became a paramedic squad, I was working on Squad 164 as a firefighter with Howard Ure. The squad responded to a reported injury at a home. When Howard and I entered with our rescue box there was a woman crying because she had sliced her hand while cooking. Howard had a way with women, so he put his arm around the lady as I began to cleanse and wrap her wound. Howard said, "Now now, stop crying, you'll be just fine." Just then the lady said, "This has been a terrible morning!" Howard asked why, then she continued, "first my daughter had to stay home from school because she has a rash on her vagina and now I have sliced my hand!" Howard, with a straight face, answered, "Well let's take a look at that little beauty; maybe we can apply a lotion to it!" Many years later, Howard was murdered when he was a captain at Fire Station 3. A woman who wouldn't pay her rent shot Howard in the head. The incident never received much publicity because it occurred while Howard was off duty.

Before going on, I have to tell you about the time I was working overtime on another shift at Station 164. Battalion Chief Jack Hinton and his driver whose name is Hayden Swingle were having Sunday brunch with our crew. Swingle had brought in a twelve inch rubber dildo; it remained at our table, just vibrating, all during brunch. Chief Clinton lost at cards, so he had to do all the cleanup work. Jack was known as being a terrible loser at anything, so he threw a trash can out of our upstairs opened window; that was shortly followed by Swingle throwing out that rubber dildo. A few of us ran to the window to see two elderly ladies walking arm-in-arm. When they approached that vibrating dildo, they both looked down, and then looked at each other, before steeping around it. It was so funny that even Hinton started laughing, then he said, "Somebody run down and pick up that damn thing before I start getting phone calls." Stuff like this was routine, so the fun helped relieve any pressure.

The Saddest Fire I Witnessed

I was still the engineer assigned to Truck164 on the day this fire occurred:

Engine 164 and Squad 164 were out on separate calls. Suddenly the alarm bell rang; then the loud speaker was telling us that Truck 164 should respond to a reported warehouse fire on Santa Fe Avenue. James Sheppard was the firefighter who joined me as we turned right on Santa Fe Avenue. We could immediately see smoke rising in the distance. I was senior but Jim was on both the engineer and captain's list, so I asked him to get on the radio and ask the location of Engine 164. We were informed that Engine 164 was on a rescue in our district, so I knew Truck 164 would be the first-in company at the fire. As we approached we noticed Sheriff Department deputies hiding behind their vehicles; then as we got nearer, we saw compressed-gas cylinders firing into the air like rockets. When we had less than a block to go, we could see Engine 164 completely engulfed in flames.

What happened, we later learned, was that Engine 164 had left their previous assignment when they saw smoke a block away. When they arrived, Captain Warr told Jim Hannum to park Engine 164 directly at the front gate so they could attack the fire directly. What Captain Warr did not know was there were gas cylinders in the storage yard that were also involved in the fire. As Captain Warr was on the tailboard, preparing to pull 1 ¾ inch hose, one of the cylinders that was blazing began spinning, and then shot directly at Engine 164. The cylinder lodged under the back wheels and continued to spew fire on our beautiful engine. Jim Hannum was temporarily surrounded by fire so he started running, but he turned to see if Doug Warr was safe; as he was looking at Doug, Jim center-punched a street sign with his hugh body and fell to the ground. Captain Warr immediately jumped off the tailboard and rolled on the ground until his turnouts stopped burning. But, every few seconds, cylinders continued to explode and fly over us, then came down like floating razor blades. Just then, Engine 9 and Engine 16 arrived, so they contained the fire to the storage yard and saved the warehouse. Engine 164 was, however, a complete loss.

The Saddest Rescue I witnessed

Willie Sanchez was working overtime at Fire Station 3 as a captain, and I was I was working overtime as an engineer the night Station 3 responded to a reported vehicle collision on the freeway just behind the station. We were informed that people were trapped. When we arrive, we saw a car completely mangled which had stopped at the side of the freeway. We didn't notice the second vehicle at first, so Captain Sanchez and a paramedic looked over the side of a hill; there they could see a truck lying on its side. After Willie came back he looked ashen, so he sat down on the running board of Engine 3. I asked him, "What's wrong Willie?" Tears were rolling down his face when he replied, "That's my brother in that truck: he's dead."

Certainly we had much-worse incidents where people were decapitated or guts were lying in the street but this is the saddest for me because Willie and I were friends who worked at Fire Station 22.

The Two, Funniest Fires I Witnessed

Nothing is really funny when people lose all their possessions or property damage forces a plant to shut down: people temporarily lose their income until the plant resumes production; but certain fires leave you laughing. The fires that followed left many of us firefighters hysterical with laughter.

The first one was a vehicle repair shop which had seventeen cars and trucks inside the building. Ernie Golphenee was one of the firefighters working on Engine 22 with Captain Don Doppenberg and me. For weeks Ernie kept asking, "Ralphie, when are we going to have a really-big fire? I can't wait to see how I do!" Well we found out how Ernie would react that night. As we approached the fire on Atlantic Boulevard, the captain radioed Station 3 to come up on Woods Street and take the west side of the fire. We stopped at the nearest hydrant and the other firefighter got off the rig to pull lines so he could connect them to the hydrant; meanwhile, after I drove up to the fire, Doppenber got off and ran around the entire building to see what else needed to be done. Just then, as I was connecting those two lines to outlets on Engine 22, Ernie ran up to me and yelled, "Ralphie, I've gotta take a shit, I've gotta take a shit!" I laughed as I said, "Ernie, I don't care if you shit in your turnouts, but first you'd better take a 2 ½ inch hose line and start protecting the north side of the building." What wasn't funny was that Captain Kenny Phillips and firefighter Ozzie Amparin, who arrived on Engine 3, were working a high-volume, water monitor on the asphalt, when suddenly the monitor began to slide and flip in the street. Both Kenny and Ozzie refused to let go, so both were hurt and bruised; they both had to receive medical treatment from Squad 3 after the fire was out. I ran over to see if they were okay, then I told everyone about Ernie. Poor Ernie just couldn't find a place to hide after that. Guys kept screaming things like, "Hey Ernie is the shit in your turnouts lumpy or runny?"

The second fire happened about 2:00 a.m. on the night I was working as an engineer at Fire Station 22. We awoke to hear that there was a building fire in our district; so, along with Fire Station 3, which included an engine, truck and squad, and Fire Station 27, which included an engine and a truck, we all responded to that fire on Olympic Boulevard. It was a combination retail store and warehouse where we had shopped for fresh bread and rolls many times in the past.

When we arrived, we found the warehouse portion fully involved in fire; in fact, the roof had already collapsed, so smoke and flames were visible from far away. Wayne Brooks was the captain; he was newly assigned to Fire Station 22, so as we approached the fire, he asked me what I thought. I answered, "Cap, the building is already lost, but there are fourteen inch water mains running all down Olympic Boulevard, so we'll have no problem with water." Captain Brooks got on the radio and told Station 3 to attack the front of the fire while Engine 22 took the back; then he told Fire Station 27 to wait on Olympic Boulevard until he had time to access what else needed to be done. I dropped off the captain and the firefighters at the warehouse door, and then I drove past the building. I approached the building from the alley. I stopped the rig next to a metal barrier; that was as close as I dare get to the corrugated-metal, roll-up door, and then I set the brakes. By this time Squad 3 was there to assist me so Lloyd Laye and the other paramedic began pulling hose to connect to a hydrant that was toward the alley.

The roll-up door had warped from the heat of the fire and was in the up position so Lloyd and I hooked two 2 ½ inch lines to the metal barrier which ran all along a ramp that descended to the roll-up door, so trucks could back down easily and unload their cargo; I told the other paramedic to go assist Engine 3, so off he ran. Lloyd and I managed to keep the fire from extending into the market area of the building while Station 3 firefighters extinguished the fire. There was so-much water flowing that it filled the entire ramp area and resembled a lake.

Assistant Fire Chief Jim Enright had been informed of the fire and was en-route to our location, but arrived after the fire was extinguished. After he walked through the warehouse portion of the building he stood at the rolled-up door and gave me a "Thumbs Up" with both hands. I turned for a second but heard a splash; when I looked back all I could see was Chief Enright's helmet floating on the water. I ran to the other side of Engine 22 and started honking the horn. As all the men began to arrive, they also saw the helmet. Apparently it was so slimy and slippery that the chief lost his footing several times. When he did finally appear, he looked at us then spit out a mouth full of black, filthy water. He looked at me and I said, "Hey Chief, you picked a Hell of a time to go swimming!" Chief Enright just glared at me and responded with, "Fuck you Mendoza!" There was nothing left to be done so, all of us just sat and roared with laughter, Chief Enright, with his turnouts dripping and his boots filled with slimy, black and filthy water, sat in his car and was about to drive away. We all got up and started clapping so that made Engright even madder. He even left skid marks as he sped away!

Jim Enright had a nephew who also attended Rio Hondo Prep., and he knew I was friends with Willie Menold. One day as we were both hitting golf balls at a range in Arcadia, Jim warned me about Menold because Jim felt Menold was callous, devious and mean-spirited. I disagreed because I had known Willie for several years on a casual basis, which is to say that we worked together a few times, but now I was working with Menold almost daily when he replaced Jim Hannum on Engine 164. At about that time John Price also replaced Dough Warr so I really liked working with both. I told Jim that the only thing I had noticed about Menold was that he would run up to the kitchen and lick each piece of meat he wanted to reserve for himself. None of us would touch that meat after seeing that, so Menold would glare at us and laugh in our faces. I guess that should have been a warning but I overlooked it at the time.

In fact, Willie and his wife Irene became our closest friends. They joined us when we took a trip to camp in Angeles National Forrest and spent the day in our trailer. We had so much fun being with them that we began taking Steve and Tina with us when Irene would invite us over for supper.

Irene was unstable so Willie had to rush home one night when Irene tried to commit suicide: she shot herself in the stomach with a pistol. Willie immediately moved out and was living in Long Beach with another firefighter. When I moved out of our Danbury home the first time, Willie said it would be alright if I roomed with them until I decided what to do about my situation with Eileen.

Willie never went back to Irene but he was lonely and wanted Eileen. I vividly remember telling Menold while we were working together at Station 164 that I had a date with a girl named Jane who lived in Dana Point. Willie and were together the night we met Jane when we were bar hopping. I told him I didn't know what to do because I had accepted an invitation from Eileen to have supper with her while Steve and Tina were at Mary's apartment. I asked Willie what I should do so he replied, "Why don't you keep both dates." So that's what I did. I never suspected that Willie was trying to take Eileen away from me, but when I was sure that something was going on between them I immediately transferred from Station 164 to Station 22.

Although I really liked working at Station 164 I decided that I could no longer work with Menold. I can remember one morning after I had that date with Jane: I heard brakes squealing in the alley behind Station 22. Eileen jumped out of her car and started yelling, "You bastard, now I know why you left so early that night! You had a date with that bitch in Dana Point!" After she left I couldn't figure out how Eileen had learned about that affair I had with Jane. Now the puzzle was starting to take shape. I'm no Sherlock Holmes, but even I could figure out what had been going on behind my back.

It was Menold who was pulling the strings like some puppeteer in the hope that Eileen and I would divorce so he could take my place. I'm also sure that it was Menold who had called to inform on me when I had that date with Jane because he was the only person I told. Jim Enright was correct in his assessment of Mendold when he said Menold was as devious as he turned out to be.

Willie became known as "Dog-Shit Menold" when we were playing golf together at Singing Hills in El Cajon, on our annual golf outing. Someone in the foursome ahead of us had scribbled a note and attached it to a rake, then planted the rake in a large pile which had probably been dropped by a dog or coyote. On the note was written, **"Here are the remains of Dog Shit Menold: looking like what he really is!"**

When Menold was promoted to captain he was first assigned to another station but quickly transferred to a spot that was vacant at Station 47 so he could be closer to Eileen. Dad and I would see Engine 47 parked at Rio Hondo Prep when we went to see Steve play in a football, basketball or baseball game; we also saw Engine 47 parked at the school when we went to see Tina play in several basketball games. We both knew that it was Menold who was there with Eileen.

After Eileen and I divorced Eileen married Menold, but he died while he was a training captain. Steve and Eileen were there when Menold died of heart failure; I later found out about his death when Rafael Ortiz called me from our dispatch office. Steve felt terrible because he was unable to save Menold that night.

It's not surprising that law-enforcement officers and firefighters lead the nation statistically when it comes to divorces in the United States: many law-enforcement officers become cynical after dealing with situations which can cause anyone to become contemptuous after dealing with what they do on a daily basis. They take their problems home with them which can cause havoc with their spouses. Firefighters, on the other hand, are away from home for long periods of time; sometimes that leads to their spouses looking to someone else for comfort.

During the time I worked as a firefighter and engineer, three men married women who had been wives of former friends. Now I was to become the fourth. I guess Captain Carrillo knew what he was talking about when he warned me about not getting too close to the men I was working with and suggested that I keep my private life separate from my career.

It is not my intent to vilify Willie Menold, but if I am to be true to my conscious I must write what follows:

Menold would lie about everything. The year after he married Eileen, I saw him with a woman in his Corvette behind our hotel at Singing Hills. The next day we played against each other in a "Derby" but no matter how much I hated him, I did laugh because he could be very funny. Later that night, while I was in the restroom, Willie entered and tried to patch things up, but before he could say a word, I looked at him straight in the eyes and said, "Menold, as far as I am concerned you died five years ago!" I think Menold knew that I had seen him behind our hotel, so I think he was afraid I would tell Eileen and the kids what I had seen the night before, so he went home and told Eileen and the kids that *he* told *me* that as far as he was concerned, I had died five years ago. I didn't learn about it until many years later when Tina and I were arguing. She said, "Dad…you were so bad that even Bill had to tell you that he felt like you had died five years ago!" I still don't understand what logic Tina used to form her opinion. I never dated or phoned Irene, even after I learned about Menold's affair with Eileen. Menold had taken my place, not the other way around, so why Tina would ever believe him instead of her father is something I will never understand.

I was to work with many captains while I was at Station 22. My regular captain was Ray Maldonado. He used to call himself, "Sexy Ray from East L.A." I don't know about that, but I do know that he was a womanizer who boasted that he had once met a nun at a gathering. According to Ray, the nun was so distant and aloof that night that Ray decided he wanted to get her drunk so he could sleep with her. I guess he succeeded in doing exactly that because he told the crew at Station 22 that he took a special delight when he left the nun asleep – complete naked – at the side door of the church the following morning.

Willie Menold had been Ray's engineer before Menold transferred to take the vacant spot when Jim Hannum left Station 164. Ray and Menold were bar-hopping buddies when they were off duty but apparently Menold got mad when Ray asked Menold to sign his first performance evaluation. In the evaluation there were words such as lazy and unreliable; those words offended Menold because he thought they were untrue, so he immediately transferred. In fact it was Menold who suggest that if I were going to leave Station 164 that I should transfer to Station 22 because he said I would really like working with Ray Maldonado.

The one thing the two had in common, I thought, was that they both seemed to delight in the misery of others. Ray's spot was frozen for about eighteen months while he went through therapy for a bad back. Ray became one of the guys I would play golf with for several years. He had a lung removed after he retired because he had developed lung cancer. He was found dead at the base of the hill that led to the golf course.

We went through over ten captains who were temporarily assigned to Station 22 for brief periods of time after Ray left. David Galindo joined our crew about this time, so we became instant friends. We used to jog up and down Grace Place, which is only a block from the firehouse. There was always a lot of change on the asphalt because lunch wagons would stop there as people purchased food. Davey and I had a contest each time we jogged; we wanted to see who would pick up the most change; so I began calling Davey "Galindostein" and he called me "Mendozavitch." David is one of the smartest firefighters I would ever work with during my time on the department. We remain great friends even now and is one of the two men I admire most.

This is where I also experienced working with a woman for the first time. Her name is Cindy Fralick; she was working an overtime shift at Station 22 on the day I met her. I had slept in my van behind the station because I had been drinking the night before and wanted to be sure that I arrived at the station in time for shift change. When I entered our bathroom I could see two small feet in sandals just behind the stall door. I immediately said, "Oops!" I could hear her laughing as I walked out. Later the overtime captain and I were sitting in his office, discussing what adjustments we would have to make, when I said, "Let's test her!" All new firefighters are immediately tested to see their reactions, so we both thought it would be fun to test Cindy.

When we returned from a normal response Cindy immediately climbed down from her seat and jumped on the tailboard. We had a button on the rail of the tailboard so that the firefighter could signal the engineer if it was safe to back in to the station. After I had positioned Engine 22 to begin to back into the barn I waited for Cindy to signal me. The normal signal is one beep to stop, two beeps to go forward and three beeps to begin to back in, so Cindy gave me three quick beeps. I looked over at the captain and said, "Let's do it now!" I placed the transmission in reverse and flew up the ramp. Cindy never removed her finger from the button for the entire time I was backing in so we could hear one continuous buzzing noise as we literally flew into where the apparatus was housed. I had a piece of reflective tape glued to the spot I would attempt to stop next to so the rig was perfectly centered. Cindy must have thought that I'd hit the back wall so she never took her finger of that button. I abruptly hit the brakes and came to the stop I had marked. Suddenly Cindy came running at me and threw her shoulder in my chest! The captain, Davey and I really started laughing so that made her even madder. She had the cooking assignment that day and she really served us two fine meals, but later that night we found it difficult to be in a bed next to a woman for the first time, so I felt very uncomfortable when she would turn in the bed next to mine and I could see her in her regulation shorts and T-shirt. I didn't sleep too well that night because I was always waking up so I could see what Cindy looked like in different positions. When I finished this manuscript I called Cindy. She is now a captain at Fire Station 17 and is about to retire. She said she remembered me and the time she thought she was going to be killed when I backed the rig into the barn. Memories like this one will stay with me forever. Cindy was famous because she was the first female to be hired by our department. They even made a movie about her life as a firefighter. The movie was appropriately titled *Firefighter* and starred Nancy McKeon.

Over the years the Los Angeles County Fire Department has always been instrumental in innovative changes. The department was one of the first to begin to explore the use of firefighters as paramedics and train EMTs in the use of defibrillators. In fact Engine 22 was one of the engine companies who received training in its use. I can't tell you how thrilled we felt after finding a person who had died, then after correctly using the defibrillator we were testing, we were able to restore a normal heart beat. I was personally involved in three incidents where, after properly using our defibrillator, a person whom we found dead was restored to life and was being loaded onto a gurney with a normal heart beat!

One of the temporary captains at Station 22 was Tom Fullerton. Tom was the engineer at Station 1 when I transferred to Station 1 as a firefighter and Ron Jones later replaced our former captain.

One day while Tom, Ron and I were working our regular shift at Station 1, Tom asked me about my wife and children. I said that I had two children and that Eileen was Irish and had gone to Washington High School. Tom looked at me and said, "Hey Ralphie...I remember Eileen; wasn't she in the Delta-Y sorority?" I answered that Eileen must have been the same girl Tom was talking about. I didn't know it at the time, but Tom was waving bait in front of me. All day he kept bringing up the subject of Eileen and what a wonderful girl she was. He said that Eileen's best friend was a little loose when it came to the boys in school but that Eileen remained pure. Finally while we were having supper, Tom finally yanked the hook when he said, "As far I can remember, Eileen was only intimate twice." I really bit when I came back with, "Oh yeah, tell me about it?" Tom answered with, "As I remember it she only had sex twice: once by the football team and once by the band!" Ron ran out the back door and I fell to the floor. I almost vomited from choking on my food, because Tom had hooked me good yet I couldn't stop laughing!

Believe me, these are only a few of the stories I've collected over the years. Some of the stories I have, I first read about in *Straight Streams*, which is our monthly magazine. I've also borrowed a few stories from the L.A. County Fire Department Golf Association newsletter that Tom Peacock sends out each month; Here's two portions of articles Dave Stone sent in; I borrowed them to show how outrageous our group was.

For four years at Singing Hills, the foursome of Jim Eaton, Keith Chausse, Larry Carroll and Bob Cross would play golf in a different costume every year...the "Cone Heads", the "Blues Brothers", the "Beach Boys", and "G.I. Joes". They were fantastic!

Here's another one.

Probably the best one of all was the golf cart in the room on the second floor of the hotel. How it got there I will never tell. The next day the cleaning lady called the office and said there was a golf cart in room 212. Impossible...I don't think so!

It seems that each year our group travels to Singing Hills we always return with new stories to tell; I know I have stored a collection of stories such as this one:

For about fourteen years my golfing foursome consisted of Gary Dennis, Larry Simcoe, Ed McGrail and, of course, me; we also used to room together. One night I went to bed early as my roommates were outside putting after midning, on a lighted green playing "Shower-Down" for a dollar a hole. I was asleep on a roll-out bed in the living room when suddenly I woke up to feel something moving: it was a large furry cat! I jumped out of that bed and ran outside, followed shortly by that frightened cat. Thank Heaven the sliding door was opened or I might had really been hurt. As I stood outside in my shorts, all the guys turned and started throwing beer cans at me! I was told the next morning that one of my roomates had placed the cat next to me then slipped out of the sliding door because that wanted to scare, not hurt, me so the culprit made sure to leave the sliding door opened.

Just before I left Station 22, our engine company was taking a class with several other companies at Fire Station 50. The paramedics from Station 3 were conducting a class on rescue in the field. I felt ill as I sat in the back of the rec room. I just couldn't stop thinking about all that had happened to destroy our marriage and cause a rift with my children. I started to experience chest pain and felt weak, so as I got up to go to the restroom, I suddenly dropped to one knee. Everyone was alarmed so the paramedics rushed over to check my vital signs; meanwhile my captain requested an ambulance. A few minutes later I was being rushed to the nearest hospital. As I lay in the back of the ambulance I looked over to the paramedic who was trying to get me to calm down, and asked him to please call Steve and Tina and tell them that if I didn't survive, my last thoughts were of them.

After the emergency-room doctor examined me, he said that I had not suffered a heart attack, but I did have a severe anxiety attack. That's about when Steve, Tina and Eileen joined me in a private room. The kids started crying and even Eileen gave me a look which said she felt bad. I tried to hide my anxiety from them but couldn't, so I began to weep. The doctor told Eileen that he was going to keep me for a few hours to observe me, but that I would not be allowed to return to duty that day. After Eileen and the kids left, I received my first dose of Xanax.

I transferred to Fire Station 40 shortly after that incident. As I wrote earlier, I spent the last five years of my time on the job working as an engineer at Fire Station 40. My first captain was one of the funniest captains I ever worked with. His name is Mark Wagner and we remain friends even to this day. On the first day I reported for duty, Engine and Squad 40 responded to a reported structure fire in Fire Station 28's area. The moment I jumped behind the driver's seat, Mark looked at me and asked, "Hey Mendoza, when's the last time you had some great pussy?" Even as we were driving up Beverly Boulevard and could see smoke billowing in the sky, Mark continued with, "You gotta admit it...huh? There's nothing like great pussy in the morning." I said, "Mark, let me concentrate; I don't even know where I'm going!" I was laughing so much that I turned right a block before I should have turned left; so we had to go around the block before we could drive up an alley to attack the house fire from behind.

Mark had to wear an ear piece because his hearing had gone bad, so he was conscious of it and became embarrassed when he had to ask someone to repeat himself. It was impossible to talk with Mark on the phone, because he couldn't hear you, so you found yourself shouting everything. One day I was working overtime at Station 3; Mark had worked overtime there a few days earlier so the guys kept telling me that they would just move their mouths but not speak. I guess Mark went half crazy trying to understand what was said to him that day! Mark finally retired so we had a few captains after him.

I enjoyed being at Fire Station 40 because my father would come by whenever he knew I was on duty, so we'd sit and have coffee and just chat. All the guys liked my father so they invited him to stay for lunch or supper many times. Dad sure got a kick out of playing cards for dishes, but none of us ever let him lose. Dad was a car painter by trade, so whenever I felt we needed to paint the undercarriage of Engine 40, we would go to a steam-cleaning shop and I would wash any oil and grease from the undercarriage, while the firefighter who was assigned to our engine that day would wipe everything dry, then my father would show up with his equipment and paint our rig.

Most days when we were out in the district, we'd stop at my father's home and spend a few minutes with him. Those were days I really enjoyed.

I bought a small puppy and named him Dudley. I used to ride my bicycle to the firehouse each day when I was on duty. I'd leave early so I could have a cup of coffee with Dad, then I'd leave Dudley with him for the day. Dad had a dog which played in his secure, back yard; so I knew Dudley would be safe for the time I was away. Other times I would take Dudley with me to the firehouse. The guys didn't mind so long as I cleaned up any mess he made before I left the next morning. Dudley and I used to sleep in our equipment room; there we had a recliner, so Dudley would fall asleep on my chest. It sure was funny when Dudley would suddenly wake up to find me jumping into my turnouts then closing the door, so I could jump on Engine 40 and head for a response.

When my father died, Captain Bobby Contreras took Engine and Squad 40 the burial services at Rose Hills Memorial Park in Whittier. Bobby sat with Ed Murrieta and a few others to say goodbye to my father; it was a very touching moment for me because Dad thought so highly of Eddie, David and the men of Station 40. Later, we all gathered at my father's home. Eddie couldn't stay but it was typical of him to stop at a market and buy four cases of beer, then drop them off before he left that day.

Before Max Everson joined our crew, we had a captain who was far-too immature to ever be responsible for the care of any men. One morning, while members of all three shifts were gathered having coffee, this child who had been promoted to captain walked in; he asked me what our scheduled housework for the day was. Each firehouse has a list of things which the on-duty personnel must complete so the firehouse will remain neat and clean, for example: if it's Saturday, then it's lawn day, or if it's Tuesday, it's window day.

He began to reprimand our crew in front of Captain Contreras and others from the other two shifts. Captain Contreras just looked at me and shook his head. Bobby was a captain who had worked at Fire Station 40 for over twenty-five years; he was one of the most-highly thought of captains on our job. I had told our new captain on his first shift that we had taken care of what was scheduled to be done that day; but since that day was only his second shift as a captain, he chose to show his authority to everyone present.

Later I cornered him in his office and asked him if he was aware of what he had just done; he sat at his desk and answered, "No...tell me?" So I said, "You just violated the first rule of being a good captain: you humiliated the men you in your charge in front of a seasoned fire captain and men from the other two shifts." I said I could just imagine the gossip that would begin to circulate among the other shifts because our crew had to be chewed out for not doing their assigned work. I asked him if he had ever, even once, come out to see what his men were doing the day he first worked as a newly-promoted captain; his answer was, "Well...no I didn't, because I was too busy learning how to complete reports." Then I recounted how on his first shift as a captain he wanted us to wait all night for the power company to come to the home we were at, to sever a downed, power line. Any captain knows that the bottom wire on any pole is always the phone line, but this child didn't even know that. So I suggested we simply cut the line ourselves and head back to the barn.

I threatened to call our battalion chief so we could have a private, shift meeting to discuss what had happened, but he declined, saying, "That won't be necessary; I get your point, so I'll never do that again." But the damage was done; fortunately that idiot was quickly transferred to another station.

My last captain was Max Everson; I had known him when he was an engineer at Fire Station 27. Max was sure fun to work with; at first he seemed very reserved, but later he became more open to the men, so we all liked Max very much. Max was my last captain and constantly helped me as my career was coming to an end.

Engine 40 responded to a reported stabbing at a local Chinese fast-food restaurant. When the three of us who were working on Engine 40 entered the front door, we saw a large swath of blood which led to a boy who was unconscious on the floor. Max began taking down information as Squad 40 arrived. Meanwhile the paramedic assigned to Engine 40 and I cut off the kid's shirt. Still we could see no visible signs of wounds, so we log-rolled him on to his stomach. Just then blood spurted into my right eye because the boy had a partially-severed artery in his back; in fact, he had been stabbed in many places on his upper back. My knee-jerk reaction was to rub my eye, so I rubbed a lot of blood into it that evening. We were able to save the kid: when Squad 40 returned from the hospital, they said the boy would survive. All went normally for a few weeks then Captain Everson called me into his office. He asked me if I remembered the boy we had saved and I answered, "Sure, I do. Why?" Max asked me to sit down then said, "We just received the results of the blood work on the boy who was stabbed – he is HIV Positive."

I sat in his office and looked so despondent that Max said that it would probably be best if I went to the emergency room at Whittier Presbyterian Hospital. I waited until another engineer arrived to replace me, then got into my car and drove to the hospital.

The emergency-room doctor drew blood from me but said that the gestation period was about six months before he could definitively learn if I had acquired the disease. He recommended that I be given a leave of absence from the department and seek a good psychiatrist to help me with any issues I might have. He finished our session by saying he would recommend a minimum of six months for me to seek help. The department backed me fully, so after I saw a doctor in West Hollywood, I went back to the emergency-room doctor and he advised me to see Dr. Charles Wilson. He said Dr. Wilson was a very-good psychiatrist and had his office in Whittier.

I received authorization from the department then saw Dr. Wilson. We discussed many issues including my feelings that I was letting the department down, so that was the first issue we discussed. I told him I was engaged to a woman but that she was hesitant to continue with our plans because she feared getting the disease so Dr. Wilson and I discussed all of the losses we all suffer in life.

When Dr. Wilson asked me about my childhood I broke down while I was reliving those terrible events of my past; finally Dr. Wilson said that we had a lot of work to do before I could begin to feel healthy again, he said, "Ralph you have to resolve your personal issues before you can deal with your departmental problems, so be prepared for a long and arduous period." Dr. Wilson then asked me what I was doing to combat any stress I felt, so I told him I was jogging two or three miles a day every week and reading a lot of great books. Dr. Wilson immediately started writing something on a note pad: it was a list of books he recommended I read to help me work through my problems. Here are only a few of the books on that list:

Looking Out for #1 by Robert J. Ringer.
Necessary Losses by Judith Viorst.
The Road Less Traveled by M. Scott Peck, M.D.
Obsessive Love by Dr. Susan Forward.
The Gentle Art of Verbal Self-Defense by Suzette Haden Elgin.

I already had *Looking Out for #1*. So I went home and began reading it for the second time. This time the book meant much more to me than when I first read it. I especially liked the chapters on overcoming *The People Hurdle, The Love Hurdle* and *The Friendship Hurdle*. Eventually I bought the rest of the books on Dr. Wilson's list and others I checked out of the Whittier library. Still, even to this day, I always return to Mr. Ringer's book whenever I feel I have a problem to resolve.

About a week later Dr. Wilson asked me what else I enjoyed doing, so I answered that I really missed playing golf with my friends. He said he would write a report to the department advising that I remain off the job for as long as it took for me to receive the results of my blood tests and resolve my personal problems. He also recommended that I be allowed to play as much golf as I wished: he thought my being outdoors would help me while I was rehabilitating.

I started seeing Dr. Wilson twice a week, then once a week,

and finally every-other week. At the last session I had with Dr. Wilson he recommended I go home and write a list of all the pain I felt inside. He said, "Ralph, you should really be thorough and include everything on that list. Then I want you to perform a ritual that many people have found to be helpful: I want you to burn that list and see all your suffering go up in smoke!"

We hugged each other on that last session. I didn't know it at the time, but I was to return to Dr. Wilson for a second time just before I retired. He continued to prescribe Xanax but warned me that it was addictive, so he would only prescribe that drug for a limited time. He didn't know that I had unlimited access to Xanax from my drug-selling pals whom I spent time with in the "Bookie Joints" I used to frequent.

After I returned to duty, things were normal for a short period of time, but one day Engine 40 responded to a reported warehouse fire a few blocks from our station. Squad 40 was out on a rescue with another company, so they were unavailable to assist us. The captain that day was Carl Allen; he was a veteran captain and I had a lot of faith in his decision-making ability. When we arrived at the warehouse yard, we saw fire and smoke rolling out of the warehouse door which was about to ignite another building and some lumber which was stacked next to that building. Carl said, "If the firefighter knocks this down right here, I can go inside the building and confine the fire to just one section of the warehouse." I had passed a hydrant about five-hundred feet away, so I said, "That sounds like the thing to do. While you're attacking the fire, I'll connect to that hydrant back there." I engaged the pump and opened the necessary valves, then, after I was certain Carl and the firefighter had water (Engine 40 carried five-hundred gallons of water) I ran to the back of the engine and began pulling 4" hose and the hydrant valve. I threw out six-hundred feet of hose to be certain that I wouldn't come up short. I threw one section over my left shoulder and another over my right and held the hydrant valve in my right hand. I struggle to a point about half way to the hydrant because I was pulling over three-hundred pounds of hose and the hydrant valve. I suddenly felt a deep pain shoot up my lower back. I was on the asphalt as the second engine company arrived so they completed connecting the hose and valve to the hydrant. Just then the other companies arrived so the fire was confined to only a small portion of the warehouse. Neither Carl nor the firefighter ran out of water because the engineer on the second-in engine took over while I was still on the asphalt. I was afraid to move because each time I tried the pain only got worse, so I stayed in one position until I was being loaded onto a gurney.

Again I was taken to Whittier Presbyterian Hospital. This time I was diagnosed with a sprained back so again I was off work for over three months. Gradually the pain lessened with each passing week; of course I was half drunk most of the time and continued to take Xanax as well as the medication the emergency-room doctor prescribed. After those three months I decided to return to work because I was missing out on a lot of overtime money. After I returned to duty, I worked for a few months but never complained about the ache in my back. I had long-ago learned not to take my personal problems with me to work because anything I said would instantly become fuel in the minds of the others and I didn't want to walk around all day having jokes made about poor little Ralphie and his personal problems.

One day Engine 40 responded to a reported heart attack in a private home. Again Squad 40 was on another response, so we were on our own. When we arrived, we found a woman wedged between her bed and a piece of furniture. Captain Bobby Contreras told the paramedic and me to extricate the woman and take her into the living room. As we were moving the woman, my back gave out again and I fell on the woman in the hallway. The ambulance and Squad 40 arrived shortly thereafter so they moved the woman into the living room and began CPR as I lay in the hallway. They were unable to save the woman even after repeated efforts. That was the last day I ever worked as a firefighter/engineer.

Once again I returned to Whittier Presbyterian Hospital. This time I was given extensive x-rays. The emergency-room doctor said that I had a crushed vertebra in my lower back, so again, I was off the job for over a year. I became extremely depressed so I once again began to see Dr. Wilson as well as an orthopedic doctor.

By this time I was fed up and the department wasn't happy either. I felt terrible when I had to file bankruptcy because I was no longer receiving overtime money to pay my bills. Finally the department told me that I'd either have to have an operation or retire. I didn't want to retire, but I was reluctant to have an operation. I was given one year while my spot was frozen before opening it up for a permanent engineer to replace me. What made things worse was that during that last year, my salary was reduced from one-hundred percent (without any overtime) to seventy-five percent and finally fifty percent. What really infuriated me is that I never applied for bilingual pay. I routinely used my knowledge of Spanish to interpret what people who only spoke Spanish would say to me so I could relay that information to the paramedics; the paramedics would then relate, via radio, to emergency-room doctors any vital information about the patient. When we were involved in non-life-threatening responses I would inform law-enforcement officers with any helpful information. That additional income would have really helped me with my financial problems during that period.

About six months before I retired, I received a call from vocational rehabilitation asking me to come in so we could discuss what type of work I could do after I left the job. I kept the appointment but when the woman who was interviewing me asked, "What do you want to do now that you are unable to work for the fire department?" I answered that I only wanted to become a professional gambler. She was stunned at first, but asked me to return in two weeks while she researched my options. After two weeks I returned and she said, "Ralph, we've never been asked by someone to become a professional gambler but there is a course you can take which will allow you to become a dealer in any casino in Las Vegas." She went on to tell me that the course was for thirteen weeks and that vocational rehab would pay for my tuition, room and board and per diem as well as pay the cost for me to return every-other week to Whittier to see both of my doctors. So that's what I did.

I had requested a disability retirement, so I had to see several doctors and had the firm of Lewis, Marenstein, Wiche & Sherwin represent me. That firm was known to be knowledgeable in disability retirements and had successfully represented several of my friends in the past. After a few months I was awarded a disability retirement. I officially retired on March 4, 1996.

I would like to write the following before closing this chapter of my journey:

Most people have an image of what they perceive a firefighter to be: each is a man or woman whose life is filled with adventure, and he or she goes around putting out fires and saving people's lives. Well, that's true, to a certain extent; but now I would like to tell you what life is really like on a year-to-year basis.

Imagine you are a firefighter who is about to go to bed. It's raining outside, and the wind is howling. Just about the time you're in bed feeling cozy and warm, the bell rings, the lights come on and some voice on a speaker is telling you of a fire you have to immediately respond to or a child who has been seriously injured, You instantly jump into your turnouts and off you go. Let's say you're out of the firehouse for two hours. When you return, the engineer and firefighters clean all the equipment you used so it will be ready for the next response and the captain begins typing endless reports and entering the details of the response in the station's journal. You want nothing more than to take a hot shower before returning to bed. One firefighter is already in the shower so you stroll into the kitchen and raid the refrigerator or go into the rec room and turn on the TV. Finally, the shower is free, so you jump up to be next in line. After you take off your freezing turnouts and take off you wet underwear, you take a hot shower, then put on some fresh underwear. About a minute after you're back in your bed it happens again! Sometimes it happens five or six times a night.

Meanwhile you think about the house you were unable to save or the child who just died and you realize that now these events affect you much differently than when you first became a firefighter. Back then everything was new and exciting.

When I left the job Squad 3 averaged sixteen responses per shift: most of those were after midnight! If you do this long enough a lot of the glamour is replaced by tedium and it only gets worse with time spent on the job and age.

Looking back, I think that Xanax was the wrong medication for me because I became addicted to that drug shortly after I began taking it. When I had a stroke in 2003, I was finally mentally-strong enough to cease taking that terribly-addictive drug.

Chapter Eight

My "Wild-Child" Years

The day I retired from the department I closed the door on another chapter of my journey. I was at a turning point in my life. I could settle down and actually work at being the father I had only talked about or I was free to do as I pleased. I suppose there are numerous ways to rationalize my behavior: if anyone searches hard enough he or she can find any number of excuses for their actions. But the plain and simple truth is that for the next twenty-five years I did things that *pleased* only *me*!

I had started going to Las Vegas on an infrequent basis; eventually I was going almost every weekend. My first real score at the tables occurred on Tina's twenty-sixth birthday. I had called her a few weeks before to ask my daughter to join me on a Saturday so we could go to watch the thoroughbred-horses race at Santa Anita Race Track.

Before continuing this story I should inform you of two, simple facts: Christine has absolutely no fear of me; and she will do anything to embarrass me!

A few days before I was to pick up The Bop, I called my cousin Lorraine who worked at Santa Anita and asked her to reserve a box on the front row, so Lorraine called me back and said she had reserved box thirty-seven for us. On the Saturday morning we were scheduled to go, I knocked on the door where Tina was living. She shouted from an area in the back of her house, "Come in Dad...I'm in the laundry room." When I found her she was folding her underwear, so I casually said, "Gee Bop, you sure have a lot of different styles of underwear." Tina never looked at me when she answered, "I know Dad... but must most of the time I don't wear any!" I chose not to respond, but did chuckle a little as I walked out.

When we arrived at the race track we stopped to say hi to Lorraine. She hadn't seen The Bop in several years so she gave Tina a few "Tout Sheets" where Tina could read the names of horses the expert handicappers thought were the probable winners in all nine races.

When we found our box Tina commented that it was nice of me to reserve a box for us. Then she said, "Hey Dad, since were sitting in box thirty-seven, why don't we make an "Exacta Box" bet on numbers three and seven!" For those of you who don't know what an exact bet is: it's a bet and by making that bet you are betting that the two numbered horses you pick will finish first and second. An exact-box bet allows you to pick the same two numbers, but it doesn't matter which horse wins as long as the horse that finished second is also a horse you picked.

I looked at the *Daily Racing Form* and realized those two horses had absolutely no chance of winning or coming in second so I told The Bop we would be throwing our money away if we made that bet. As soon as the first raced finished, Tina hit me on the arm, then said, "Dad...you never listen to me. See number seven won and number three came in second!" She really went crazy when the payoffs were announced. A four-dollar exact-box bet returned over fourteen-hundred dollars if you picked numbers three and seven.

I just laughed when Tina said, "Let's try it again in the second race," I again looked at the form and said there was no way numbers three and seven could possibly win back-to-back races, when all four horses were long shots. Well, you guessed it! Number three won and number seven came in second again; this time the payoff was over one-thousand dollars. The Bop just gave me one of her goofy looks and said, "Dad...I see a couple of boys from RHP over there; do you mind if I go sit with them for awhile?" I said I didn't mind so after Tina left I decided to pay a visit to a pal of mine named Greg Gross who worked in the valet section of Santa Anita. Greg had been on the USC Trojan golf team along with Craig Stadler; both played for Coach Stan Wood while attending USC. I was surprised when Greg invited me to play a round of golf with Craig and him but I gladly accepted then said that I had to return to our booth because my daughter was waiting. Tina returned just after the end of the fourth race. As she walked over, she said, "Dad, I really have to get home because I have something planned for this evening." So I answered, "Fine. Let's make a bet on the fifth race, and then watch it before I take you home." As we were in line to make our bet, Tina again said, "Come on Dad...It's only four dollars! Let's make one bet on three and seven at least once today!" I shook my head and said, "No way Bop!" When that damned race finished the winner was number seven and the second horse was number three! The payoff was over twelve-hundred dollars. Tina tells that story whenever we're together with people who haven't heard it before so I suppose she'll even tell that story at my funeral. God, I hope she doesn't!

Just before leaving with Tina on her celebration trip I kept that golf date with Greg and Craig. I was stunned to see Stadler drive the first green with a 1 iron; in fact both he and Gregg drove the first green that day. I duffed my drive and had to use a pitching wedge to reach the green. A few holes later I was so frustrated that I snapped my driver. Suddenly I realized that I had sliced my left hand so it was bleeding profusely. For the remainder of the round I had to have my hand wrapped in a towel and only took the towel off to a swing any club. That incident probably remains one of the most embarrassing moments I have ever experienced while playing the game I love so much. I was so embarrassed that I didn't join them for a drink but jumped into my car and sped away!

Two days before leaving for Las Vegas I called the maitre d at Stefano's restaurant which is inside the Golden Nugget Hotel & Casino in Las Vegas and asked him to put on something special for my daughter's birthday. He answered, "No problem, Mr. M. everything will be paid by your host and ready at 6:30 p.m. on Saturday." I called Tina and she asked if she could bring Mike along so I answered yes. Very early that Saturday morning I picked up Tina and Mike then headed straight for Las Vegas.

We arrived shortly after noon then immediately checked in. A few minutes later we were down in the casino. Tina and Mike were playing the slots while I was at the craps pit. All of us lost that afternoon so we all agreed to shower and change, then meet at 6:00 p.m. for our celebration party. When we arrived at Stefano's the maitre d was there to welcome us. He took us to a nice table, and then summoned the wine steward over to our table. The maitre d said, "Happy Birthday young lady, I have reserved a special wine for your celebration," so the wine steward formally presented Christine with an expensive bottle of wine. The Bop just looked at the maitre d and said, "No thanks...all I want right now is a long-hard-screw-against-the wall." No one said a word; both the maitre d and the wine steward looked at me, I looked at Mike, Mike looked at Tina and everyone started laughing. Meanwhile, Tina never even smiled, but continued to stare straight ahead with another goofy look on her face! I apologized to the maitre d and the wine steward. Thank Heaven everything went normally after that. Stefano's had a group of singing waiters so they came over to our table and dedicated a song to Christine. We had a fabulous meal that night which included that bottle of wine. When we returned to the casino, it was almost 8:00 p.m. so Mike and Tina continued playing the slots while I was at the black-jack pit. About midnight they both came over to say they were tired and were going up to our room.

At about 4:00 a.m. I was throwing the dice and had just made a bet of one-hundred twenty-five dollars on a two-way "Yo" bet; which means I was betting one-hundred dollars for myself and twenty-five dollars for the dealers that my next roll would be an eleven. I turned just before I threw the dice to see The Bop dressed in a sweat shirt, jeans and sandals, and she was crying. I threw the dice and waited; suddenly the people around the table began shouting and clapping. I had rolled an eleven so the house paid me fifteen-hundred dollars for my wager and the dealers received four-hundred dollars. I knew that I had not received the correct payoff so I said, "Take me down." So my dealer added another one-hundred dollars to my stack. I was on fire that night and had over seven-thousand dollars in various checks (chips) in front of me. It took some time for the dealers to pay all those people who were betting as I was, so I looked at Tina and asked, "Why are you crying Bop?" Tina had stopped crying by now and said, "Hey Dad...throw me a "Hunskie" which meant she wanted me to toss her a black check worth one-hundred dollars. I did, so she grabbed it and stuffed it into her jeans. Again I asked her what was wrong. Tina answered, "I was worried about you when I woke up so I called security." "You did?" I asked, "what did they say?" Tina waited while I made a few more bets then threw the dice again. Then she said, "The man asked me who you were, so when I said you were Ralph Mendoza, he said not to worry because you were either drunk under some table or getting laid." I just laughed, but since Tina was no-longer crying, she stayed with me while I stayed hot for another five minutes. When I cashed out, I was paid eight-thousand nine hundred dollars. I finished my beer then Tina and I walked up to our room. We woke Mike up and we all sat around for over an hour just talking about how lucky I had been that night.

But the story hasn't ended yet! The next morning we checked out of our room, had breakfast and returned to Los Angeles. All along the way I felt great because I had won. I turned to The Bop and Mike and said, "You know...I think I'll return tomorrow and see if I can do it again." Tina said she didn't think that was such a great idea and said, "Dad...why don't you just accept what you won and forget it?" But I couldn't!

Tina was then working for the Los Angeles County Federal Credit Union, so early Monday morning I walked in and deposited seven-thousand dollars in my account. Before leaving I stopped at Tina's desk and we talked for awhile. Sylvia remains one of Tina's close friends and her desk was next to The Bop's so I walked over and said, "Sylvia, Tina did it to me again!" When she asked what I was talking about I told her the whole story about embarrassing me in front of the maitre d. Sylvia answered by saying, "That's nothing Mr. Mendoza, when Tina and I go out, she orders a blow job!" I threw up my hands, turned around and walked out, as Tina's was laughing up a storm. She had set me up once again!

I called Willie Ramirez who was a friend and was always available to take any trip as long as he wasn't paying. Coco (whom I will write more about) used to say that Willie would go to Hell if the Devil was serving a free meal. I knew that, but I liked Willie anyway. He was a friend of my father's whom I met when I first started playing golf at Montebello golf course. So Willie agreed to join me the next morning so we could return to Las Vegas, but first I had to arrange for someone to cover my spot at work. I picked Willie up and we returned to the Golden Nugget. One of the reasons I enjoyed Willie's company is that he really was a wise old man, when you took the time to understand him. I'm not exaggerating when I say that I took Willie to Las Vegas over one-hundred times from the time I met him until I moved to Henderson, Nevada. I would speak Spanish and he would correct me because I had asked him to help me to speak the language correctly and he would also do some of the driving as I gulped down beer after beer. Willie didn't like the fact that I smoked too much, but that was the price he had to pay for receiving all that he did. That night I hit the casino for an additional eight-thousand six-hundred dollars. In some ways I think it may have been better if I had lost several times when I first began gambling:

maybe I would have walked away from gambling in Las Vegas forever. But it didn't work out that way, so that's just the way things went for almost twenty-five years.

Now I was playing golf every day at Montebello when I wasn't working. We had a locker room that was private, so those of us who wanted to exercise, take a sauna and shower, had to pay a yearly fee. We had a key to the locker-room door and one for our locker. There, I had several changes of clothing as well as some cash stored so I was ready for anything. Our routine was to play golf in the morning, then go into the sauna for about thirty minutes, then shower, shave and head for Santa Anita or to a bookie. In the evenings we returned to our lockers and cleaned up before going to a Mexican bar/restaurant called La Casita or walking upstairs to the Quiet Cannon.

I guess I spent over twenty-five years sitting on a bar stool. If anyone spends as much time as I did sitting on a bar stool he quickly learns how alcohol and drug abuse can change a man. Some men become mean and wanted to fight anyone when they get drunk, but I always stayed mellow when I drank too much. I was involved in so many fights during the first two of my Wild-Child years, that I can't possibly remember them all. Eventually I found the answer I had been searching for. Whenever someone approached me wanting to argue, I immediately knew that the argument would lead to a fight, so I'd say, "Sorry pal if I've offended you but I've been involved in ten fights in my life and lost all ten, so before you punch me in the nose why don't you let me buy you a drink and we can just forget this argument." I guess I was doing exactly what my brother Tony had done; I learned that if I could get some drunk to laugh he'd soon forget what the argument was all about.

Sometimes, when I drank too much, I would park my van behind Station 22 so I wouldn't be late for work. That was fun because if I picked up a girl and didn't want to drive home or rent a motel, I could park my van behind the station, have some fun, then fall asleep! When I'd walk into the station some guy would say, "Look at Mendoza; he's been at it again!"

Dad only played on Saturday mornings, so I would join him. Steve even joined us a few times. He rode with my father and Willie Ramirez and I shared a golf cart.

Coco is a great friend of mine who is naturally funny and a very-stylish dresser. He is a bookie whom I first met one evening when I went to search for my father at a bowling alley in Montebello. I was impressed because, there sitting with Dad and Coco, were four beautiful Mexican women. Coco used to flash his wad of money: his roll of cash was so large that he used rubber bands to hold it together. All the ladies liked being with Coco because he paid for everything.

On a day much like any other, I was playing golf with Willie and Coco. We were getting ready to hit our second shots on Montebello's ninth hole when I received a message saying my mother had died. I immediately stopped playing and took our cart to the pro shop. There I received a phone number requesting that I call immediately. When I called the number, it was Grandma Mendoza's hospital nurse who answered. She asked my name and said she remembered me from my frequent visits to see Grandma Mendoza during the last years of her life. I was relieved that Mother hadn't passed away but sorry that I had lost one of the most influential human beings I was ever to know.

I remembered those many times when I would visit Grandma after a round of golf. Of course I reeked of beer and cigarettes, so Grandma would always say: "Por favor Ralphie, no bebe ni fuma demasiado." What Grandma was asking was for me not to drink or smoke too much. Her last year was terrible. She had already had one leg amputated and was scheduled to have her other foot amputated a few weeks after her death. On those days when I returned from Las Vegas and felt like I was a "Big Shot" Grandma would always say a Mexican phrase she used many times when speaking with me: "No escupas tan alto que no te pegue en la cara!" In her kind and gentle way she was warning me, "Never spit so high that it doesn't fall in your face." Grandma Mendoza was always there to gently correct me when I seemed to be losing my way. Her death affected me much more than others I had known and loved during my journey through life.

Grandma Mendoza was given a beautiful funeral and is now at rest in a cemetery in San Gabriel. Grandma Navarro rests in peace just a block from the house where Mom and I were so happy at while we lived on Second Street in East L.A.

One afternoon my cousin Joanie called to tell me her family was giving a surprise party to celebrate Aunt Emma's wedding. I really wanted to go because most of the Navarro side of my family would be there. I thought this was a perfect time for sweet revenge so I decided to play a prank on Joanie because she had once scolded me for wearing tan socks with a white outfit. So I wore a green shirt and shorts with a pair of horrible-looking purple socks. When I went to the backyard, I saw Joanie sitting with Aunt Emma. I had brought a bouquet of flowers for Aunt Emma, but Joanie never noticed them, all she could do was gawk at my purple socks. Joanie still tells the story of me and my purple socks!

That party was the last party we were all destined to gather together before loved ones slowing began to die. Aunty Virginia (my father's sister) had lost all four of her children in less than a year. These were the cousins I used to sleep with in the upstairs bedroom of Grandma Mendoza's unit at Ramona Gardens. Albert, Armeda, Theresa and Joe all died in a short space of time; I can't imagine the depression Aunt Virginia must have felt. Jo Jo, as we called him, is Steve's godfather, so he was always one of my favorites. Earlier in his life, Jo Jo worked with Ann Margaret and later with Helen Reddy on stage in Las Vegas. Jo Jo invited Grandma Mendoza, Aunt Virginia and a whole group of our family to the Helen Reddy show; he also invited me and a friend to fly to Las Vegas, so I took a woman I was dating at the time. We had a wonderful time. Jo Jo used to joke that Grandma Mendoza would walk so slowly that if she entered the hotel on Sunday she wouldn't reach her room 'till Tuesday!

Shortly after Grandma Mendoza died I learned Mary had died too. I attended her funeral services where Eileen and I exchanged a few emotional moments. I remembered how Mary never abandoned either my father or me while Eileen and Menold were at the same games our kids competed in. Mary always took a few minutes to sit with Dad and me. I also recalled Steven and Christine giving a piano recital at Rio Hondo Prep. Mary was beaming that night; we all were! When I walked out of the funeral hall that night I felt that I had lost another wonderful woman whom I truly loved. Mary, like Grandma Mendoza, was irreplaceable.

Both my father and I were living in San Gabriel, so I would jog down to his home and we would have a beer or two together. This is about the time when Dad and I started to become close. We would see each other at his home, at the firehouse or at the golf course. Dad became one of my best friends from about that time until his death on December 9, 1991. He was to continue to counsel and guide me although the first person

I always turned to for advice was Ed Murrieta. It's ironic that they should share the same first name.

One day my father came to Station 22 and introduced me to a woman named Elena. Dad said he was in love and wanted me to be his best man at their marriage. So a few days later we were headed to Tijuana, Mexico. We had a great day as Dad and Elena took their vows, then we partied all evening. Many years later I was again to be my father's best man when he married Decy here in Las Vegas; that happened only six months before Dad died. I'll bet I'm the only person you know who was the best man at his mother's wedding once, and his father's weddings twice!

I met two girls one night whose names are Sally and Kathy. I met them when I was in the upstairs bar above the Montebello golf course. The name of the restaurant and dance hall is The Quiet Cannon. I first met Sally so we danced together and eventually became smitten with each other. Kathy was also there on a date with a Latino named George. Sally said she wanted to see me later than night, so I said I was scheduled to leave very early the next morning on a skiing trip to Mammoth Mountain with a group of firefighters, but said I'd leave my door unlocked so she was welcome to come but could not stay the night. I jotted down my address, then left. A few hours later I woke up to find Sally in bed with me. We stayed up until dawn exploring each other so I had reason to believe that she was a woman I would continue to date.

But, as often happened to me in those crazy days, I spent the four days dreaming about Kathy. When I returned, I heard the phone ringing as I was inserting the key into the lock. Sally was on the phone asking when we could meet again; but I felt terrible when I said, "Sally, I like you, but I really hope to date Kathy." There was only silence on her end, but she finally said, "Well, if that's the way you feel, we can still remain friends. Let me call you back after I talk to Kathy." An hour later Sally called again to say she had spoken with Kathy. She said Kathy was reluctant to date me because I had slept with Sally first. I asked Sally if she would give me Kathy's phone number so we said goodbye shortly after she gave me Kathy's number.

I had a few beers to get up the nerve to call Kathy then finally I called. When she answered, she asked, "Why did you invite Sally to sleep with you if you wanted to be with me?" I answered that I thought she had been on a date with George that night. She laughed when she said, "George and I are old friends; we're not dating. I was hoping you'd ask me to go with you that night." Kathy agreed to date me once to see if we were compatible. Kathy lived in an apartment in Whittier, so the next Friday evening I picked her up and we went to a party. We were dancing and having a great time until Sally walked in; that was an awkward moment, so I asked Kathy if she would mind if I left early. She knew I wanted to leave because Sally was there so she said, "Sure, I'll ask Sally to take me home." We walked out to my car and had our first kiss that night. Within four months Kathy moved in with me. We remained living in San Gabriel until we scrimped up enough money to buy a condo in Whittier. When we moved in we both felt like this was the place of our dreams. My father thought we were moving much-too quickly; after all, he said, I had only been divorced from Eileen for less than a year. But I didn't listen to my father because by now I was in love with Kathy.

Kathy worked for Mt. St. Mary's College in Los Angeles so I would travel with her when she would take business trips to San Francisco, San Diego or Phoenix to recruit high-school seniors. We had some great times because she would drop me off at the nearest golf course, then visit several high schools in the area. She was quite good at recruiting so we had great times together when she signed a few girls to attend the school. I really liked San Francisco the most because I had never seen that beautiful city before. Kathy had an expense account, so we would stay at nice hotels and dine at some of the finer restaurants which seemed to be everywhere. One night we stopped at a restaurant which specialized in sea food. We had some of the best stuffed trout I have ever eaten; in fact, we ordered two extra orders and ate them later that night.

In all, Kathy and I stayed together for over two years. Slowly things began to change. She was always happy to go with me to Santa Anita or Hollywood Park because she loved watching the horse races. We made it a habit to always stop for supper at the Original Pantry Café in downtown Los Angeles because they were famous for serving great food and had only closed their doors once in over forty years. Dad and I loved eating there too. Sometimes when Kathy was away, I'd take my father there for supper. We had some great times together and Dad and I became more like what I thought a loving father and son should be as time went on and all those painful memories began to slowly fade away.

On the spur-of-the-moment, Kathy and I would head to Las Vegas. One weekend we drove to the Golden Nugget because Joe Williams was appearing and was one of my favorite singers from my father's era. That night Joe put on a great show for all of us. Since everything was free we had a front-row table reserved for us.

But Kathy was resentful because I was away for so many days. We began to quarrel often. One day, as I was returning to our condo, I stopped and bought fresh flowers, Champagne and Chinese cookies. I had left two-days earlier so I wanted to make up and enjoy that one evening together before returning to work an overtime shift at Station 163 in the city of Bell. When I got off the elevator I saw the door to our unit open so I walked in. I couldn't believe it: our condo was completely empty! She had taken everything in those two days when I was on duty. I found my clothing on the rug and some treasured pictures torn to pieces which she had thrown on the floor in our condo. I called my father and told him how I had found the condo so he immediately drove over. He said, "I told you I thought you were moving too quickly; now see what you have to deal with." He said I should go to Mt. St. Mary's the next day to confront Kathy; but I didn't. There was no way that I was going to give Kathy the satisfaction of begging for my stuff back. Fortunately, I had stored a few pieces of furniture and a box filled with pictures and other valuables in my father's garage. About three months passed while my father and I moved my furniture and other things into the condo, and slowly I replaced my kitchen table and other items; finally I had a bed to sleep on instead of my rug.

Another few months passed before I was to once again see Kathy at the Quiet Cannon. Tito Puente and his Latin band played there each Wednesday and Saturday night, so the place was packed with some of the greatest salsa dancers I have ever seen. When Kathy and I exchanged glances, I motioned to her to follow me outside to the terrace. When we were there we both tried to be pleasant but I eventually I asked her what she had done with my stuff. She replied that everything was placed in a storage garage and she told me she was now living at her parent's home. We got into a terrible argument that night; she began to say some things which I felt were uncalled for, so I finally left.

The night was cold and foggy, so it was difficult to see anything as I drove up Beverly Boulevard. I heard a car whiz by me then heard a terrible crash. As I slowly drove up I could see five cars that had been hit and were strewn all over the street.

Then I saw Kathy's parent's car: it was upside down and there was steam coming from the engine compartment. I guess I panicked so I parked my truck and ran to the car. She said she was unhurt but her head was pinned inside the car. People began to gather, so I asked one of them to call for an ambulance and a rescue squad. I was worried that someone might be smoking and ignite the gas that was dripping onto the street, so I yelled at everyone to stop smoking and ran and grabbed a garden hose while we all waited.

A few minutes passed before we could hear sirens approaching. Squad 28 and Engine 17 arrived before the ambulance, so they extricated Kathy and placed a neck brace on her. She asked me to call her parents just before the ambulance transported her to Whittier Presbyterian Hospital. I left my truck where I had parked it because it had a flat tire from driving over glass and twisted pieces of metal. When I entered our condo, I called Gus who is Kathy's father. He was really pissed when he learned what happened to Kathy and his car. We agreed to meet at the hospital an hour later.

I sat on our terrace and had a few beers and a couple of cigarettes so I could calm down; I even downed two or three Xanax tablets. I returned to my truck and changed the flat tire as Engine 17 was cleaning up the street. I thanked those I knew, especially the captain whom I had known for several years. When I arrived at the hospital, Gus and Lou (Kathy's mother) were there; they were shortly followed by Sue and

Vince (Kathy's sister and brother-in-law.) We learned that Kathy was unhurt, so we were allowed to enter the area where she was recovering. For some reason Kathy asked me to return with her and her parents to their home, but everyone was mad at me because they felt that the accident had been my fault. I returned with the family that night and slept with Kathy in her bedroom. A month later, Kathy moved back in and brought all my stuff with her. Kathy's other sister, Cookie, had helped Kathy the day she stole all of my things and callously destroyed my pictures, so Cookie and Kathy hired a moving company to return everything. I still don't know where she stored my things because I was on duty the day they returned everything.

My father just hollered, "What?" when I told him everything; he said, "If Kathy did it once, I guarantee you she'll do it again." Less than six months later, Dad proved to be correct. But this time Kathy only took her things and didn't maliciously destroy any of my stuff. I vowed to do two things from that day forward: first, I would never allow another woman to hurt me or fall in love again, and I would never have anything to do with Kathy.

Somehow I had lost sight of my obligations, other than financial, to both The Mick and The Bop. Tina says that when I did have them over, I was always drunk and would fall asleep while they sat in the living room and talked on the phone with Eileen until morning. I hated that I had become oblivious to the needs of my children, but I always thought that as long as they had Eileen and especially Mary, they didn't really want or need me in their lives.

I had become a regular player on a group known as "The Montebello Rabbit." Our group played together weekly and included some very-good golfers. We had monthly and yearly tournaments with some large prize money handed out to the winners.

One year I was on the winning team and had David Galindo's father for my playing partner. What made that day memorable was that Mr. Al (as I called Mr. Galindo) had left the hospital earlier in the week so he could play in our match. We had a back-and forth tussle and were all square when we walked onto the final tee. I innocently mentioned to Mr. Al that he had played wonderfully, especially since he had left his sick bed to play in our match. Our opponents must have heard what I said because we actually won that match when Mr. Al hit a two-iron on to the green with his second shot. After our opponents drove their tee shot they couldn't stop talking about how wonderfully Mr. Galindo was playing. They were now concentrating on my partner's play instead of their own, so they each duffed their second shots and didn't reach the green until their third stokes. There were many people resting and drinking on a large hill to the side of the eighteenth hole at Montebello golf course that day; the group included my father and his current lady friend. As Mr. Al drove up the final hill which approached the green, I walked over to my ball. Dad gave me a quizzical look which meant that he wanted to know how our team was doing. After I hit and 8-iron onto the green, I extended my hand, then after pausing for dramatic appearances, I gave him the "Thumbs Up!" Everyone stood up, yelled and clapped as we walked onto the green. Dad just sat on the hill and smiled at me.

In about 1982, Fernando Valenzuela, who was one of the greatest pitchers who played for the Los Angeles Dodgers during the '80s, came to Montebello golf course. He was looking for a place where he could play in peace and not have people constantly asking for his autograph or free tickets; he found what he was looking for at Montebello golf course.

Fernando amazed us with the distance he could hit a golf ball and would later become our long-ball-driving champion. I was playing with Fernando one day when we approached the fifteenth hole. Fernando almost drove the green that day but seemed unhappy. I hit last and, as I was walking back to our golf cart, Fernando said, "Hey Rafa (the nickname he gave me) give me your driver. I wondered why because Fernando did everything left handed. He took a few practice swings, put another ball on the tee and hit the ball past where he had hit his first ball! His "Babe Ruth" looks were deceptive because Fernando was a great athlete.

I played for years with Fernando who would often bring other

Dodger players with him: famous players like Kenny Landreaux, Enos Cabell, Bill Russell and Alejandro Peña routinely played there too because they were treated no differently than anyone else. What I liked best about Fernando is that he was so unassuming: except for the Corvette he drove, you wouldn't know he was a very-wealthy man.

Alejandro *Peña*, who also pitched for the Dodgers, was my favorite of Fernando's pals. One day Fernando, Alejandro, Willie Ramirez and I were playing the third hole which is a par five of over five-hundred yards. Alejandro knocked the ball over the green using first a driver, then a 5 iron! Willie and I couldn't believe that anyone could hit the ball that far; yet Fernando could hit it further! Alejandro was also a modest person who left the golf course after we had lunch; he wouldn't stay and drink with us like Fernando did. One afternoon he invited me to his home for supper that evening, so I gladly accepted. When I entered his home, there was a case of Budweiser on the table. He said, "That's for you Ralphie!" I drank almost all of that case of beer that night.

The Rabbit began to have contests with a group of black guys who belonged to a group called the "Fun Lovers." This group included Alejandro Pena and other great athletes. Player like Enos Cabell, and Kenny Landreaux of the L.A. Dodgers, Jim Brown of the Cleveland Browns, Joe Morgan of the Cincinnati Reds, and Fred Williamson of the Oakland Raiders routinely played on Sunday mornings with the Fun Lovers. O.J. Simpson tried to join that group but was rejected. Easily my favorite was Dr. Hal "Candy" Carroll. Candy and I would have some of the most competitive matches against each other for several years.

Typically an "A" player would be joined with a "B" player on each team; Candy and I were the "B" players on several of our three-day matches. It seemed that each time "The Rabbit" played against "The Fun Lovers" Candy and I were always pitted against each other. We played for a "Wolfing Towel" which each team carried for six months until we had our next match. Candy was so much fun to be with; he was the definition of the word gentleman. One day I asked him, "Hey Hal, how did you get the nickname Candy?" He just smiled, then winked at me, and said, "Girls call me Candy 'cause my kisses taste so sweet!" Before I retired and moved to Nevada, Candy and his wife moved to the Sacramento area so we lost touch.

I can't even begin to tell you about all the bets we made during those three-day battles, but they included large bets on the outcome of the contest, daily winning teams, and individual bets. You could easily lose five-hundred dollars at the end of our matches. Alejandro *Peña* was sitting on the dais on our Sunday-evening-award banquet, so, in his broken English, he announced the winners. The winners bought supper and the losers bought the drinks. I had the woman I was dating drive us home because we drank far into the night during those special matches I will never forget.

During all this time after divorcing, I also continued to play golf with the L.A. County Fire Department Golf Association. We had monthly tournaments, a yearly tournament and a special tournament which was a four-day event at the Singing Hills Resort in El Cajon, California. It's a wonder I wasn't fired or disciplined because I was constantly juggling my time so I could do all of these things. But in my defense, when I was on duty I was considered a fine engineer who drove better than most and took pride in keeping his equipment in perfect condition.

Ed Murrieta and I seemed to always be opponents, and I would want to kill him when, after closing me out, he would pull out a cigar and ceremoniously unwrap, light, then blow smoke in my face from that damned cigar! I guess Eddie beat me fifteen to twenty times in our fierce matches. One day I said, "Eddie, one of these days I'm gonna whip you then stick that cigar up your ass!" Ed fired back, "Mendoza...you haven't seen the day you could ever beat me!"

Just before Eddie and Virginia were to celebrate their twenty-fifth wedding anniversary, I was invited to their surprise, celebration party. That night I asked Eddie if he had any special plans to celebrate the occasion, he answered, "I think I want to surprise Virginia with a cruise." I replied that it would be wonderful to surprise Virginia with a cruise and asked if I could join them so Eddie said, "Why don't you bring a girl with you," so I invited a woman named Lynda to join us.

Eddie and I booked a ten-day cruise on "The Love Boat" which included stops at Mazatlan and Acapulco on our way south, then Ixtapa/Zihuatanejo, Puerto Vallarta and Cabo San Lucas on our return trip.

I don't know how it happened, but somehow Lynda and I became engaged to be married. I must have been drunk when I proposed. One day Eddie and I were playing at Brookside golf course. I asked him to be my best man as we sat in the bar after he beat me to a pulp again! He said he would be glad to be my best man if I were ever to marry again. Eddie said, "Mendoza...you're someone who will probably remain single for life." I didn't realize it at the time but what Eddie said that day proved to be my Achilles' heel. Some people call it marriage but I preferred to call it deceived at the time because I had allowed Kathy to deceive me twice.

While at sea Eddie and I booked a morning to play golf at a private golf course on the day we would spend in Acapulco a few days later. The first few days were wonderful. We would spend the morning having breakfast at sea and after lunch we would lounge around the pool and dress for dinner then eat some of the greatest meals I had ever experienced. But Lynda seemed unhappy because I wouldn't join her when she worked out or went to the theater to see a movie. She was unhappy with all the time I was spending with Eddie and Virginia and wanted me to devote all my time to her. After arriving in Acapulco we divided; Lynda and Virginia did some shopping and sightseeing and Eddie and I had a fabulous day playing at one of Acapulco's finer golf resorts. We were about the only two people playing that morning, so we each hired a caddy. Eddie had his tequila and cigars, and I had several bottles of Budweiser and Marlboros I placed into my rented bag; then the four of us took a leisurely stroll over the rolling hills of that lovely golf course. I hit a drive on one hole which landed a few feet from a lake. As we were approaching the water, my caddy said, "Ningún Sr. Mendoza, no va cerca de ese lago porque hay cocodrilos que ocultan en el agua!" My caddy was telling me that there were crocodiles hiding in the water so we should hurry away. Eddie allowed me to drop another ball without taking a penalty stroke, so we continued playing. If you ask who won our match, I'll refuse to answer the question; although my clothing reeked of cigar smoke after we finished!

That evening the four of us found a café on the second floor of a hotel which was just above Acapulco's main street. We sat on the terrace and called for a group of Mexican mariachi musicians to sing and play for us. Lynda started to object because Eddie, Virginia and I were enjoying the Mexican music and she couldn't understand Spanish, so she said, "If you're not going to include me in your fun, I'll take a taxi back to the ship." I answered, "You do that to embarrass me and our engagement is over!" A few minutes later Lynda was gone, so the three of us continued enjoying our evening until we heard the first whistle from our ship, alerting us that the ship would be leaving in one hour. We finished our drinks and hailed a cab, then returned to The Love Boat. We spent the entire night enjoying the view as our ship left Acapulco Bay. The view was so beautiful with all the lights reflecting off the water, so we remained there until the bay disappeared from view. Lynda and I cancelled our engagement after we left Acapulco. She was really upset because I hadn't come to ask her to join us on deck as we left Acapulco Bay. Well I didn't see it that way so we quarreled. We began to verbally throw rocks at each other! I said that I felt like a one-legged man at an ass-kicking contest because I felt that everything I was doing was wrong from Lynda's point of view. I had repeatedly told her that she was welcome to join us, no matter what we did, but we became distant after cancelling our engagement. I thought to myself, "With any luck at all we'll never see each other again."

When we returned to Los Angeles, Lynda and I didn't speak to each other, even though we lived in the same condo complex. Her condo was in the next building from me, so it was hard not to see each other. She started bringing a doctor who worked in the same building with her over in the evenings so the situation became awkward. Less than five months after returning from our cruise, Lynda married that doctor she was seeing! Some Love Boat...huh?

The following year I again took that same cruise; this time I took Elizabeth. She remains one of the nicest women I would even know as I went from woman to woman. She worked at La Casita so we spent a lot of time together. I gave her a key to my apartment and would often find her in my bed when I'd wake up. She would give me an aspirin and rub worm, wet towels on my face. I think she knew me and accepted me for the man I was. Looking back I think she was probably the perfect woman for me. Even Eddie thought she was exactly the woman I was looking for, but I wouldn't allow myself to get too close to any woman after what Kathy had done to me.

Elizabeth and I had a wonderful time just resting on the deck and swimming in the sunken pool while at sea. In Mazatlan we went parasailing and in Ixtapa/Zihuatanejo we went banana-boat riding. I was seated at the front of the tube and would catch a wave and try to fly as high as I could. When we returned Elizabeth and I joined a whole group of people and purchased tickets to see Luis Miguel. This was supposed to be a fancy, dress-up occasion, so I rented a tuxedo and we all attended his performance in Beverly Hills. Luis had his parents flown up from Mexico especially for that performance which donated the profits to the American Cancer Society. We had a fabulous evening, but later, when the subject of marriage was discussed, I would remember what had happened between

Kathy and me so I again found a way to end a perfectly good relationship.

One evening while Dad and I were at La Casita I introduced my father to Elizabeth and Dad said that she was probably the one I should have waited for instead of rushing into my relationship with Kathy. When Elizabeth and I split, Dad asked, "Son…what's wrong with you? I don't think you know what you're doing. You just let a wonderful woman walk out of your life and I think this time it was your fault." Years later I tried to contact Elizabeth but she had moved from Monrovia and now had an unlisted number.

David Galindo and I were partners for several years in our golf matches. We played as regularly as Eddie and I did. A game of golf with Davey was different from a game with Eddie: our matches were less competitive and we just enjoyed our day together while we told stories and drank beer.

Davey and I took a trip together with about fifty other firefighters and spent three days along the Kern River. Everything was included in the price so we ate a great lunch when we arrived then had a cook-out in front of a fire pit later that first night. We spent two days white-water rafting down the Kern River and had a totally relaxing experience. Our host was a guy who boasted that there had never been a group of firefighters who had ever depleted the camp's supply of beer. We showed them otherwise on those three days!

For the period shortly after divorcing, I was involved with all these activities and more. I squeezed in as much golf with Dad as I could and even took him for three years in a row to play at famous Rivera Country Club as his birthday gift; we would celebrate his birthday by first playing Rivera in the morning and spending our night at La Casita where just about all our friends drank each night. When I wasn't working at Fire Station 22 or 40, Dad and I would meet for breakfast each Saturday morning before we played golf. He had a friend named Art Nogales in his group so we became friends too. A good friend of mine was Bobby Miranda. Bobby was the maitre d at the Frontier Hotel & Casino in Las Vegas, so one day he invited Art, Dad and me to join him so we could play at the famous Las Vegas Hilton golf course.

We all met on the morning we were scheduled to play and had a sumptuous breakfast before playing golf. We were having a great time as we approached our third shots on the eighteenth hole. It was Dad's turn to play, but as he was about to swing, a woman, who must have been a showgirl, came out of her home which was to the left of the eighteenth green. She took off her robe and was totally naked; but what was funny was that there was a boy lying on the grass, who was reading a magazine. Dad was distracted, so he kept looking at the woman, then the boy, before he took his third swing. When Dad shanked his third shot into the lake, which was to the right of the green, we all laughed, but when Dad shanked his next shot too, his face turned a deep read. Bobby and Art started to clap as I was on the grass laughing until I almost cried, then we all laughed as the boy got up and walked inside his home. Apparently he had seen that woman naked before so it was no longer a novelty for him.

While I was on disability leave from the department, Dad joined me every time either Steve or Tina played any game. The last night we were together, we went to see Steve play in a basketball game. The next morning, as I was in the shower, I heard my phone ringing. When I answered, Captain Allen was on the line; he informed me that Engine and Squad 40 as well as Squad 28 had just returned from my father's home. Carl said, "I'm sorry Ralphie, but your father died before we could save him." I rushed over to Beverly Hospital and sat with Dad and Decy as Belinda and Laura arrived.

Probably the finest compliment our father would ever give me was when I learned that he had left everything to me. Decy felt as though she should have received Dad's possessions because she was his wife. We each hired an attorney because Dad had not left a Living Trust or a Will so his home was intestate; but the court allowed me to keep the funds in my father's checking and savings accounts because he had me as his only beneficiary; I was also made executor of his property. Dad is buried at Rose Hills Memorial Park in Whittier. On his headstone there is an image of Dad swinging a golf club. Decy and I agreed that she would remain in my father's home until she died; I even helped her financially to fix up my father's home and paid the few debts Dad had. I sold Dad's home after Decy's death, and I divided the remaining money with Belinda and Laura.

When I officially declared that I wanted to retire instead of having a back operation, Dudley and I moved to Las Vegas for thirteen weeks. I didn't want to become a dealer, but I wanted to have all the knowledge the pit bosses and others knew about playing the games of craps and black jack. We studied for twelve weeks learning to deal craps and one week learning black jack. On the fifth week I was there, I went to the Rio Hotel & Casino and hit them for just under twenty-thousand dollars. That was followed on the ninth weekend by again winning more than five-thousand dollars at the Rio, then doing the same thing at Golden Nugget.

When I returned, some of my friends held a surprise, retirement party for me; then I sold everything I owned and moved to Henderson, Nevada, where I would continue to play in casinos daily.

During the period after Eileen and I finally divorced, I lived a life only few people experience. It was truly a roller-coaster ride. I had more money than I had ever dreamed of one week and was flat broke the next week. I used to have to beg Steve to wire-transfer me enough to make it to the end of the month when I received my retirement check. But I also continued to receive many comps so for about the last ten years before

I quit gambling I attended Christmas, New Year's Eve and Super Bowl parties as well as being invited to play in golf tournaments. When I couldn't find a date I would always ask Willie Ramirez to join me, or if he was unavailable, I would invite someone I had become friends with at Montebello golf course.

When Oscar De la Hoya fought Julio Cesar Chavez in September of 1996, the casino host at the Golden Nugget Hotel & Casino invited me to that fabulous boxing match. When I asked him if I could bring two guests he didn't hesitate. He said, "No problem Mr. M., I'll reserve three tickets for you and you can pick them up at the VIP desk." Again I took Willie Ramirez with me but also invited Al Chavez. So the three of us drove up and everything was paid for by the Golden Nugget. I lost heavily at the Golden Nugget the first night so I hoped to change my luck by gambling at the Rio where I was also comped before having supper, then the three of us would go to see the boxing match. But I just continued to lose, so I took out a five-thousand dollar "Marker" in the hope that I could recoup my losses. My luck suddenly turned for the better so I won back all I had lost at the Golden Nugget and the Rio and was almost ten-thousand dollars ahead. That night remains one that I'll never forget. Willie, Al and I were having supper at the All-American Steak House which is located inside the Rio Hotel & Casino. When we were about to leave I asked to be excused because I wanted to speak with my casino host at the Rio so I could make arrangements for my next trip, so I gave Willie five-thousand dollars and my player's card then asked him to pay off my marker. Willie looked at me and said, "Mendoza...I've never even seen five-thousand dollars before!" Al and I just started laughing. That fight was probably the finest I had ever witnessed which includes all the boxing matches Dad, Uncle Jimmy and I would attend in Los Angeles. Dad, Willie, Al and I all new Oscar, if only on a casual basis, and were hoping he would win.

Oscar had grown up in Station 3's district but when he wasn't in training he played golf at Montebello golf course so I had met him a few times and we would each say hello as we passed each other. I never became friends with Oscar as I had with Fernando Valenzuela or Alejandro *Peña* but all of us at Montebello golf course took a special interest in Oscar's career because he was a local boy. One day Tina met me for lunch at the golf course, so as we passed the pro shop, I introduced Tina to Oscar. So Tina was smitten with Oscar's good looks and still talks about the day she met Oscar De La Hoya.

Willie Ramirez joined me when I was ready to move to Las Vegas. Willie always called me Mendoza because he knew I didn't like the name Ralph. When I was a child in school, kids used to put their finger down their throats and say *Ralllf* as they pretended to vomit; so I grew to hate my name. After I leased a home in Henderson, I drove Willie back to Montebello and picked up the rest of my belongings and drove back.

I thought, "You know what: this is the perfect time to change my name." Casino dealers, hosts and pit bosses only called me Mr. M. so I thought of several different nicknames I could use when I introduced myself to the new people I would meet. Eventually I thought about the movie, *The Morning After.* In one scene Alex (Jane Fonda) is riding in a battered, old convertible with Turner (Jeff Bridges) who is an ex-cop from Bakersfield. When Alex looks mockingly on the car Turner is driving, Turner notices her look, so he says, "Oh this... this is an investment. Take your Beaners... they'll fight with machetes for a car like this." In another scene Turner pretends he's answering a phone so he says: "Spade, Beaner and Spick... Good Morning!"

I knew from the moment I thought about those two scenes that I would introduce myself as Ralphie, Rafael or The Beaner, but definitely not Ralph for the rest of my life.

Chapter Nine

Life after Learning

In 1999, I was fed up with the life I was living. I had gambled myself into ruin. My weight had ballooned to two-hundred sixty pounds: the result of gluttony, alcohol and Xanax and I was smoking four and a half packs of cigarettes each day. My children, as well as my friends, were a long-distance away so I only had Dudley to console me when I felt lonely.

I was beginning to experience blackouts and didn't remember anything I did for weeks at a time. Christine brought a few of her family members from Ireland to see Las Vegas. Tina swears that I spent over four hours with them one Saturday morning. According to Tina we spent at least two hours having brunch but I don't remember even seeing her.

Here's another good example of my blackout period: I have four pictures where I am with a lovely woman. Since we are both wearing different clothing I am assuming that the pictures were taken at different times, but I can't remember to this day what her name is or where we first met.

After taking a day to thoroughly examine the life I had lived for over twenty-five years I was certain that I had to leave Las Vegas or suffer the consequences. When what follows happened I felt that I had received a warning so I was preparing to return to a more-normal life.

One day, as I was going to gamble for the day, I was driving my truck when I began to approach a stop light. There was a car stopped at the light so I tried to move my right foot from the accelerator to the brake but couldn't. I slammed into the back of that car which had a small child seated in the back seat. The Henderson police arrived, gave me a sobriety test and handcuffed me. Thank Heaven the child was uninjured and neither was her mother. I said to myself, "Well you haven't learned a damn thing over the years...have you?" I kept remembering seeing Roy hauled away many times in my youth and felt I was no better than he. I had almost killed a child that day, so I felt terrible.

I was booked, finger printed and placed in a cell for over four hours. While I sat there I started thinking. I was certain that I hadn't been drunk; it was only about 10:00 a.m. when we had that accident, so I knew I had only had one or two beers that morning. After I was released from jail, I saw an attorney who specialized in cases such as these. His name is Harvey Gruber. Mr. Gruber represented me when I appeared in the Henderson Court House. The judge was sympathetic so he released me on my own recognizance but ordered me to return. The second time I was before the judge he ordered me to enroll in an alcoholic-rehabilitation class. I explained that I was about to leave on a two-year trip so the judge allowed me six months to complete the course on-line and ordered me to return.

I had previously leased my home to a family and bought a new F-250 diesel pickup truck and a new, fifth-wheel trailer. I tore the guts out the interior, had the trailer carpeted and arranged as I wanted, then moved my desk, computer, printer and scanner into it. I also took my complete collection of CDs and about fifty books.

Dudley and I hit the road for over two years and had the most wonderful adventures I had only dreamed of. We stayed in the Southwest, for the most part, and visited places around Reno and Lake Tahoe then we traveled to Mammoth Lakes where we stayed for over a month. All along the way, we stayed in campgrounds and along streams for weeks at a time; I had no set schedule, so I had nothing I had to do except complete the course the judge had ordered.

When we stayed along a brook or stream, I would put out a chair and sit under a tree, then just read one of the books I brought with me. Dudley would play in the water and chase the fish or romp around. After lunch, we'd do about the same. It was so relaxing that I was beginning to lose weight and reduced my smoking to less than a pack a day; I even reduced the number of beers I drank to about three or four a day. That's when I first read Charles Dickens' *The Pickwick Papers*; I enjoyed reading the book so much that I bought every Dickens' book I could find. Now I have a complete collection of all his novels and short stories. I did the same thing when I first read Agatha Christie's *Spider's Web*. I really liked the way she wrote, so I began shopping for her books on-line. Now I have ninety-seven of her books and plays, most in a hard-bound matching set.

When we stayed in trailer parks, I would work on completing the course the judge had ordered. I would also work with my music collection and store all my music in my computer. That wasn't as easy as it sounds because I first had to buy an audio rectifier, so I could covert my LPs and audio tapes into information my computer could understand. I would often take an hour just to get one song the way I wanted it, then type the title of each song and store it in a file in my computer. When CDs came along it was much easier. I only had to place the CD in the CD-ROM drive in my computer, then the computer would do the rest.

Over the years I've continued to include music in my computer. I now have over eight-thousand five-hundred songs stored in my computer, and I have a stack of CDs I haven't found the time to include in my music collection. I'll get to that when I finish with this manuscript.

Music has always been a part of my life. Without question the song *Smile* has always been my favorite because the words reveal some of the heartache I have suffered during my journey especially when I reflect on my failure as a father. But the song also offers hope; so I hope there is still time for me to correct my past failures.

I also began to reproduce Thomas Kinkade photos. Later, I sent away and bought eight Thomas Kinkade photo albums which were richly embossed. I wrote a synopsis of Mr. Kinkade's history then included it as a Forward to each album. Each was meant to be surprise gifts for Mother, Steve, Tina, and some of my friends. I made eight sets in all, and then gave each one away; I sure wish I had saved one for myself!

Dudley and I would stay on the Pacific Ocean in an RV park for a month or two at a time and then drive to Ridgecrest, California to visit Mother. Ramon, his second wife and her children also lived in Ridgecrest, so I was finally able to spend months with my youngest brother.

I marveled at his mechanical skills because Ramon could do anything from chiseling figures out of wood to repairing electrical or mechanical equipment. Once Ramon saw an ad for a suction device used to suck wood shavings from a work area and then deposited them into a filtered bag. Ramon said, "Hey Bro, I'm not going to pay that much money; Hell, I'll make one myself!" A few days later I went to visit Ramon, and sure enough, he had made his own device. On another day I saw an old, beat up radio, which was in three sections, stacked in the dirt in his back yard along with other relics Ramon had collected. I said to Ramon that I thought it was a shame that something which once was so beautiful had gone to ruin. Ramon just smiled then said, "Let's see what I can do with it." Two weeks later, Ramon had joined all three sections, sanded, stained and varnished everything. He even replaced all the wiring and tubes so now it actually worked. I have kept that beautiful radio for many years and still have it in my townhouse today. It will always remind me of the brother I never really got to know until much later in our lives.

I would visit Mother during this time, but she was now deeply into religion, so we would have disagreements then I'd leave for a few months. I loved staying at an RV park in San Dimas; we had a large space with a view of the lake. Dudley would chase the rabbits and I sat and read book after book. That's about the time when I began collecting books by John Grisham, John Sanford and several others. I had the books sent to my mother's trailer, where she would save them for me. Each time I visited Mom, I replaced the books I had read with new books; soon I had a collection of some the finest books ever written so I continued to enjoy reading great books because I was learning things I had never known before.

One night as I was talking with Tina on the phone, she laughed and said, "Dad, I just got back from spending a weekend with

Grandma." I asked what she was laughing about, so she said, "Grandma's car didn't have any gas in it, so I told her that maybe we should stop to buy gas before going to church. Grandma said not to worry because Jesus was watching out for her, so Jesus would be sure we made it to church." Then I asked, "Well what happened after that?" Tina was laughing so hard when she said, "Jesus must not have been listening that day, because we ran out of gas before getting to church!"

Tina could always make me laugh even when we disagreed. I guess I used to lecture both Steve and Tina so often that they memorized all of my lectures. One day I was beginning another lecture to Tina because she was wearing combat boots with her dress. That was the fad at that time, and Tina was going along with it. I began to give her one of my stock lectures when Tina cut me off. She said, "I know, I know...you hate people who copy others. So you always say 'If it becomes socially acceptable to walk around with a light bulb up my ass, you think I'll do it...right Dad?'" I couldn't control myself because I was laughing too hard. Then Tina continued, "Then you always say that if a blue light bulb is no longer in vogue, but a red bulb is, I'll start walking around with a red bulb up my butt...right?" By this time both Tina and I would both be laughing so hard that it hurt. I wasn't being dishonest when I said The Bop has absolutely no fear of me!

I returned to Henderson when I completed the course and Mr. Gruber said I wouldn't need to appear before the judge because I had satisfied his order. So I spent the day gambling then returned to Ridgecrest.

One year I called Mother to see what she was doing for Thanksgiving; she said she had nothing planned because Ramon and his wife were spending Thanksgiving with her parents. So I told her I was really in the mood for a good, old-fashioned Thanksgiving supper with all the trimmings.

I asked her to make reservations at one of Ridgecrest's finer restaurants so I could treat her to a great meal. When we arrived at the restaurant, I asked our waitress to bring us two Thanksgiving Day specials. The waitress, who knew Mother asked, "What will you have Irene?" Mom just looked at her and said, "I don't care what he's having; I want waffles!"

As hard as we tried, Mother and I just couldn't adjust to each other. She had a ritual where she would preach outside a market or mini-mall each day and ask people, "Do you know Jesus?" One day the manager of a market stopped me and asked, "Are you Irene's son?" I answered that I was, and then he said, "We have a problem. Your mother keeps screaming that everything in our market belongs to Jesus Christ, so we have no right to sell it, but should give everything away. I can't allow this to continue." I knew Mother went overboard on just about everything, but this was too much even for her. I apologized to the manager and said I would attempt to correct the problem. That night I asked Mother, "If Jesus

Christ owns everything, why don't you leave this trailer and move out? Doesn't Jesus Christ own this trailer too?" She said that her situation was different because Jesus wanted her to spread his message.

I knew for a fact that Mother did senseless things. Once, when I was still at Fire Station 40, I returned from a gambling trip in Las Vegas. I had over seven-thousand dollars in winnings. Mom had driven down to visit me and some of the Navarro family. Mom especially liked staying with Joanie and Larry whenever she came to Los Angeles so she stopped by the station on the way to Joanie's. It had taken her so long to make the trip because her car kept breaking down. There was a combination truck and camper shell that was for sale behind Fire Station 40, so I took my mother to look at it. When I asked her if she would like to have it, she replied, "Of course I would...who wouldn't?" Well, I bought it for her as a gift. Later I learned that she had picked up some hitch-hikers who were now living in her camper. Mom did countless things like that. Both Ramon and I knew we couldn't do much, other than to love her as much as we could.

Ramon and I scheduled an appointment with Pastor Mark Godfrey who was the pastor of our mother's church. When the three of us arrived, both Ramon and I told him about what our mother was doing. I said if she didn't stop, I'd be forced to place her in a home. Mom jumped out of her seat and looked at me, then said, "Before I let you do that, I'll commit suicide!" So neither Ramon nor I did anything but hope she would change her ways before it was too late.

I have chosen to exclude other painful incidents which I have stored in my memory because I now believe that they serve no useful purpose other than to portray our mother as a bad person. She certainly was neither bad nor hurtful during our youth: misguided maybe, but certainly not bad or hurtful. There were times I can still remember where our mother did selfless things such as the year when she worked so-many additional hours to send me to St. Catherine's Military Academy, and the time when I took my first trip to a summer camp. There was a large gift on the platform that day and all of the children kept hoping that the gift was for them. I almost fainted when my name was called, because the gift was meant for me.

I was beaming inside as I passed out the candy and other treats Mother had surprised me with. I don't doubt that she had done the same for Eddie, Tony and Ramon, but when Eddie, Tony and I lived with our mother she was at her worst. I had chosen to judge her by only recalling the ugly things that happened in our lives, yet forgotten that she was wonderful in the sense that she loved us deeply and *never* consciously did *anything* to be cruel to her three sons.

But to be honest I have to admit that our mother was totally different from what people perceive a mother should be.

Now I realize that I was no shining example of what a father should be so I can understand much better about some of the seemingly insane things she did along her journey, because I have also done things that may have seemed insane at times. You know, forgiveness is a word we often use; but do any of us really apply the word in our daily lives?

If I ever hope to be forgiven for my past sins, I must first forgive the sins of other, especially those of my parents. So now in 2009, I have chosen to "Judge Not" as the Bible instructs because I hope not to be judged for only the sinful things I did in my past, but rather be judged for the human being I am constantly striving to become. If I had ostracized my father when he was at his worst, I would have never experienced those wonderful times we had during the last twenty years of his life. So now I believe that the word *forgiveness* is one of the most healing words in our English language.

Eventually, I bought a home in Ridgecrest which was within a block of where Mother lived in Ramon's trailer. I would walk over each afternoon toting two beers with Dudley by my side. Mother had quit drinking and smoking; she even ceased having epileptic seizures when she found religion, but now she seemed to reluctantly tolerant it when I'd pop a beer or light a cigarette in front of her. Now our mother was getting older so I wanted to do something special to thank for sending me to St. Catherine's for a year. A few months before her birthday, I asked her, "Mom, if you only had one thing you wanted to do before you go to Heaven, what would it be?" She said that her lady friends who were called Women Aglow were planning a three-week trip to Israel and if she only had one wish remaining in her life, it would be to join them. I said, "Mom, I can't do this every year, but I'll send you on that trip and pay for everything. You just get your passport and I'll take care of the rest." I concluded by saying, "Next year I'm taking you to McDonalds for your birthday!" Mom jumped up and hugged and thanked me. I used to take Mom out to supper about four times a week, so later that evening we went to a restaurant and found several of her Women Aglow friends there. Mom took me by the hand, then introduced me, she said, "Everyone, I want you to meet my eldest son Ralphie; he's taking me to McDonalds for my birthday!" Mom went on that trip and brought back pictures of rocks and palm trees. I just couldn't stop myself from laughing because who would ever want to just sit and look at a picture of a rock or a palm tree? Not me! But Mother also said that her trip was the best experience of her life.

I also leased a townhouse near Tropicana and Jones, in Las Vegas so, when Dudley and I weren't traveling, or living in Ridgecrest, we stayed in our townhouse. One week I phoned Ed Murrieta to see if he were available to play golf. He said he had no special plans other than to play with his brother Javier and Bob Erickson. Bobby is always fun to be with and is our mutual friend so we play golf together whenever we're together. On June 26th Dudley and I returned to Ridgecrest. It had been my plan to leave Dudley with Mother then go to supper at Ed and Virginia's home on the 27th before playing golf with Eddie, Javier and Bobby. Dudley began to fuss just after I passed Baker, California, so I pulled off the freeway so Dudley could urinate. As I was having a cigarette, I became disoriented and slid about fifty feet down a slope, then slammed my head into a large rock. About six hours later I awoke to find Dudley resting on my chest. I was covered with blood on my head, face and clothing. We somehow climbed the slope, got into my truck and continued our journey. I can't believe, to this day, how I managed to avoid an accident because we still had over two-hundred miles to drive.

When I walked into Mom's trailer I began to sway and slobber, so Mother thought I had been drinking; but I hadn't. She told me to take a shower then go bed as she was entertaining Sherry who also belonged to Women Aglow. The next morning Mother could see the cut on my head, so both she and Sherry thought that it would be better if Sherry drove me to Los Angeles. We left shortly after I dressed. I was glad to have Sherry along because I had left Dudley with Mother again. We checked into a motel, showered and then drove to Ed and Virginia's home. When I went over the threshold of their front door, I collapsed in their hallway.

Eddie had to call his brother Pete to come and help him load me into Ed's truck; from there they took me to St. Jude's Hospital in Fullerton. I remained in a coma for eleven days.

The only thing I remember is having horrible nightmares. There were two nightmares in particular I continued to have during that time. The first was that I could see Steve, Tina, Ed & Virginia, and David & Kathy dragging chains to beat me with for having been such a self-serving father. The second was that somehow I was able to open a door to the Earth, and then was suddenly sucked through space, where I could see molten lava and the Devil waiting for me.

During the time I was in the coma, doctors began testing me for various illnesses because they wanted to know what may have contributed to the state I was in. I awoke on July 9th to find Steve and Tina in tears. I guess I kept muttering in my coma, "Basically my life is over," and "I don't deserve to live." I looked around and saw Ed and Virginia sitting there as well. I could see the pain in their faces.

Eddie was in no condition to be there that day because he had just had an operation to remove a benign tumor from his head. I can vaguely remember seeing a piece of his hair shaven with stitches in the bald spot. But Eddie is not the type of person who worries about himself when a friend needs help, so I just accepted it and was thankful for their concern.

One afternoon Willie and Coco came to visit. Coco said, "Hey Mendoza...all the guys said to say hi when they learned that Willie was coming to visit you so I decided to join him. I wanted to see if you'd pull through, but after seeing the way you look, tomorrow I'm setting the morning line at eight-to-five that you don't live another week!" The three of us just laughed in the hallway. Willie seemed uneasy. He said he was always frightened when he was in a hospital and wanted to leave before I had an MRI. I guess Willie had his demons like the rest of us. I was one of the few people who saw the worth of Willie Ramirez. Unlike Willie Menold, who briefly passed through my life then drifted away like the smoke from my cigarette, Willie Ramirez was a decent human being; one whose friendship I would continue to share for a few more years.

Steve and Tina told me that my doctor had only given me a few days to live, but I had somehow survived. They also told me that my doctor had found a tumor in my chest, but was hesitant to operate until I was stronger; so we had no choice but to wait. Steve flew back to Sacramento and Tina took care of Dudley, as well as seeing to it that all of my bills were paid. She visited me several times a week and Steve called whenever he could. On my birthday, Mom, Tina and Dudley as well as a few others came to visit me. But since Dudley was not allowed into the hospital, I was wheeled outside. The moment Dudley jumped out of my truck he dashed at me and jumped on my chest so hard that I almost toppled off my wheelchair.

Before I could have my operation, Dr. Wong had my lie on my stomach while he injected three large needles filled with purple dye into my back so he could mark my tumor. That was some of the worst pain I was ever to experience, but I got through it. My operation was scheduled for July 17th so Dr. Wong came in to see me the day before. He asked how I was doing, so I answered that I was doing as well as could be expected. He said, "Ralph…you have two ways to go: you can either refuse to surrender or die. If you fight as hard as you can, I can assure you that you'll beat this cancer." The next day I was ready to fight, so Dr. Wong said he wanted me to count backwards from one hundred as the anesthesiologist injected a drug into a tube. I only remember counting to ninety-four. When I awoke, Dr. Wong asked how I was feeling, and then showed me what looked like a small rock. He asked me if I wanted to keep it; but I declined because I felt as if he were holding death in his hand. Dr. Wong told me that my tumor was malignant but it had been found so early that I would not even require radiation or chemotherapy.

Steve and Tina had talked about what I should do after leaving the hospital; then Tina came to talk to me about it. She said, "Dad, I've found a rehabilitation center that is close by, so Eddie, Virginia and I can visit you often. It's a three-month program, so you'll have to live there." I was totally against the idea of going to a rehab center; I wanted to return to Ridgecrest or Las Vegas and recuperate there, but finally I conceded to my children's wishes.

On July 28th I reluctantly hobbled into the Oasis Treatment Center. It was nice enough, but I felt I needed help with smoking and riding myself of Xanax; this place was mainly for alcoholics. I realized that I drank far-too much and too often, but I considered drinking beer to be merely a habit I started as a youngster then continued for several decades. On the first day at the center anything that contained alcohol was taken from us and we began to take courses designed to help us in beginning an alcohol-free lifestyle. I learned that our instructors were previous addicts who had no formal training. As far as I could tell, they were just ordinary people who had abused alcohol so much in their lives that they had been force to choose this path or die. One of our instructors even had his sister and mother enrolled in that center in the past. Our day began with mandatory kneeling and praying: asking for Devine guidance, that was followed by hours of classroom sessions which were boring and, for me, unproductive.

I was forced to kneel in a sandbox and play with another patient: we each had model cars which we used to simulate children at play. I was positive that Dad would have gotten up and spit in an instructor's face before he would degraded himself by playing like a child. I wanted to leave after the first day, but I had promised the kids that I would remain for the ninety-day course, so I stuck it out for as long as I could. After I was there for two weeks, Steve flew down to attend a conference with the owner. Also at that meeting were Tina and Ed Murrieta. We were forced to hold each other's hands while they told me how much I meant to them then I had to respond, by telling each of them, in turn, how much I had changed. Well, to me, that was bull shit. I got mad then slammed my hand on the sofa while I was speaking with Tina. Steve asked, "Dad...why don't you try doing that with me?" I immediately knew that I had exaggerated the situation but it was too late; the words had already been said in anger. This would probably have been the perfect time to say to everyone, especially to Steve and Tina, that I had never physically hurt them; but the moment passed without me uttering a word. We could feel the tension in the room so I asked Steve to go with me to the room I was sharing with three other patients so I could give him a few items so that Tina could save them for me. In all, that was a very unproductive session. I define an unproductive session as being one where everyone walks away unhappy. Well, everyone walked away unhappy from that session.

Tina, Eddie and Virginia would often visit me. One weekend my cousin Joanie and Larry came and spent the day with me. Bobby Erickson and his wife, along with Virginia's sister and brother-in-law also paid a visit so I felt that I still had at least a few friends who were concerned for my wellbeing. On the last weekend, Ruben and his second wife whose name is Yvonne came as well as a few other friends. Eddied and Virginia attended my thirty-day celebration where all the patients were awarded a pin. Eddie and Virginia were forced to say a few words. Being Eddie, he said, "Well...at least your eyes have cleared!" There were some chuckles after he said that. Virginia stood and seemed very uncomfortable then said, "Ralph...there will be a pot of your favorite beans waiting for you when you're ready to leave." Eventually I had to give a speech saying what the Oasis Treatment Center meant to me. I felt like a hypocrite because I hated the place.

Ramon phoned me to say that our mother had been diagnosed with intestinal cancer. Mother had earlier decided to keep her cancer a secret from her sons: Mother had intestinal cancer several months earlier but thought it had been found in time to save her from death so she never told any of us about it. Mom didn't want her sons to know because she thought we would be forced to stop what we were doing and devote too much time to her.

I told the owner that I was leaving immediately. I walked out of the Oasis Treatment Center knowing that I was not an alcoholic because I had lost my craving for beer after coming out of my coma but I still yearned for cigarettes. Fortunately Tina had left my truck at the center because after thirty days each patient was allowed to leave the compound to seek employment. I threw all my belongings together and went to Tina's house. She had a vial of Xanax in her hand when she asked me, "Dad, what do you want me to do with this?" I replied, "You can flush those damn pills down the toilet, for all I care."

As I was driving to Ridgecrest I thought of the one good thing my experience had revealed: I hadn't been drunk the day I had the vehicle accident. Later, after returning to Las Vegas, I called Mr. Gruber. He arranged to have my record amended to show I had not been drunk but had suffered a minor stroke. Later I learned I had been cleared of drunk-driving charges!

When I arrived in Ridgecrest I went directly to the hospital where our mother was staying. She was groggy from the morphine she was given, so I don't think she remembers me being there. Later, Mom was transferred to Beverly Manor. I thought it was ironic that my father had died at Beverly Hospital and our mother was about to die at the Beverly Manor. She stayed there until she was transported back to the hospital and at 3:15 a.m. our mother died. All during this period I was commuting back and forth from Las Vegas. Ramon and I were with our mother the night before she passed away. The next morning we were informed of her death so I began to make arrangements for her funeral and put my home on the market.

Tony and Sabina came as well as many of our Navarro family. We had a nice service for her and after burying some of her ashes under a tree next to her church, Tony, Ramon and I divided the remaining ashes. I still have the ornamental urn in my living room. Actually I bought an urn for each our mother's surviving sons. Here is an article which was written by our mother's best friend:

Goodbye to a friend:

On Saturday, September 20, Ridgecrest lost an 81 year-old lady, Irene Reyes, who went home to be with her Lord Jesus. Most people knew her by her waist-length gray hair, her little hats and her hugs for everyone.

She met people at Albertsons, Wal-Mart and other stores and asked them, "Do you know Jesus?" and "Do you have any un-forgiveness in your in your heart?" Hard-of-hearing, she may not have exactly heard the reply, but she was always ready to pray and share her Jesus. She lived below the poverty level, yet she always made sure her church got her tithe money first. Her favorite expression was, "Another blessing from the Lord!" If you asked her how she was, she always answered, "I'm blessed of the Lord."

That was true enough as she lay dying of recurring cancer. And so as she lived meagerly, she also lived abundantly in the Lord. During her last month of life, she was asked if she lived alone. Her answer was, "No, I live with the Father, the Son and the Holy Spirit."

As I watched her strength and system shutting down, she would come out of a coma-like state to minister to someone who had stopped by to share a hug and kiss. After a prayer of praising God with them, she would slip quietly back to sleep. Wherever she was, nurses, aides and visitors prayed and sang with her.

On her last good day with me just before she left the hospital to go to Beverly Manor, her last words were, "It's all in God's hands." She repeated this three or four times during our hours together. When I left her bedside on Friday, September 19, after praying with her and singing to her, I said, "Goodbye Irene, until we meet again. Remember, it's all in God's hands. She slipped away from us and into His hands about 3:15 a.m.

"Goodbye, Irene, until we meet again at the feet of Jesus." I know she will be waiting.

Marci Crabtree, Ridgecrest.

After the service was held Ramon's wife took all the food back to their home and invited everyone but me to attend. I was really hurt because she always invited Tony and Sabina to stay in their home whenever they were in Ridgecrest, but she never invited me. I used to have to stay at the Motel 6, which was just before I bought my home in Ridgecrest.

To me, not being invited was a slap in the face. We parted with harsh feelings on both sides. When I returned to Las Vegas I received a box filled with our mother's unpaid bills that Ramon's wife had sent. The box was only addressed to Ralph with no last name on the address label. Of course I paid each of them in time, but I never got over being humiliated by Ramon's wife after Mom's goodbye service. I have not spoken with Ramon or his wife since that day in 2003. That is regrettable but I understand Ramon's position: his wife must come before his brother. I might well do the same if I were confronted with the same option.

In the movie *The Natural* there is a scene in which Iris (Glen Close) is speaking with Roy Hobbs (Robert Redford). In one of the later scenes Iris is reflecting on the bizarre things that cause people to change. Iris looks at Roy and says, "**We have two lives.**" Roy interrupts with, "**What do you mean?**" Iris answers: "**The life we learn with, and the live we live with after that.**"

I can certainly attest to that! I had done some incredibly stupid things during my journey; now was the time to change my life or prematurely die. My relationship with Steve and Tina had suffered greatly because of my inability to think of others; I had to face the sober fact that since well before my divorce I only thought of myself. Even Ed Murrieta once told me I had one – and only one – chance to turn my life around or he would discontinue any association with me. That was a very-difficult thought to accept because Eddie is like a brother to me and a man whom I admire very much.

Was this what lay ahead for me? Did the sixty-plus years I had lived not taught me anything? I didn't honestly know at the time but prayed that I could turn things around. I said to myself, "Ralph...there is nothing you can do about the past but be sorry, but being sorry alone will not change a single thing you've done thus far." What was needed was a change in the way I behaved when dealing with others, so I was resolute in my determination to turn my life around. I knew that if I made any changes, neither my children nor the people I truly love, would accept any changes in me unless they became normal and permanent.

On page 140 of Agatha Christie's book, *An Autobiography,* she wrote:

"On reflection, though, I think that you are what you are going to be. You indulge in the fantasies of, "If so-and-had happened, I should have done so-and-so," or, "If I had married so-and-so, I suppose I should have had a totally different life." Somehow or other, though, you would always find your way to your own pattern, because I am sure you are following a pattern: your pattern of your life. You can embellish your pattern, or you can scamp it, but it is *your* pattern and so long as you are following it you will know harmony, and a mind at ease with itself."

I am not making excuses for the way I had lived in the past, but I realized it had become my pattern: that was changeable. So from the time I realized that, I have not allowed anything to sway me from the path I am now attempting to follow. Peace of mind has replaced my desire for overindulgence and forgiveness has replaced revenge. I only pray that those who are an important part of my life will someday read, understand and accept the hurt I feel inside for having caused them so much sorrow.

Chapter Ten

Life in Boulder City

Now that I was determined to change my life, living in Las Vegas was no longer an option so I drove out to see Boulder City. The last casino I passed was the Railroad Pass Hotel & Casino. I traveled several miles before coming to the first stop light. The town is so small that there are only two stop lights in Boulder City. I spent most of the morning exploring the town then I went to see a realtor. He said he had some excellent properties that I might be interested in buying. As we drove down Highway 93 I could see Lake Mead just a few miles away and enjoyed the tranquility of the area: it was totally different than any-other place where I had lived before. When we turned on the block which led to the townhouse, I could see a park on the side of the street and there was a "Beware of Big Horn Sheep" sign as we drove, so I asked him about it. He said that between April and October, Big Horn sheep as well as other small animals, graze in Hemmingway Park. The tenant wasn't home, so the realtor used the lock-box key to open the front door. I immediately liked the townhouse, as we took our time exploring every room. We sat on the balcony, which had a nice view of Lake Mead, though the view was partially obstructed by the first row of townhouses. When he told me the asking price and said that owner needed a buyer as soon as possible so she could purchase another home, I asked, "What's the lowest price I can buy this townhouse for?" When he told me the probable price, I said, "Let's make an offer today!" So that's what we did. A few days later the owner accepted my offer. A month later Dudley and I moved in and I have never regretted my decision. My unit is at the end of four units so I have a nice little yard for Dudley to play in and he enjoys chasing the rabbits which are always at our front door.

When Steven married Michelle I flew to Sacramento to attend their wedding. Because both Steven and Christine care so much for Eddie and Virginia, they too were also invited so they drove to Sacramento. Eddie, Virginia and I spent three days enjoying Sacramento and attended both functions along with Christine, Eileen and Paul. Paul is a wonderful person who has been with Eileen for many years. We had an exciting time and were there for our son's wedding. Steve and Michelle chose to go to Hawaii for their honeymoon so the next day Eddie took Virginia to Carmel for a few days of relaxation and I drove to Reno to spend a few days with Larry and Judy Simcoe. Larry Simcoe's career was similar to mine in that we almost always worked in the East Los Angeles area and worked around each other on a daily basis. We played golf for a few days then I flew back to Las Vegas. A year later Michelle suffered a tragedy when her mother and grandmother died on the same day so again I drove up to be with them during their grief. Now it was important for me to actually show both Steven and Christine, and now Michelle, that I wasn't just talking about changing my life; I was actually thinking of others more than I was thinking of myself.

Later, when Christine was engaged to be married, I also drove to Los Angeles so I could be with her; but a few days before their marriage Tina's fiancée was involved in a serious vehicle accident and had to be hospitalized, so they postponed then later cancelled their marriage. Tina was the first to see that I was making changes in the way I dealt with others, so she thanked me several times. Eventually I returned to Boulder City feeling good about myself for the first time in many decades.

While I was still living in Las Vegas I joined on on-line dating service because I was lonely for my children and all of my friends who live in the Los Angeles area, but most of all I wanted to find a woman who would complete me as the man I was trying to become.

For whatever reason, things never did turn out the way I hoped. But I met a few women who are now very-close friends. Women such as Mary Ann; we have remained friends even after she chose to returned to Carlsbad, California. Mary Ann was once an assistant editor for the *Carlsbad Journal*, and she also wrote a social column which appeared weekly.

I asked Mary Ann to help guide me when I began finishing chapters of this manuscript. She has proven to be very helpful in spotting errors and advising me when she thought changes or additions should be made.

I have been much-too busy with writing this manuscript and giving Mickey & Molly the attention each deserves to start searching again for the woman I wanted to spend the remainder of my life with. I bought Mickey & Molly shortly after I had Dudley put to sleep. But I guess the real reason is that women and I haven't had a great history of success.

Are you familiar with some of the quotes by Albert Einstein? Of all Mr. Einstein's quotes, I have saved this one in my *Insightful Thoughts* folder because I like it best:

"The definition of insanity is doing the same thing over and over again and expecting different results."

I had been doing exactly the same thing over and over where women are concerned; so I had used no logic in assuming things would turn out differently. I've gone through women like lost money: when I look around, the money is gone and so are the women!

But I hoped everything had changed when I met Maria: I was positive Maria was "The One." Just before leaving on-line dating for what I thought was the last time, I met and began dating Maria for many months. She is a wonderful woman;

we had so many mutual interests that I thought she was the woman I was destined to marry. Maria is originally from Mexico; she speaks, reads and writes Spanish well. She also loves to travel, but most of all, I started to care for Maria because she is both beautiful and humble.

I proposed to her and actually bought her an engagement ring. I had hoped to not spend too-much money on her ring or our wedding; but instead hoped to use the saved money for our lavish honeymoon. But, when I took Maria to Jared's, she fell in love with a ring. The price tag was four-times what I had hoped to spend but when I looked into her eyes, I thought, "What the Hell...she's worth it!" So I bought her ring then and there. Maria picked up the ring when it was set but did not wear it until I performed the ritual all women hope for; so, in front of Maria's mother, I got down on one knee, and humbly asked, "Maria, will you marry me?" as I placed the ring on her finger. She smiled and answered, "Yes Rafael; I will."

We were planning our wedding and honeymoon a few months before I began feeling terribly sick. During that period, I gradually began to feel worse then I went to see my doctor. When the blood-tests results returned, they showed that my blood-glucose level was over four-hundred. Only six months earlier, my blood-glucose level was only one-hundred and twenty. I learned that I was finally a diabetic but never mentioned anything to Maria. Finally I became so weak and lethargic that I stayed in bed for over seven weeks. I only left my townhouse to see Dr. Leovy, do some marketing or see Maria; but when I did see Maria, I felt so sick that I think she started to believe that I had begun to have second thoughts. I never mentioned a word to Maria about my diabetes until it was too late.

I had hoped to get well first then tell Maria everything. I didn't want her to feel obligated to marry a man who might never recover then continue as planned because she felt it was the honorable thing to do.

One day, when I was at her house, she said she wanted to break off our marriage plans as she returned the ring. I felt too-much pain to talk further, but later we talked on the phone. We agreed to keep our relationship platonic and only speak to each other on the phone and through email. Slowly our calls became fewer and emails were no longer answered. It's been months since we've either written or spoken.

Now I had to eat my words because I had spoken with Michelle, Steve and Tina, and written to everyone telling them all about Maria and sending her pictures via email. Now I have safely saved all those pictures so I can look back some day and see the face of the woman I asked to be my wife.

Life in Boulder City is just about the same as any other small town in America. People are much-more friendly than people you may find in larger cities such as Los Angeles. Everything is within a ten-minute drive from my townhouse and people wave at you as you drive by. A trip to one of the two larger markets can be a great experience. Often people stop me, or I stop them, and we just stand and chat for ten or twenty minutes. I know most of the employees by their first names and they often say, "Hi Ralph," as I walk by.

Boulder City Municipal Golf Course and Boulder Creek Golf Course are the two courses I routinely play. The other golf course is Cascata Golf Club which is the private course where Michael Douglas serves as host at his annual celebrity golf tournament. Each year Cascata holds a "Boulder City Appreciation Day" where our residents are allowed to play golf and enjoy a fine lunch at a very-reduced rate.

I've belonged to a group of fellows who meet each Monday, Wednesday and Friday since I first moved here. We play in a "Skins" game where we each give DW our money; DW is our leader who figures out all the score cards and distributes the cash to the winners. Our group often plays in three and one half hours; not like the five, six or even seven hours which is common in larger cities. We like it this way, so if we tee off at eight a.m., which is our custom, I'm often home by twelve-thirty, even if I've spent an hour having a beer or two with my pals. In Boulder City, my pals call me Bean, The Beaner or Nevada Bean. I know they do this with affection, and I like it!

Over a year ago we had a surprise golf and birthday party

for our group's eldest member; his name is Homer. We had a great outing of golf and fun then had Homer's surprise ninetieth birthday celebration. A week later, Homer made the first hole-in-one of his life. Homer had to buy each of us a drink; that is the custom everywhere, so I've known about it since I first started playing golf. I was in Albertsons market one morning, when suddenly I heard, "Hey Bean!" There was Homer, with his lovely wife, shopping at the other end of the market. I walked over and kissed Homer's wife on the cheek, then said, "Homer, if you can still make a hole-in-one after you're over ninety years of age, what do you plan on doing after you reach one-hundred?" Homer just smiled at me and said, "Well Bean, my wife and I have discussed it so when I reach one-hundred, we plan on cutting our sex life down to once a week!" Homer's wife just blushed as I stood there and laughed.

Homer and another friend whose name is Kenny are two ole rednecks I really enjoy playing golf with. Often telling redneck and Mexican jokes is more fun than our game of golf. One day I brought out a new driver and was showing it to all my pals. One of them yelled, "Hey Beaner, how many lawns did you have to cut to pay for that thing?" I replied, "You rednecks wouldn't know a gentlemen's club if you saw one!" That's just our way of having fun!

I met Rich and his wife Karen just after I moved to Boulder City. One Sunday they invited me to go to Mass at St.

Andrew's Catholic Church. There I met Father Joe Annese. I instantly liked Fr. Joe's Homily. He had a way of speaking with his congregation that I admired. When Fr. Joe was delivering a Homily he would always include a story which related to that week's message from the Bible. His stories were funny as he told of his experiences while living in or around Boston. He had come from a poor, Italian family so he always included a story or two about the joy and the pain he and his family had experienced. After Mass people always gather in the community center to have coffee and cookies or pastry, so I mentioned to Rich that Fr. Joe was a gifted speaker; he replied that before deciding to become a priest, Fr. Joe graduated from college with a drama degree. So I'm sure his previous experiences helped him when speaking before his congregation.

For about four years I attended Mass twice a month. On day, when I had not attended Mass for several weeks, Fr. Joe asked, "Ralph, what has kept you away so long?" I answered, "Well Father Joe, it's like this: each time I start to come to Mass, I always make a wrong turn, so I end up at some bar! But I want you to know, Father Joe, that each time I finish a beer I'm thinking of you." Father Joe just smiled, and said, "Wait for me after Mass and I'll join you for a few!"

Each spring we celebrate The Feast of Saint Joseph with a seven-course dining experience which includes some very-fine wine. That event is our fines event of the year. Mary

Ann was my last guest. She enjoyed herself very much while all the men were flirting with her. Women like that kind of adoration! Richard is in charge of selling tickets for over thirty prizes. Then, after giving the prizes away, there is an annual auction for an evening with Fr. Joe. The bids I have witnessed have gone for as high as five-thousand dollars. Fr. Joe is said to be a fantastic cook and those who have paid for the evening have raved about their experience. Things just weren't the same after Fr. Joe retired; I have only returned to Mass once since he left.

Karen is also a fabulous cook who likes to make several delicious dishes for her guests. She started inviting me to what she calls "Our Lonely-Hearts Dinner." She only invites widowed or divorced men who she thinks might need a laugh or two. Those are always special to me.

Once each year Boulder City hosts an art festival in a park just across the street from our only post office where most of our residents spend a leisurely day enjoying the works of many artists who show and hope to sell their art. It's a fun and relaxing afternoon: people just stroll through the park. You will often find families having a picnic or people buying food from the vendors who set up for the day. The chili cook off is another delightful day where many people from all over the Southwest come to enter their chili in the contest. For me, it's a day to gorge myself with all different sorts of chili, all of which are delicious!

Keeping what I was writing was beginning to create problems. I totally missed sending Christmas cards and gifts to those people whom I yearly exchange cards with. I also forgot to send a birthday card to Michelle, Steve and others I truly love so I had to begin telling lies. At first I said that diabetes was keeping me from returning to golf; later, my excuse was that I was recovering from the emotional experience I endured when Dudley passed away. For fourteen year, from the day I bought Dudley when he was only eight weeks old, until February 17, 2009, the day I had Dudley put to sleep, Dudley was with me daily. Willie Ramirez died on March 17, 2009. That date is also the day our son, Michael Phillip Mendoza, died although that was in 1964. I immediately called Coco. We spent over an hour telling stories about Willie and how tight he was with his money. Coco really made me laugh when he said, "Willie may not have died with the first dollar he ever made, but he still had change!" Willie Ramirez was a great human being – but Willie was simply Willie – so he never made excuses for being so tight with his money. Shortly after grieving over Dudley and Willie Ramirez I learned that Eladio Carrillo had also died. His death hurt me deeply because he was my mentor for over thirty years. We had briefly spoken on the phone just two weeks earlier. I immediately stopped what I was doing and wrote Tim (his son and current engineer on our department) and expressed the pain I felt for having lost another wonderful human being.

The final excuse I used for being a hermit for so long was when

I said that I had begun to use this time to begin a project: one which I preferred to remain my private secret. I began feeling better because I was now telling the complete truth. From before Thanksgiving, what I was doing was writing this manuscript. When I finally said that I would probably return to playing golf in about September my friends began to accept my answer.

About two weeks before I was ready to print every chapter I began phoning a few men I had worked with; some I was able to locate, but for others, I had to leave messages for with mutual friends, asking them to return my call. Frank Brown was one of those men who returned my call. We exchanged old, war stories about our time on the job. I told Frank that I was involved with a surprise project I was putting together as a gift for Steve, Michelle and Tina. Brown said, "Hey Mendoza, remember to include the story about the baby you delivered on Atlantic Boulevard and the bowling-alley fire where you got chewed out for posing for KTLA." I laughed as he continued, "I think you thought you were Eric Estrada while you were posing for the TV cameras, and Vic Ramirez thought he was Superman while he was climbing Truck 3." So here are those two stories:

Engine 22 and Squad 3 responded to a reported woman in distress at Dunkin' Doughnuts on Atlantic Boulevard. We arrived before Squad 3 because they were on another response. We saw two women sitting in a VW in that mini-mall with a large crowd looking inside the car. The woman seated in the passenger seat was obviously about to have her baby any minute. I had delivered five of the seven babies I personally delivered before I retired, so to me it wasn't anything to sweat as long as everything went normally. David Galindo grabbed an OB kit and a rescue blanket so that we could provide as much privacy for the women as possible. We covered the VW and, after I slid under the blanket, I asked the woman to turn sideways so I could help her. After removing her wet underwear and spreading her legs, I could see the baby "Crowning" so I knew it was only minutes before she was going to have her baby. I didn't need to calm her down; the driver seemed more excited than this woman was. Before Squad 3 or the ambulance arrived I had severed the umbilical cord and everything turned out perfectly. The woman thanked me and the driver wouldn't stop crying because she was so thankful. I got up from under the rescue blanket and began bowing to the crowd just as Chief Brown was pulling up. Chief Brown just shook his head and sped away. So that's the first story. Here's the second:

I was working with David Galindo and Paul "Opie" Oyler, the two firefighters who were assigned to Engine 22, and Jim Padgett was the overtime captain on duty that day. We received an alarm of a reported bowling-alley fire in our district. Padgett was considered to be brain-dead as a firefighter, engineer and captain by everyone who had worked with him; it was just our misfortune to be working with him that day. As we left Fire Station 22 we could see a large plume of smoke in the distance. Fortunately, Ed Murrieta was the captain on Engine 3 and Vic Ramirez was the captain on Truck 3. Also on that fire was Captain Billy Miller. Billly Miller was a friend and a captain in whom I had a world of confidence.

When we arrived at the scene, we hadn't even brought lines with us, so Davey and Opie had to mule hose to a hydrant over six-hundred feet away while I engaged Engine 22's pump and was connecting lines to outlets. Padgett was busy drawing a diagram like some coach on the cement walkway with a piece of chalk as the roof of the bowling alley suddenly caved in. To most of us it was a "No Brainer"; we just had to "Surround and Drown" the fire. Eventually Murrieta, Ramirez and Miller took control so everything worked out just fine. In the meantime Battalion Chief Frank Brown arrived. Other chiefs from headquarters also saw the fire because headquarters sits high on a hill which is only a few miles away, so eventually Division Assistant Fire Chief Bill Zeason arrived to find me without my helmet or turnouts on and Captain Ramirez high up the ladder, also not in safety apparel.

It must have a slow day in Los Angeles because CBS, NBC and KTLA sent film crews to cover the fire. After everything was over, Zeason turned to Brown and asked, "Who is that goofy, Mexican engineer who isn't in uniform?" Brown answered, "That's Mendoza. I've been too busy to reprimand him, so why don't you?" Zeason never said a word to me that day, but Brown was able to get a copy of KTLA's coverage of the fire. A few shifts later, all who were involved were ordered by Chief Brown to report to Fire Station 3, so we could critique that fire. The video showed me strutting around in front of the building, smiling at the cameras with no helmet or turnouts on and Vic Ramirez on top of the extended ladder of Truck 3; he too had no turnouts on. Chief Brown began to chastise both of us for not being dressed properly, when Ramirez got up and took over the critique. Captain Ramirez got nose-to-nose with Chief Brown and an argument ensued. We were all embarrassed because Monterey Park's engine was also at that critique, so they looked startled to see a fire captain haranguing a battalion chief. Chief Brown said, "That's it... this critique is over!" He and Captain Ramirez went into the captain's office, so we could hear them continuing with their squabble. So those are the two episodes Frank Brown wanted me to include. The least that SOB can do in return is to buy a copy of this after it is published!

Vic Ramirez called me when he heard through the grape-vine that I was now a diabetic. We had some fun on the phone rehashing some old stories. Now maybe you will begin to realize what a great group of men I had the honor of working with for some of the best years of my life.

On May 1st we had a Navarro family reunion in Las Vegas. We gathered to watch the 2009 Kentucky Derby and renew friendships. I saw friends and cousins I hadn't seen since I left Yuma. I took quite-a-few pictures during that two-day gathering that I now have safely stored in my computer. I have one picture of Joanie lifting her boobs and smiling at the camera. If you remember, she is the person who first thought I had a gift for telling stories. Her confidence in me led to my writing this manuscript.

I thought I had completed the manuscript when I received a message from my Uncle Joe on my answering machine. He is my father's only surviving brother who is now eighty-two years of age. He is also a diabetic who takes better care of his health than most people do so he's only one-hundred and forty pounds; he keeps his weight down by continuing to work out three days a week and takes nightly walks. Uncle Joe had suffered a great deal during the final years of my Aunt Stella's (his wife) life. When he was informed that Aunt Stella had Alzheimer's Disease Uncle Joe refused to have Aunt Stella confined to a home; so for two years he fed, bathed and clothed her daily. He is a man I admire greatly because he remained with her until her death.

I had been shopping for supplies so I missed his call. Uncle Joe hadn't left any information other than he was staying for one night with a group of senior citizens who had chartered a bus and were staying at the Hacienda Hotel & Casino just east of Boulder City. I tried to reach him by phone and left several messages but was unable to make contact. So I thought I'd surprise him with a visit.

Thirty minutes later I was in the lobby having him paged. Eventually I found Uncle Joe while he was searching for me. We sat in the casino because neither of us was hungry. I told him about my surprise gift for Steve and Tina then said I was preparing to see a lawyer to obtain a copyright then a publishing agent, so we began to tell each other stories of life in Ramona Gardens. Uncle Joe thought it was ironic that we both had lived in Ramona Gardens and attended Murchison Street School. We started to reminisce about my father and Grandma Mendoza. He had tears in his eyes when he recalled his mother and his brother as well as his two other brothers who had been killed in the Korean War. He said Grandma Mendoza never really recovered from the deaths of my Uncle Lawrence and Uncle Pointe. I had never really considered Grandma Mendoza's heartache because she hid it so well. Each time I learn something I never knew before about Grandma Mendoza, such as the grief she kept silent, it only makes me love her more for putting aside her grief and devoting so-much time to me.

We spent a few hours just chatting about how life seems to pass us by so quickly and we thereafter carry around scars from some of the wounds we suffer as we each continue our journey. He said my Aunt Virginia's scars were too deep for her to accept the death of her four children in less than a year. Uncle Joe said, "You know Ralphie, I was at Armeda's, Theresa's and Jo Jo's bedside on the day each of them died. I never knew about Albert's death until it was too late, or I would have been there too." I thought: "There sure is a lot of ugliness people are forced to live with."

When it was time for him to return to his room, we embraced and said goodbye. As I was driving home I thought about all the injustice each of us must pay as the price for living: maybe it's not right but I guess we all have to live with it and somehow go on with living our lives.

Of all of my paternal cousins Jo Jo has remained my favorite. We've had some great times together when he was appearing here in Las Vegas. Jo Jo never married, but chose instead to travel all around the world; he really loved exploring different countries and meeting different people.

When I look back many years from now and remember those who are now gone I will think of Grandma Mendoza most. I have a picture which was taken on Grandma Mendoza's eightieth birthday. In that picture it shows her toasting everyone, so that's how I'll end this chapter. So I am raising a glass and sending a toast to all of you. I hope your journey is filled with wonder!

Epilog

Now that I have completed this manuscript, there still remain a few things I must do. I hope to surprise Steven & Michelle and Christine with my book as a special Christmas gift. My hope is that after each reads what I have written they will know the soul-searching I went through for those long sessions in which I would write for ten hours each day only to delete what was written and begin again. Now maybe they will understand why I missed birthdays and sending Christmas card for almost a year.

You may be wondering what is ahead for me: I don't have a clue! Since before Thanksgiving, 2008, I have not played a single round of golf, so I hope to begin practicing a few times a week, so when I do return to our group, I won't embarrass myself. I haven't read a book since that same day, although I continue to collect books which are not in my library; so I will resume on chapter three of Barack Obama's book *Dreams from My Father* and picking up where I left off reading *The Wicked Wit of Charles Dickens* and *The Wicked Wit of Winston Churchill*. Mr. Churchill's eloquence was truly a gift from above. I like what he wrote about dying. He wrote: **"I am ready to meet** my Maker – but whether my Maker is prepared for the great ordeal of meeting me is another matter."

When I stopped everything I had been doing so I could concentrate on only writing this manuscript, I was reading those-three books I have just mentioned. In Dominique Enright's compilation of Mr. Churchill's famous sayings, the following is written:

During his long life, Churchill – a boy noted for failing exams – received many honorary degrees. In 1946, at the University of Miami, on being awarded his doctorate of law, he remarked, "Perhaps no one has passed so few examinations and received so many degrees."

From the day of my divorce so many things have changed. After my stroke and lung cancer and later when I finally decided to change my life or die there seems to have been a moment in time where I arrived at my personal "Age of Reason." Thomas Paine was a gifted writer who wrote about that subject. I have read what he wrote so now I am attempting to apply his wisdom to my life.

Over the years I learned so much through movies, reading great works of literature and researching the Internet almost daily. Now I feel as though I know a few things. Subjects, in which I don't have knowledge, but a desire to learn about, are only a web site away.

I now have over six-hundred and seventy-five films in my collection, and the number continues to grow each month. Reading wonderful books has taught me many lessons from the first book I casually read to those I now study in my desire for more knowledge. Knowledge is a goal which is attainable simply by reading great books and researching subjects via the Internet. I guess I have over three hundred or more books in my collection. I now love reading so much that I figure if I read an average of three books a month for twenty-more years, I still have seven-hundred and twenty wonderful, new and exciting adventures to share with the author.

I would also hope to include a trip to play St. Andrews golf course because I've seen many great tournaments played there, not the least of which is the British Open on TV; I've also read about this course which is credited with being the birthplace of golf. Of all the books I have read about golf, none are better than *The Complete Golfer*, which was edited by Herbert Warren Wind, and *The Story of American Golf*, which is a book Mr. Wind wrote; so visiting St. Andrews is definitely on my list.

I have decided to abandon my search for "The One!" I think finding the woman whom I was destined to share the remainder of my life with has long ago drifted away like a cloud that is visible one moment then is slowly blown away by the winds of chance. It's funny that I could never find the woman I wanted here in Boulder City, Henderson or Las Vegas since there are so many to choose from. But if I eventually do find that special woman we both must realize that we are accepting a person who has not succeeded in previous relationships or marriages; however, in another way, our relationship will be just beginning to grow, so we won't have to suffer from the corrosion which has damaged the relationships and marriages of some couples.

Recently, I was watching the move, *First Knight*. In that movie there is a scene where King Arthur (Sean Connery) is speaking with Lancelot (Richard Gere). As Lancelot begins to walk away, King Arthur says, **"Lancelot...just a thought: A man who fears nothing, is a man who loves nothing. And if you love nothing, what joy is there in your life?"** I have known both fear and love along my journey, but somehow having someone to share the remainder of my life with still remains important if I am ever to have a balanced life.

Ed & Virginia and David & Kathy deserve my special thanks so I plan to do something very special for them. It's important to me to actually show the four of them how thankful I am for having put up with me in situations too numerous to count.

I suppose I could think of other things I would also like to do, as I head toward my final years: the end of my journey. But those remain vague; so while there is still time, those I have just included are what are important to me now.

Do I have another book to write: I can't answer that question.

Who knows what tomorrow may bring? But this book is all I can think of which I know enough about to write anything worth reading.

Two Final Thoughts

I had a folder in which I wrote over sixty pages of thoughts I wanted to include in this manuscript; some of those thoughts have been included in previous chapters. I didn't want to change this manuscript from my original dream: which was to tell a story. But, after reading those pages, I realized that I was beginning to pontificate; so I deleted everything. However, there remain two subjects which I feel I must write at least something because each is extremely important to me. Here they are:

To all those who have always dreamed of doing something special in your life, I say this: If you have a dream of what you want to someday do, such as the dream I had of writing this manuscript; I will first say that all the evidence you will ever need is staring you right in your face: my book. But dreaming alone will not get you once inch closer to achieving your dream.

As I see it, there are two things each of you must ask before deciding to turn your dream into a reality; those two questions are: is my dream *realistic,* and am I willing to do whatever is *necessary* to achieve my dream. It's unrealistic for a blind person to dream about becoming a world-class speed racer;

therefore, that person must accept that his or her dream is unattainable; but there are other dreams a blind person can achieve: have you ever heard of George Shearing, Stevie Wonder or Ray Charles?

Conversely, it is not unrealistic for someone who had the misfortune to be born without arms, or was involved in a tragic accident and was forced to have both arms amputated to dream of becoming a celebrated painter. There are many stories and articles of people who have learned to paint with their toes! So, if you feel your dream is realistic there remains the second question you must ask: am I prepared to do what is *necessary*? All people who have achieved prominence in any endeavor had to be willing to do whatever was necessary to achieve that dream. If you are unwilling to do what is necessary, forget that dream and find a dream for which you are willing to pay the price for your achievement.

Finally, I would like to write something to those who, in one way or another, feel they don't symbolize the image of a real American. When they look in a mirror they realize that they don't look, talk or behave like what some Americans perceive *all* Americans should symbolize before each is entitled to be called an American. Our Founding Father's made it clear that anyone born in America, or anyone who took those actions necessary to become a citizen, were *all* Americans.

I'll only use people who originated in Mexico as an example

because I have at least some knowledge of that subject. People whose forefather's came to America from Mexico have been called many names; not all of them have been flattering, but now they are generally called Latinos or Mexican-Americans. Here is where I completely disagree. Please don't misunderstand me: I love my rich heritage and Mexico's food, music, customs and traditions. But, although my last name happens to be Mendoza, in no way do I feel that I am any less American because my name isn't Smith or my skin happens to be brown in color.

I proudly call myself an American. If someone disagrees, I will sometimes say, "Okay, I'm an American of Mexican ancestry." I feel that I am both entitled and responsible for all I have *earned*, so I refuse to take credit or blame for something which happened through the years – something over which I had no control! Why people choose to call themselves names such as Mexican-Americans, African-Americans or Asian-Americans implies that those people feel less-worthy from what an American ought to symbolize. If you fall into this category: be proud of your ancestry and treasure your forefather's beliefs, customs and traditions; but always remember that you are an American; and as worthy of all America's promises as anyone!

I will close this work with a passage I read from R.B. Rubenstein's biography: *Thomas Jefferson.*

Thomas Jefferson's exposure to Europe had affected him and forever changed his opinion of most of those countries where "Monarchy" and "Aristocracy" rule. In a letter he wrote on June 17, 1785, he urged James Monroe to visit Europe; in this letter he wrote:

"The pleasure of the trip will be less than you expect but the utility greater. It will make you adore your own country, its soil, its climate, its equality, liberty, people and manners. My God! How little do my countrymen know what precious blessing they are in possession of; and which no other people on Earth enjoy! I confess I had no idea of it myself ...."

The End